Mass Media in Revolution and National Development

The Romanian Laboratory

Mass Media in Revolution and National Development

The Romanian Laboratory

PETER GROSS

Iowa State University Press / Ames

TO VERA, ERIC, NICK, KATY AND SONYA

Peter Gross is professor of journalism at California State University–Chico, where he directs training programs for journalists from Romania and Russia. In 1992 Romanian-born Gross established a journalism program at the University of Timisoara, Romania.

Authorization to photocopy items for internal or personal use, or the internal or personal use of specific clients, is granted by Iowa State University Press, provided that the base fee of $.10 per copy is paid directly to the Copyright Clearance Center, 27 Congress Street, Salem, MA 01970. For those organizations that have been granted a photocopy license by CCC, a separate system of payments has been arranged. The fee code for users of the Transactional Reporting Service is 0-8138-2670-5/96 $.10.

∞ Printed on acid-free paper in the United States of America

First edition, 1996

Library of Congress Cataloging-in-Publication Data

Gross, Peter
    Mass media in revolution and national development: the Romanian laboratory / Peter Gross.
        p.   cm.
    Includes bibliographical references and index.
    ISBN 0-8138-2670-5
    1. Mass media—Political aspects—Romania. 2. Press and politics—Romania. 3. Journalism—Romania—History. 4. Romania—Politics and government—1989-   . I. Title.
P95.82.R6G76   1996   96-22614
302.23'09498—dc20

Last digit is the print number: 9 8 7 6 5 4 3 2 1

CONTENTS

PREFACE

Twenty days after Nicolae and Elena Ceausescu fled Bucharest on December 22, 1989, signaling the end of the communist nightmare and the beginning of a new era for Romania, I arrived in Timisoara by train from Vienna, Austria. Timisoara, the westernmost Romanian city, is situated less than 30 miles from Yugoslavia's border to the southwest and Hungary's to the northwest. An ancient city, it grew out of a settlement whose existence was noted in eighth-century European chronicles. It was the capital of Hungary for a short spell in the 16th century; occupied by Turks until its liberation in the 18th century; and a prosperous, multiethnic city in the Habsburg Empire until World War I. Today it still retains some vestiges of cosmopolitanism and quiet civility that centuries of Western influence and intermarriages between its Romanian, Hungarian, German, Gypsy, Jewish, Czech, Slovak and Serb citizens have brought to it. A city of around 400,000 inhabitants, home to a university and a polytechnic, it is the community which gave birth to Romania's anticommunist revolution in mid-December 1989. It also happens to be my birthplace.

This trip was to be the first of four back to Romania in 1990, followed by three in 1991, two in 1992, one each in 1993 and 1994, and two in 1995. (They were coupled with trips to other East-Central European countries and former Soviet republics—Albania, Bulgaria, Hungary, Poland, Slovenia, Croatia, Serbia, Russia, Belarus, Moldova.) These were working trips sponsored by the U.S. Information Agency (USIA) and the Voice of America's (VOA) International Training Program, the International Media Fund (IMF), or the Freedom Forum (FF). They gave me the opportunity to observe and to discuss media-related matters with print and broadcast journalists, editors, publishers, politicians, government officials, academics and other Romanians from one end of the country to the other. I was able to gather information and data on all aspects of the mass media and journalism's transition from their communist days. In the process, I developed close personal and professional relationships with many in the mass media, government, parliament, and universities.

East-Central Europe has undergone momentous change, starting in 1989. This transition from communism, whether on the political, economic, social, cultural or mass media level, is without precedent. Therefore, there is no model, no theory, to aid in its charting or explaining. Indeed, while there is a transition from socialism or communism, there is as yet no clear understanding of where this transition will lead.

Ralf Dahrendorf, in a spring 1990 interview published in *New Perspectives Quarterly* (pp. 41–43), pointed out that the "open society" the East-Central European countries joined in 1989 does not qualify as a system but "an opportunity." Thus far, East-Central European political parties and politicians seem to have used this opportunity to jockey for power. They applied a mentality that says democracy means simply someone else's (rather than the communists') turn to dictate or one that says individual hunger for power and attendant opportunities for acquiring wealth are paramount. Governments have been slow to privatize the economy and quick in their attempts to control the mass media. Nationalism has overtly reasserted itself, and historical claims and counterclaims have resurfaced. East-Central European nations have proven Dahrendorf's characterization that no system per se was joined by them in 1989. So, how and to what end are the East-Central Europeans using this opportunity won after 40-plus years of literal and figurative incarceration?

Since 1990 I have tried to learn and understand how the Romanians used their opportunity after freeing themselves from Ceausescu's communism to establish and develop their mass media and journalism. I sought to discover the nature and effects of the elements impinging on this process and what influence they had at every stage of leaving the old system and embarking on and contributing to this uncharted transition.

In 1991 I was asked to present at an international colloquium held in Minsk, Belarus, a paper dealing with media as facilitators and impediments to public opinion formation in Romania. The paper was subsequently published in an edited volume of articles in Kiev, Ukraine (Manaev and Pryluk 1993). Together with an article dealing with the small and large roles of mass media in Romania's 1989 revolution, completed in 1992 and finally published in 1995 (Paletz, Jakubowicz and Novosel 1995), it served as the seed for this book.

This work provides a panorama and explication of the nature and influence of the mass or news media, their journalism and their relationship with what has occurred in Romania before, during, and after the December 1989 revolution. It supplies one small part of an overall puzzle of the landscape of the new Romania and therefore also of the new East-Central Europe, in which the mass media figure so very prominently. The work offered here is in the spirit of a profusion of articles written since 1989, on the newly freed mass media in East-Central Europe. It is also kin to a number of books dealing with various aspects of mass media and their journalism in that region's countries, which are in the process of being completed or have recently been published. Most notable among these are Slavko Splichal's *Media Beyond Socialism* (1995) Tomasz Goban-Klas's *The Orchestration of the Media: The Politics of Mass Communication in Communist Poland and the Aftermath* (1994) and Svennik Hoyer, Epp Lauk and Peeter Vihalemm's *Towards a Civic Society: The Baltic Media's Long Road to Freedom* (1993).

Romania is an interesting and rich laboratory in which to study mass media and journalism in the context of the transition. It was the second in the region to enact a postcommunist broadcasting law (after the Czech broadcasting law of 1991), and its print and broadcast media (on a per capita basis) are the largest in East-Central Europe; its precommunist media history is brief, rich, yet preprofessional in nature; what its postcommunist journalism lacks in professionalism it makes up in vigor, diversity and controversy. Other than Albania, Romania is the one East-Central European country to have experienced an extreme communist regime, and it is the only one to have foregone a "velvet revolution" for a violent one to end it. Both factors are affecting the changes occurring there now. The Ceausescu regime cultivated a personality cult more akin to North Korea's Kim Il Sung and controlled every facet of life in the country in an undeniably Stalinist way. Journalism, as the noncommunist world understood it, simply did not exist. The mass media were under complete control and, unlike in other East-Central European countries, there was no underground or (indigenous) alternative press. In the aftermath of the Ceausescu regime's destruction, where does one begin the remaking of society and its mass media? What kind of journalism and mass media can be established? How and what can they do to contribute to the transition? What effects does the transition have on journalism and mass media?

The recognized power of the new means of global and national communication and the wide-reaching, lighting-speed conveyor belt of huge amounts of information create "social intimacy on the global scale—overcoming time and distance" (Brzezinski 1993, 76). Overwhelming testimony in the post-1989 period, from Vaclav Havel and Lech Walesa down to ordinary citizens, made it clear that this global media network aided the struggle for freedom and even the psychological balance of East-Central Europeans. It informed and entertained them, providing a window to the world that prevented their figurative blindness and asphyxiation. Now their own mass media are free yet struggling for economic survival and guaranteed access to information; they battle to attain a degree of professionalization, credibility and influence; and they fight against new attempts to curtail their freedoms, attempts spearheaded mostly by the new East-Central European govern-

ments whose attitudes vis-à-vis mass media "were also a depressing re-
minder of how much still needed to be done" (Brown 1994, 34). Romania's
mass media share this new reality with their regional counterparts.

All across the new East-Central Europe, the mass media function in and
contribute to societies in which "combative, not competitive, politics" dominate, as Brown has succinctly put it (1994, 34). Print and broadcast journalists were not professionally prepared to report and explain to their audiences the complex social, political, cultural and economic issues at the core
of the transition from communism (see Paletz, Jakubowicz and Novosel
1995). Furthermore, the mass media were faced with immense political, economic, legal, cultural, technical and managerial pressures they were ill-pre-
pared to handle. The communist and precommunist legacies of all East-Central European nations also weigh heavily on remaking mentalities and
reconceptualizing the philosophy of and approach to journalism.

The principal focus of this work is the print and broadcast news media
and their journalism, and the principal theme is their struggle to remake
themselves at the same time they are called upon to play a role in the remaking of society. The entertainment media, or the nonnews segments of the
media—the religious, pornographic, intellectual, student, professional-inter-
est, scientific press, and so on—are not specifically examined here. Neither
are the ethnic minority print and broadcast media in Romania, which account for a significant number of outlets in Hungarian, German, Armenian,
Bulgarian, Czech, Slovak, Gypsy (Roma) and Macedonian languages. They
constitute an important ingredient in this diverse society and in the transition
and should be the subject of some future work.

Romania is to some degree no different from all other former communist states. It must simultaneously resolve several severe social, political,
economic, educational, cultural and national psychological problems. It
must create a degree of stability to move ahead. In some sense Romania
needs to begin where it left off in the 1920s, with its incipient moves to eliminate feudalism, its first steps toward the professionalization of journalism or
mass media, and the initial phase in preparing Romanians to democratize
their society. But the nation has to deal with the legacy of the intervening 60
to 70 years and the problems presented by the present transition itself.

In my opinion, it will take 40 to 60 years for the country to arrive at that
exalted stage of a truly open society, now in utero. Such a relatively long
time will be necessary not because Romanians lack the intelligence or in-
dustriousness necessary to work toward that ultimate goal, but because it
will take more than one postcommunist generation to change deep-rooted
mentalities and modes of behavior that are inimical to an open society. For
Romanians to be allowed the opportunity to make these transitions, to complete the gestation period and successfully give birth to an open society, they

will also have to be spared serious upheavals in the country, the region, or the world. Many things can derail progress.

Only 10 to 15 percent of Romania's population of 23 million can be considered middle class. Ten and a half million today live below the official poverty level, and nearly 12 million more are daily concerned with the possibility of joining the former. At least half the people live in the countryside or are first-generation city folk, but literacy is relatively widespread. The economy cannot be classified as a truly market one. A civil society is barely mushrooming, and the legal system is slowly reforming but is by no means independent, and it has yet to instill the rule of law. The political culture is ill-developed, showing only a patina of tolerance for any kind of pluralism, and the concept of citizenship is in its infancy. And, unfortunately, there are yet no new leadership cadres sufficiently knowledgeable, competent, and politically mature to serve the stated desideratum of reaching a liberal democracy or a truly open society.

The people's democratically oriented sociopolitical and cultural re-education, a function the mass media and the sociopolitical leadership have thus far been unwilling or unable to carry out, remains a slow, trial-and-error, autodidactic one. To put it another way, the mass media have not been able to contribute to what Dahrendorf (1990, 105) calls filling "the gap between the state and the people—sometimes, as in Romania, one of frightening dimensions—with activities which by their autonomy create social sources of power." Until this is done in East-Central Europe in general, and Romania in particular, "the constitution of liberty and even the market economy, social or otherwise, will remain suspended in midair."

Yet, to reiterate, Romania is not an aberration among the former communist states. Unfortunately, thanks to foreign media coverage, Romania is often seen as the poor relation of East-Central Europe, the hopeless enfant terrible, the Balkan entity embodying all the negatives of the region. The foreign media first presented their audiences with the senseless barbarism of a bloody, confusing revolution and the summary execution of the Ceausescus. Then came stories of the Dark Ages–like conditions of Romania's orphanages, endemic corruption and dishonesty, poverty, nationalism and xenophobia, miners periodically invading and rampaging through Bucharest, and the stereotyped Gypsies as the representatives of the country. Last but certainly not least, there was the image of Romania as a country still led by communists, whether the "ex" or the "reformed" variety. For some reason Romania's retention in power of former or reformed communists seems to have been painted in far darker terms by the world's media than the return to power, or the acquisition of a share of power, or the retention in power of their Hungarian, Lithuanian, Ukrainian, Belarussian, Russian, Serbian, Croatian, Bulgarian or Polish counterparts (many of them relabeled socialists). Altogether, it was and still is a decidedly shallow, limited, one-sided presentation of Romania.

More specifically, many American organizations aiding journalism education and mass media evolution in East-Central Europe view Romania's news media as being uniquely immature and unprofessional and their progress particularly slow and troublesome. In travels to other East-Central European countries and examination of their news media, I found little divergence. And, allowing for strictly cultural and historical differences, there are strong similarities between Romania's news media and journalism and those of Poland, Hungary, Albania, Bulgaria and other East-Central European and former Soviet states.

Acutely aware of their image abroad, Romanians find that the negative news coverage of their country accentuates their general, national and individual tendency of alternating between a habitual Schopenhauerian view that life for them consists only of suffering and victimization, on the one hand, and a perspective of the most extreme hubris, on the other hand. The latter viewpoint is ultimately also tied to a kind of martyrdom or at the very least self-felt isolation from the rest of the mere mortals populating the near or distant environs. Yet as individuals, as a nation and in the situation in which they find themselves, they are neither as negative as they often perceive themselves and are perceived by others nor as exceptionally positive or unique as is their own view sometimes.

But there is the harsh, daily reality of their political and economic existence, and Romanians deal with it with a mixture of resignation, anger and humor. In 1990, when it became clear that former communists were predominant in the new government, that a former communist occupied the presidency, and that they were not going to be dislodged from power, a new group was formed alongside the Association of Former Political Prisoners: the Association of Future Political Prisoners. Yet Romania's present situation and near future are not quite that bleak, and incremental improvements have been recorded since 1989 in various aspects of society.

To make any progress toward an open society, Romanians must completely dismantle the communist system, rid themselves of communist mentalities, and install a new generation of leaders at every level of the economy—the political, judicial, social, cultural, educational, and mass media hierarchy. They must close that gap between the state and the people and between the intellectuals and other societal strata. Furthermore, they must mature as a nation, a process sidetracked and delayed by history numerous times since the mid-19th century, when all but the Transylvanian province which they claimed a part of their historical patrimony were united in an internationally recognized nation-state. Last but not least, they must develop a mass media system whose character is consonant with that of an open society and its requirements, reflects it and contributes to its maintenance and growth.

I am optimistic about Romania's chance to eventually evolve as a democratic nation. Its potential is certainly great when the available human and material resources are taken into consideration. Furthermore, I am optimistic about Romanian mass media's positive evolution in the next decade or two. In my view, they have the potential of reaching the same advanced level as the strongest and best of Western European mass media.

I have many people to thank for their direct and indirect contributions to this work, as well as the U.S. Information Agency, Voice of America, Freedom Forum, and International Media Fund for providing me with the opportunity to carry out research, consulting, teaching and lecturing in Romania. My thanks go to the press and cultural attaches and public affairs officers who served with the U.S. Embassy in Bucharest during the 1990–95 period and extended to me a helping hand and their friendship. My gratitude also goes to the hundreds of Romanians who have shared with me information and insights on the subject under consideration.

For their contributions to the substance of this work or their review of, advice on, or editing of the manuscript, I wish to single out Mihai Coman, Stefan and Dorotea Niculescu-Maier, Lia Trandafir and Gabriel Stanescu in Romania; and Ken Starck and Hanno Hardt (University of Iowa), Owen Johnson (Indiana University), Ray Hiebert (University of Maryland), Jerome Aumente (Rutgers University), Ion Manea (former Agerpres journalist now living in California), and Nestor Ratesh (Radio Free Europe) and the editors at Iowa State University Press in the United States. My wife, Vera, has my undying gratitude for her advice, editing and overall support. Any errata contained in this work are due to my shortcomings and not of those who have contributed to its completion. The majority of the translations from Romanian into English are also my doing, and I take full responsibility for them.

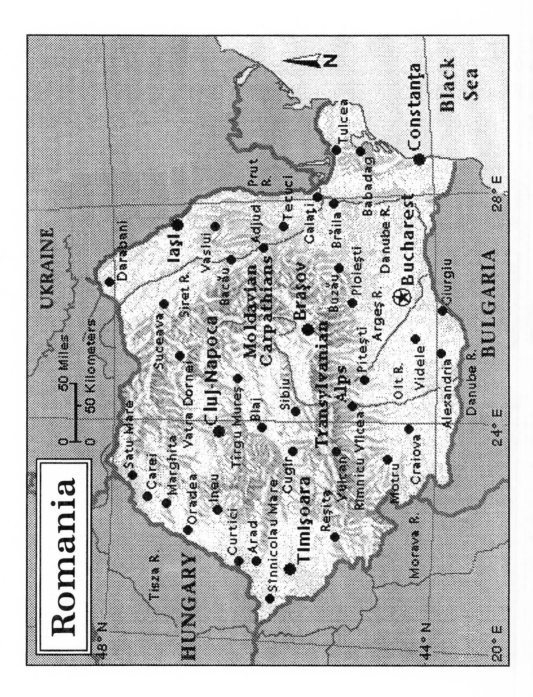

Mass Media in Revolution and National Development

The Romanian Laboratory

CHAPTER 1

The Legacy

As Romania's postrevolution journalists, journalism and mass media attempt to remold themselves in order to serve the perceived exigencies of the transition from communism to a would-be democracy and market economy, they are burdened by a historical portmanteau that encompasses a short yet tempestuous 170 years. During these years there was almost continuous censorship of one degree or another, and the journalism practiced seldom exhibited a professional quality that reached the world's highest standards of the day. The Romanian press and its journalism suffered the harsh vicissitudes reserved for those under direct or indirect physical or ideological foreign occupation and tyranny and the struggles for national unification and evolution from feudalism.

The legacies to present-day Romanian media, journalists and journalism are derived from three general time periods: (1) the 1821 to 1918 period, when the first Romanian-language newspapers, magazines and journalism were established and began evolving, (2) the 1920s, when the Romanian press and journalism achieved the most growth, freedom and (quasi) professionalism to date, and (3) the communist years, 1947–1989, when they virtually disappeared as viable, bona fide institutions and whose last decade constituted the nadir of their short history.

The Precommunist Legacy

For nearly a century before World War I, Romanians battled against foreign occupation and their feudal, monarchist system and strove to unify Romanian provinces into an internationally recognized nation-state. Their press mirrored the sociopolitical turmoil and nationalistic aspirations

3

of the people as well as the cultural and intellectual evolution in the Romanian provinces.

The Romanian press in these provinces was the young cousin of French, German, and Hungarian-language publications established in the 18th century, testimony to ethnic diversity and sociopolitical and cultural developments (Gross 1988). The rich history of the ethnic press in Romania includes publications established in the 19th century in Serbian, Bulgarian, Yiddish, Turkish, Albanian, Greek, Polish and Russian languages. They contributed to the rich cultural, political and social life of the region so gloriously described by Claudio Magris in his *Danube* (1989) and provide the theme of a separate study. The focus here is on the Romanian press.

1829–1918: A Brief History

From 1829, the year the first Romanian-language newspaper appeared in Bucharest and Iasi (Ivascu 1964; A. Ionescu 1913; Hanes 1927), to 1859, when the principalities of Wallachia and Moldavia were united under one Romanian banner, the infant press gave expression to a national consciousness and provided a forum for the discussion of Romanian problems. It supported and encouraged the legitimacy of Europe's 1848 revolutions, which in Romania had the additional goal of liberation from foreign subjugation. It also articulated nationalistic sentiments, informed its readers, gave journalistic life to the Romanian language and literature and served as a catalyst and mobilizer for national unification. Romania's new press showed considerable vitality and staying power despite prolonged periods of censorship—the practice of suspending newspapers that displeased the powers that be and imprisoning editors and journalists who were considered politically dangerous in monasteries or exiling them to foreign lands (Antip 1979).

The 1859–1918 period saw the introduction of the first press laws in Romania (1862), which proclaimed the right of individuals to express ideas through the press without fear of censorship. It was to be a short-lived period of press freedom, with the press being censored again and many newspapers and magazines being silenced altogether by 1864 (Ionescu-Dolj 1914). Between 1866 and the outbreak of the Franco-German War in 1870, when yet another conservative government was installed in Romania, the press again experienced relative freedom and prosperity.

The press of 1866-70 was a primarily political press, a party press whose main theme was independence from the Ottoman Empire. Autonomy was finally achieved in 1877. Romania became a kingdom and both political and journalistic life picked up, with a diversity of sociopolitical opinions being expressed in a growing number of newspapers and magazines (Olson 1966, 400–54; Antip 1979, 119–22; Chendi 1900).

This post-1877 press addressed the needs of Romanians at every point of the then-contemporary political spectrum, as well as those with specific professional, academic, intellectual and artistic interests. It was still primarily a political, polemical press. Yet in the last two decades of the 19th century a small number of newspapers made their national debut and gained respect for their political independence and impartiality. *Universul,* launched in 1884, and *Adevarul,* which began publication in 1888, were the first examples of newspapers that concentrated on news reporting rather than sociopolitical and personal polemics and partisan politics. *Adevarul*'s morning edition, *Dimineata,* first published in 1904, gained a reputation as the *New York Times* of Romania (Olson 1966, 402).

In Transylvania, a region yet to be incorporated into Romania, publications such as *Gazeta Transilvaniei, Telegraful Roman, Tribuna, Albina, Familia* and *Foaie pentru minte, inima si literatura,* among others, played a key role in nurturing Romanian political aspirations, language and literature.

The growth of the press at the end of the 19th century and in the first two decades of the 20th also brought a competitiveness that spurred an expansion in staffs and the establishment of a corps of foreign and domestic correspondents and stringers (J. Georgesco 1936). That era also saw the establishment of the first news service, Agentia Romana (Kruglak 1958), a modernization of printing plants (Antip 1979, 143–47), and the formation of the first Organization of Journalists in 1822 and the first Union of Journalists in 1900 (Caliga 1926). C. A. Rosetti, one of Romania's premier journalists, editors and publishers, envisioned a press staffed by professionals becoming a Fourth Estate in a civilized nation (see Rosetti 1889; Sept. 27, 1881).

The principal themes in the fin de siècle period and up to the end of World War I expressed in and by the press included land reform, social unrest and the plight of Romanians still living under the heels of the Russian, Ottoman, and Austro-Hungarian empires. Romania entered World War I on the side of the Allies on Aug. 18, 1916, but the country was quickly overrun by German Kaiser Wilhelm II's army. During the war anti-German newspapers were suspended and freedom of the press was sharply curtailed in those areas of the country occupied by German troops. The end of the war saw one cherished Romanian dream come true when Romania was given Transylvania, Bucovina and Bessarabia at the 1919 Paris Peace Conference, finally gathering under its banner all provinces claimed as its own.

For a brief moment in the aftermath of World War I, Romanian journalism began its attempt to professionalize. It was an attempt that was to spill into the 1920s. The dissemination of information, while still heavily mixed with the opinion of journalists, was at least one of the goals of some newspapers whose majority counterparts were party publications owned and staffed by highly politicized proselytizers for one or another political outlook or program (N. Iorga, 1922). The Romanian press between the two

world wars was not a mass media, with even the so-called national publications being distributed mainly in Bucharest and written by an elite for the so-
cioeconomic and political elite.

The 1920s, 1930s and World War II

Radio Bucharest-Romania began broadcasting on Nov. 1, 1928, and the
Rador news agency was established on June 16, 1921, an outgrowth of the
Agentia Romana launched in 1889. Most important, it was the 1920s that
brought the Romanian press to its furthest point of evolution and freedom
ever. The press experienced tremendous growth. One thousand and ninety
publications were in circulation in 1922 when the National Liberal Party
came to power. By 1936, about 2,300 publications (118 dailies, more than
1,200 weeklies, and almost 950 other publications) were offered to the reading public (J. Georgesco 1936, 147).

The proliferation of political parties was one reason for the explosion
of newspapers and magazines in what was still overwhelmingly a party press
system. Circulations increased, too, and the financial growth experienced by
many publications also allowed for investments in technical advances and
the modernization and multiplication of printing facilities (Antip 1979,
219–23). New publishing houses were established, adding to Romania's ca-
pability to produce more newspapers, magazines, and books. *Universul* acquired the first modern printing plant in Romania, a facility still functioning
in 1996.

The increasing number of journalism associations and unions signaled
a heightened concern with the professionalization of journalism, both for
professional education and standards and for the expansion and protection of
press freedoms and journalists' rights (Antip 1979, 223–29). These journalism organizations were instrumental in lobbying for changes in the press
laws that strengthened press freedom and enlarged the rights of journalists.

It was a journalistic era graced by Romania's 1923 constitution, one of
the most liberal in all of Europe, guaranteeing press freedom and banishing
censorship (Articles 5, 25, 26, 105). A press law was fine-tuned in 1922,
1923 and 1925, clearly defining press freedom and recognizing the need for
the free expression of diverse ideas and thoughts. At the same time, the ruling National Liberal Party government passed the Laws for the Repression
of Infractions against Public Order (known as the Mirzescu law) in 1924,
augmented in 1927 and 1933, legalizing official censorship in contravention
to the constitution and the operative press laws (Watts 1993, 166).

Reading the newspapers of those days[1] reveals that the journalism practiced in this nation whose elite was overwhelmingly Francophone was
highly subjective, polemical and partisan. Continuing a standing tradition,

the crème de la crème of Romanian arts and letters, of its vibrant intellectual class, was intimately involved with politics and the journalism of opinions, analysis and testing of ideas. Writers like Liviu Rebreanu and Mihail Sadovenau, university professors like Nicolae Iorga and Nae Ionescu, to name just a few, were the stars of Romanian journalism. They commented on all of the major issues and happenings and thus brought information and views to the readers. However, news reporting that steered away from the subjectivity of political partisanship, that did not include editorialization and polemics, was not to be found in the great majority of Romania's press. Yet the concept and the practice of objectivity were growing. The older independent newspapers, *Universul, Adevarul* and *Dimineata,* were joined by a few new ones that practiced a form of nonpartisan journalism geared to neutral reporting and its separation from editorials and polemics (J. Georgesco, 1936). The political Left was represented most prominently by *Cuvintul Liber,* edited by Tudor Teodorescu-Braniste. It was a forum for balanced presentations of sociopolitical opinions, politically pluralist in nature, quite unlike other leftist publications such as *Santier, Era Noua, Manifest, Reporter,* and *Bluze albastre* (Ierunca 1994, 36–37).

The brief period of press freedoms, journalists' rights, and evolution of professionalization came to a halt with the growth of fascism in the early 1930s and the establishment of a royal dictatorship. The brief royal dictatorship was followed by the neofascist dictatorship of Gen. Ion Antonescu. In 1937 the introduction of new censorship measures allowed for the banning of newspapers, among them three major national newspapers, *Adevarul, Dimineata,* and *Lupta.* Former Prime Minister Armand Calinescu, who was anti–Iron Guard (the fascist group active in the 1930s and the early 1940s), is quoted in Watts's revisionist work (1993, 167) to have said that General Antonescu, at that time the minister of national defense, "requested the removal of censorship" with the resulting removal of the ban on the three newspapers. Adding to the controversy surrounding Antonescu, his role before and after he assumed dictatorial powers in 1940 and, indirectly, his commentary on the contemporary, controlled press and its journalism, Watts (1993, 277) quotes the general as having told his minister of propaganda that he

> no longer wanted to see in the journals descriptions of crimes which excite the bestial sentiment of men. And then there are the sensational trials. No one had need to comment upon them in the press, but rather to recount, pure and simple, the sentences handed down as is done in England, not to fill whole columns of newspapers with frivolous commentary.

The reality of the 1930s and the 1940s, up to the end of World War II, was that the press became harried, timid, highly censored or muzzled altogether. Finally only the neofascist press retained a free hand (Gross 1988), despite cries for a free press as the very basis for a free society and as a guarantor to other freedoms. A mixture of restrictive legislation and economic hardship shrank the press down to 970 publications in 1941 (Gheorghiu 1991, 11), nearly a 58 percent loss since 1936.

George Silviu (1936, 3), writing on behalf of the Union of Journalists against the new laws suppressing freedom of the press, argued,

> Its [freedom of the press] presence constitutes a guarantee for progress. That is why we are rising, with all our energy, to the defense of this principle which is freedom of the press! ... [E]ach freedom protects the other freedoms and, together, they protect our spiritual and physical integrity.

In a move not to be matched later during the communist period, journalists and printers who were not contributing to the fascist press during World War II brought out underground newspapers whose journalism sought to mobilize democratic elements to resist Romanian fascism and German Nazism. Many of these underground publications were financed by the Comintern (Communist International) and had their own agenda quite separate from fighting Nazism and fascism. Their journalists were relentlessly hunted by Romania's security forces as well as by the German gestapo, and many were shot or sent to concentration camps. (Olson 1966, 406)

The end of World War II saw an almost immediate return to the prefascist days of a diverse, vigorous, freewheeling press, protected by the reinstituted liberal press laws of the 1920s and the democratic 1923 constitution. It was to be only a very brief return to the promising start of an evolving press and journalism serving a would-be democracy.

The Communist Era

Backed by Soviet troops stationed in Romania, the small (an estimated 1,000-strong membership in a nation of 17 million) Romanian Communist Party took over the government in 1947. Any hope of retaining the freewheeling, diverse press that returned after World War II concluded and the 1926 constitution that was reinstituted along with the liberal press laws vanished with the installation of Petru Groza's communist government.[2]

The Ministry of Propaganda, first instituted by the neofascist government in the mid-1930s and abolished after the war, was reinvented by the communists. A Press Directorate was set up in the ministry to oversee the Romanian media. Censorship became the natural order of things (Boila 1956). At first the communist press, embodied in *Scinteia,* had to compete head-to-head with the remaining independent press. Silviu Brucan, one of the first editors of *Scinteia,* writes in his memoirs, *Generatia Irosita* (1992, 50), that for a time some noncommunist newspapers appeared, "some of them professionally very well made, we were forced to compete. The battle for readers was fierce." Ultimately the battle for readers was less important than the political battle, won by the communists, who killed off all media other than the communist one. Only the journalists who were willing to abide by the new Marxist-Leninist definition of journalism were allowed to write. It would get worse.

Control over Mass Communications and Information

The communist era can roughly be outlined as follows:

First Stage (1947–1965). Closure of the old and attempts at stabilizing the newly established communist regime.

Second Stage (1965–1971). Attempts at softening the face of communism, a degree of openness to some Western media, books, and the like.

Third Stage (1971–1978). Romania's version of China's cultural revolution, with a highly nationalist theme and the push to create "the new socialist man." (Its culmination came in 1976 with Cantarea Romaniei and Daciada.)

Fourth Stage (1978–1989). The dominance of an ever-increasing personality cult and Stalinist dictatorship.

Nicolae Ceausescu came to Romania's presidency on March 19, 1965, and until he consolidated his power at the end of that decade there was a thinly veiled attempt to put a human face on the totalitarian system. During this period the mass media, journalism and entertainment experienced a slight easing in censorship and a loosening of the (tight) reins controlling them (Fein and Bonnell 1965, Gaspard 1965). The jamming of foreign broadcast had already stopped the year before Ceausescu came to power (Paulu 1974, 217), there was a small trickle of incoming foreign press, and foreign books and films not overtly anticommunist were available.

By the time Ceausescu returned from his visit to China and North Korea in 1971, the mask of liberalization began to fall off, and the Romanian version of China's cultural revolution was launched alongside a fast-growing personality cult (Shafir 1985, 176–80). A Reuters news agency dispatch from Vienna (July 7, 1971) discusses Ceausescu's new directives calling for "stronger revolutionary propaganda in all reaches of society, especially in schools and the entertainment and cultural world." The directives also called for the enhancement of "the educational and socialist role of radio and tv programs."

Communism in Romania, as elsewhere in East-Central Europe, became "merely a question of power," as Kolakowski writes (1978, 465), and attempted control over all means of communication and information (Kolakowski 1989). The informational isolation imposed on Romanians extended from the nonconvertibility of Romanian money, the leu (plural, *lei*), and the closing of the borders restricting Romanians from traveling abroad to forbidding free association, contacts with foreigners and religious freedoms. It also included the official closing of borders to Western books, new movies and music; hypersecrecy encompassing even the most banal data and information; and the theoretical and real possibility of being incarcerated for listening to Western radio. The inefficiency of the Romanian telecommunications system—the telephone, telegraph and such—as well as its monitoring and control by the communist authorities further contributed to the informational isolation of the population. The Romanian people no longer had control over their own lives, and therefore their society was unable to steer itself. As Deutsch (1966, 129) characterizes totalitarian societies in which the information flow is highly controlled, Romanian society became "an automaton, a walking corpse" for lack of information about the outside world, its own past, and "itself and its own parts."

The Securitate, the Romanian version of the Soviet KGB, sifted through incoming and outgoing foreign correspondence and monitored all foreign telephone conversations and many domestic ones. Radio-Television and Agerpres (the Romanian news agency) were owned by the state (Decree 690, 1973 and Decree 474, 1977). All publications were owned by the state, the Communist Party or one of their organs or by community groups, which were themselves controlled by the party.

By the early 1970s the lines between state and party became highly blurred with the establishment of organs of double nature (state-party). The supremacy of the party in all walks of life and endeavors became the sine qua non of Romanian society (Vlad 1972, Ceausescu 1972, Radulescu 1973, Anghene 1974, Busuioc 1974). The function of the media and their organizations were officially under the direct leadership of the party and state (Ceterchi, April 4, 1974), with the party leadership being in de facto control and serving as what Lendvai (1981, 25) calls "the supreme board of directors of gigantic multi-media" company.

The means of information and communication production—the television and radio studios, the printing and publishing resources—were all centralized under state-party control, specifically the Press Section of the Central Committee of the Communist Party led by Dumitru Popescu, secretary for press and propaganda. According to Mihai Coman (1994), dean of the new School of Journalism at the University of Bucharest and himself a former contributor to communist-controlled *Tineretul Liber,* the media received "by centralized decision—the needful [*sic*] shares for paper, electricity, salaries, materials facilities. All the costs were subsidized, so that the prices of production and distribution were lower than the real expenses."

By 1975 the multimedia monopoly in Romania controlled by the party could boast of offering Romanians, including the various coexisting ethnic groups, 472 publications, among them 57 dailies. It also had 47 radio stations broadcasting 40,329 hours of programs and Romanian Television with its two-channel format broadcasting 4,642 hours of programs through 27 television outlets using 180 transmitters (Horlamus 1976, 177).

The reorganization of the mass media in 1974 resulted in tighter control by the Communist Party and a relative shrinking of the size of the Romanian media. Illyes (1982, 251) writes,

> Various publications were merged, changes in content were introduced, and censorship was increased. This measure was accompanied by mass dismissals of editorial personnel. Those viewed as "liberal" were replaced by conformists: retaining one's job was based on "loyalty," and the degree of governmental control over the press was thereby increased.

Stringent party control over the media was codified in the 1974 press law (*Buletinul Oficial,* no. 48, April 1, 1974) and slightly augmented and altered at the end of 1977 (*Buletinul Oficial,* no. 3, Jan. 19, 1978). The law outlined everything from the sociopolitical function of the media to its organization and relationship with state, public organization and organs, and citizens, as well as the duties and rights of journalists. To some degree, from time to time, the literary, sport, scientific and student publications were able to deviate from a strict observance of the law, thanks in large measure to individual efforts and the uneven monitoring by responsible personnel.

The organization and function of radio and television were further defined by Decree No. 473 (*Buletinul Oficial,* Dec. 24, 1977). Ceausescu and his regime achieved the establishment of what Jakubowicz (1990) calls a "monocentric system of uniformizing communications," only in Romania it was taken to an extreme. Ceausescu's socialist system perfected and tightened an already stultifying Marxist-Leninist mass media system described in the harshest, most unforgiving and uncompromising ways by Buzek (1964), Kecskemeti (1950), and Schramm (1956), among many others.

In his analysis of the Romanian communist press law, the Romanian-born German attorney Leonhardt (1974) writes that with the exception of the

Romanian constitution, there was no legal document which more clearly expressed the party's totalitarian claim than the press law. Seven years after its enactment, its intent was reaffirmed when it was pointed out that it "serves the primary purpose of establishing party control over the entire press, legally linking it to the politics of the party, to raise the people's consciousness and *to thwart the development of any liberal tendencies*" (Cismarescu 1981, 83, emphasis added).

The press law was written under the "direct leadership" (Ceterchi 1974) of Ceausescu, who further involved himself in the approval of editorships, reporters' assignments, foreign travel and even the content of the media (Lendvai 1981, I. Manea 1986). Article 2 of the 1974/77 press law spelled out the party's control by stating that the mass media "carries out its activities under the leadership of the Romanian Communist Party—the leading political force of the entire society." Whether dealing with freedom of the press, organization of the press, the press's responsibility and politico-ideological and educational roles or the journalists' responsibilities, rights, duties, education and certification, Romania's press law emphasized the party's dictatorial rule (Leonhardt 1974), which extended even to the work of accredited foreign correspondents (Gross 1990b).

By 1977 all media operations were placed under the authority of the Council for Socialist Education and Culture (*Buletinul Oficial,* Nov. 8, 1977) which, de jure, was subordinate to both the Central Committee of the Romanian Communist Party and to the Council of Ministers. De facto, the Communist Party was in control of the Romanian mass media, which were, in Ceausescu's own words (Sept. 10, 1977) and viewed as a single entity, "an instrument of the party and has to disseminate the party's policies in all of its spheres of activity."

Agerpres, Romania's national news agency, was reorganized into eight departments in 1977.[3] It was responsible for covering the national scene and for disseminating all Communist Party documents and news to the domestic media, whose space and time it successfully monopolized, severely cutting down or eliminating other news items. Agerpres was the gatekeeper of all incoming foreign news reports as well as the official disseminator of all Romanian news (precensored) to foreign news agencies with which it had reciprocal agreements. The agency was also responsible for hosting all foreign correspondents accredited to Romania, for publishing a number of foreign-language magazines for distribution abroad and for publishing foreign news digests, or special bulletins. The latter products were distributed in three versions: a yellow bulletin to a select few party and state officials and some editors in chief, a red bulletin to a larger circle of party and state functionaries and editors and a green bulletin containing mainly economic reports.

Control over the mass media increased in the 1980s as the views of

Ceausescu and his Communist Party became more doctrinaire and defensive in the face of changes gradually taking hold in other East-Central European communist countries (Banta 1988; Echikson 1989a; Reichman 1988; Tagliabue, Dec. 2, 1987; Willey and Nagorski 1987). Glasnost was rejected in no uncertain terms by Ceausescu and his regime (Willey and Nagorski 1987, Banta 1988).

As the 1980s came to an end, the number of dailies had fallen to 36 (National Statistical Commission 1992), only nine national and local radio stations were on the air, and Romanians had only one television channel. Broadcasting only three hours per day, Romanian Television's Channel 1 reached 90 percent of the country, while its Channel 2 reached 18 percent of the nation around the capital city of Bucharest (Media Monitoring Unit 1992). Ceausescu is reported to have said that the highly restricted broadcasting schedule was due to his concern that people not stay up too late because "I did not want to tire the population" (Bohlen and Haberman 1990). The truth was that this significant decrease in the number of indigenous mass communication outlets, and in television's case the reduced broadcasting hours, was due to the nation's economic woes brought about by a centrally (mis)managed economy and the regime's focus on paying off its foreign debt as well as to the exigencies of tighter party control.

In large measure, audiences tuned out their indigenous media. Only 22 percent regularly watched Romanian Television, and 43 percent regularly read Romanian newspapers; Romanian Radio, however, attracted 69 percent of the population (USIA Research Memorandum, June 14, 1990).

Journalists as "Party Activists" and "Communist Fighters"

Ceausescu (1972, 249–50) insisted that the Romanian journalist be "a communist fighter" and that all journalists be "party activists" in the media sphere. Regardless of whether the journalists did or did not accept this designation, there was no alternative available to them given the media monopoly enjoyed by the Communist Party and state. They were, as a Hungarian journalist working for the *Financial Times* of London characterized his would-be counterparts in East-Central Europe, the "victims of a system that often treats them as cogs in the vast propaganda machine" (Lendvai 1981, 103). According to Silviu Brucan (1992, 51), one of the editors of *Scinteia* in its first postwar years, all journalistic zeal was lost a few years after the establishment of communism, and journalists became "functionaries." Whether they ever had any journalistic zeal is questionable. They did have politico-propagandistic zeal and that, it seems, was lost by the old guard and never acquired by the young one.

The profession of journalist and, according to former Agerpres employee Ion Manea (1985), the right to practice it, had ceased to exist:

> Those who are enlisted on payrolls under this category (journalist) are actually treated as a kind of "bureaucrat" on the lower rungs of such a ladder. They must have no personality at all; they must possess the ability of transcribing *ad litteram* the orders received from the Press Department of the Communist party; and, last but not least, they must be endowed with a professional mask to hide their own feelings and ideas.

At the rare press conferences held by Romania's supreme leaders, the questions to be asked by the journalists selected to attend were given them by the Press Section of the Central Committee of the Communist Party. This was not a matter of professional socialization and social control in the newsroom as may be the case in Western democratic societies (Epstein 1973, Gans 1979, Tunstall 1971), or even a professionalism based on a commitment to an established order. Rather, it was the kidnapping of a profession, its emasculation and its exploitation for propagandizing and mobilization purposes as defined by the ruling party. A 1992 article in *Cotidianul,* the newspaper published by Ion Ratiu (an émigré who returned to Romania after the revolution and was the presidential candidate of the Peasant Party in the May 1990 elections), characterized journalism under communism as a "defiled profession." It was a profession in which the journalist had to become the "accomplice or ally" of the party that used the media as "an instrument of moral genocide" (Ionescu, Oct. 2, 1992).

These journalists, "bureaucrats" (I. Manea 1985), "functionaries" (Brucan 1992), or "public officials" (Kecskemeti 1950), came from different educational backgrounds. Most of them were university graduates in a variety of social and humanities disciplines, yet some held only a high school diploma. Fewer than one-third of working "journalists" were graduates of the Communist Party's Stefan Gheorghiu Academy journalism program, where the curriculum consisted of 45 percent political and ideological indoctrination and 55 percent literature and linguistic course work (Gross and King, 1993).

Romania was a signatory to the 1975 Final Act of the Conference on Security and Cooperation in Europe (the Helsinki Act), which called for, among other things, an improvement of the circulation of, access to and exchange of information and cooperation in the field of information. It also called for an improvement of working conditions for journalists. However, this act made no difference to the work and working conditions of Romanian journalists who, beginning in 1974, were made subject to the new press law. That law clearly spelled out the limits of their professionalism.

Romanian journalists were held strictly accountable to carry out their duties in accordance with the new law, under threat of being punished with "disciplinary, material, civil or criminal penalties" (Art. 90). Article 40 of the press law outlined those duties as consisting of, among other things,

a. contributing with all ... abilities to the achievement of the sociopolitical functions of the press as established in the law and in RCP documents;
b. devotedly serving the cause of socialism and communism, and fighting to set into practice the internal and external policies of the party and state;
c. fighting to promote the revolutionary spirit in all facets of socialist life and to fight against "statism, conservativism and routine" and against everything that might "curb the forward movement of society"; and
d. proving ... ethical and professional standards, ... objectivity and responsibility, to respect the laws and secrets of the state, and to fight for truth.

These professional and ethical standards were defined by the state, or rather by the controlling Communist Party as represented by Ceausescu. Romania's journalists-bureaucrats were obliged to obey Article 69 of the press law that forbade them to publish or broadcast any materials that:

a. were hostile to the Constitution of the Socialist Republic of Romania;
b. contain attacks against the socialist order, against the RCP and the SRR's principles of foreign and domestic policy;
c. defame the leadership of the state and party;
d. encourage disrespect for the laws of the state or those that encourage the commitment of deeds which constitute infractions of the law.

The political, ideological, and educational roles of the Romanian media and the journalists were dictated in Articles 7 through 16. Journalists more or less faithfully carried out their duty, even if the majority were not zealous supporters of the regime or of Marxist-Leninist ideology. After the 1989 revolution, communist-era journalists explained that during 42 years of communism they had to learn to cover up real, meaningful, truthful information. Over the last 25 years they also had to learn to be "two-faced" about their feelings and professional standards.[4]

Control over and punishment of journalists for not following the letter or spirit of the law resulted in the loss of licenses, absence of advancements, denial of foreign travel permits, demotions, firings or imprisonment (Gross 1990b, c). In order to avoid to some degree the straitjacket imposed upon them, those who wished to practice at least a (restricted) form of bona fide journalism gravitated to sports reporting, or to some literary magazines.[5]

Some also gravitated toward Romanian Radio. Ceausescu, for some reason, considered radio less than important. Consequently, radio journalists, albeit also within certain narrow parameters, had the opportunity to practice a relatively more professional journalism.[6] Furthermore, Romanian Radio also employed students and, therefore, was able to school them in a (quasi) professionalism absent in the corps of journalists serving television and the print media. Many others who might have entered the field of journalism chose other careers only to give them up after December 1989 and pursue their journalistic interests (see chapters 3 and 4). Those who continued to work for Romania's communist press and television toed the communist line and used the approach, form and language prescribed by their political bosses.

Overall, Romanian journalism completely disappeared as a profession by the end of the 1970s. Eugen Preda, the director general of Romanian Radio from 1990 to 1995 and a Romanian journalist with extensive experience as a foreign correspondent in the West, argues that the Ceausescu regime's policies destroyed whatever professional culture still existed. It was impossible to practice real journalism, he said.[7] All Romanian foreign correspondents were recalled in 1977 after a series of defections; contacts with Western journalists in Romania were forbidden, and foreign newspapers and journals were no longer available to Romanian journalists for perusal.

Foreign journalists were also held accountable by the communist regime for their work while in Romania, work that was also judged on the basis of the 1974/77 press law (Gross 1990b). They were severely handicapped in a variety of ways in their pursuit of news stories (Lendvai 1981, 238–47). The barriers to reporting in Romania were, in some respects, more difficult to overcome than in other East-Central European nations, save perhaps Albania and Bulgaria (Klebnikov, Feb. 8, 1989; Echikson, Jan. 31, 1989b). Expulsions were not uncommon. In the two years preceding the December 1989 revolution, two French Television reporters and a correspondent from *Le Figaro* and *Le Nouvelle Observateur,* as well as an American correspondent for the *New York Tribune,* were kicked out of Romania for attempting to talk to dissidents Doina Cornea, Mariana Botez and a few others who began to openly voice their opposition to the regime in the 1980s. The expulsions of foreign journalists, the refusal of entry visas to them and their harassment continued into the last few weeks before the revolution (Riding, Nov. 21, 1989).

The absence of foreign correspondents as witnesses and recorders of the unfolding events in the December 15–22, 1989, period contributed to the world's confusion regarding what was transpiring in Romania in the first days of the revolt in the city of Timisoara. Exaggerated stories about the number of dead, rumors and other unsubstantiated, unverifiable information were passed on to the global audience by foreign media who received their information only secondhand at best. By the evening of Dec. 22, foreign journalists had entered Romania in droves and, as Robert Kaplan writes in his 1993 political travel book (*Balkan Ghosts,* p. 98), "for the first time since January 1941, journalists once again filled up the rooms of Bucharest's hotels." They also filled hotel rooms in other parts of the country and paid the price of reporting from a war zone. In Timisoara, four correspondents were shot and wounded (Associated Press, Dec. 25, 1989). Audiences all across the globe began to get better acquainted with Romania and what was happening in that country.

Censorship and Self-censorship

In the 1970s censorship in Romania became all-pervasive. With the advent of the 1974 press law, censorship changed from the positive and aggressive mode to being, as Gyorgy Konrad (1984) observes, "negative and defensive. Before, it used to tell you what to say. Now it advises you what not to say. ... In a totalitarian situation, censorship cannot be formalized."

Indeed, in 1977 censorship was officially abolished by the Central Committee of the Communist Party after the 11th Party Congress. The official censor, the Committee on Press and Other Print Media, was dissolved by Decree No. 472 (*Buletinul Oficial,* Dec. 27, 1977). There were two major consequences to this "democratization."

One was the institutionalization of censorship at the micro level of the individual newspaper, magazine or radio or television station, as demonstrated by the assignment of censors from the Committee on Press and Other Print Media to the leadership councils of individual media (Gabanyi 1978; Index on Censorship, No. 6, 1978) and to the Council of Socialist Culture and Education (I. Manea 1985). The latter was given the responsibility for media matters. Lendvai writes (1981) about this council,

> It is in fact the council which now acts as the supreme censorship body in fact if not in name, with political and ideological responsibility for publication, imports and control of the "lists of data and information supplied to papers which according to law are not permitted to be printed." The council has also the power to confiscate the offending issues prior to legal proceedings, to allocate paper, to appoint journalists and to control their activity.

The second consequence was the internalization of self-censorship (already exercised to one degree or another since 1947) to a much greater extent than before. It also heightened mutual surveillance or "collegial censorship" under a system of "collective leadership" and "self-responsibility." As the parameters of what could and should be published and broadcast shrank and the megalomania of Romanian leadership increased along with its pathological defensiveness, paranoic self-censorship became more acute. It was safer to choose only those subjects which were on Ceausescu's informational menu of the day and treat them in the stultifying newspeak of communist rhetoric which served the communist ideology and its goals. Ceausescu (June 30, 1977) considered the prescribed Marxist-Leninist orientation of all journalists to constitute in itself a form of self-censorship:

> We do not have, I repeat again, more than one philosophical conception in Romania. We only have one: dialectical and historical materialism. This is actually the only kind of censorship and we have no need for any other. It has to assure the elimination of everything which does not correspond to our conception of our world.

The "abolition" of censorship, the new means of controlling what, in what form and with what meaning was published or aired, was still not enough. By the 1980s, censorship was further strengthened. It was "doubled, tripled, diversified, while the 'purification'" of journalistic and literary texts "took on new and ever more duplicitous methods" (N. Manea 1992, 68). It increased the involvement of colleagues to make them more responsible for each other but also lessened responsibility by allowing them to "pass the buck" if something should ultimately not please the Ceausescus. Before publication an article could pass through the hands of as many as six people: the editor, the assistant editor, the section editor, (and on the day of publication) the individual responsible for the particular issue, a party activist who acted as supervisor, and the copyreader.

As a result journalism and journalists utterly failed to survey the Romanian or global environment for their readers, listeners and viewers. Only the ruler's views and visions of society and its many facets were presented, destroying any norms of truth and reality. Former Agerpres journalist Ion Manea (1985) describes the process of "newsreporting" in the following manner:

> Every Tuesday afternoon he who is responsible for the direction of the Romanian Press summons all the chief editors of Bucharest for a long meeting. He gives a detailed address as to what is to be written and what is not to be written during the following week. He dictates a series of articles on several subjects.
>
> On that same evening the Party newspaper sends them to be printed exactly as the way [sic] they had been dictated. The "normative" articles are being printed in the pages of the other papers by the second day. It is quite possible that at the meeting of the following week, the same person

> may vehemently criticize the articles of the preceding week, including those that had been dictated by himself. ... Everything takes on the appearance of a scene from Kafka.

Censorship and self-censorship did away with any notion of seeking out accurate and complete information for purposes of presenting a truthful panorama of Romanian society in all its facets. Truth was that which served Ceausescu and his regime, thereby the Orwellian lie was firmly entrenched, along with the language designed to serve it, in every so-called news, feature, analysis and opinion piece that was published and broadcast. This multitude of self-censored "journalists," in Codrescu's inimitable words (1990, 26), "were hallucinations of the bureaucracy whose existence served only to give the hallucinating censors something to measure loyalty by."

And it was not only words that were censored and self-censored. Photographs of current events as well as historical photographs were also tampered with before publication to suit the images desired by the leadership. These doctored photographs created a visual counterpart to the "wooden language" which descended like a heavy fog over the journalists' and the public's consciousness (see the subsequent section of this chapter entitled Orwellian Newspeak).

It was a classic case of totalitarianism, with its attendant pervasive censorship, in which truth was defined by the totalitarian regime, its censors and self-censored journalists. Truth, by way of a multitude of verifiable information and diverse views, was dangerous to a regime whose legitimacy was never firmly established and whose need to keep up the myth of the infallibility of socialism, of the nation's leadership and of its popular support was all-important.

The combination of a censorship apparatus *and* a system of self-censorship allowed very little leeway for journalists to act as bona fide reporters and was, to the degree that self-censorship was exercised and combined with prepublication or prebroadcasting censorship, unique in East-Central Europe. Hungary and Bulgaria had a self-censorship system, while in Poland the communist regime applied prior censorship through a formal censorship system (Curry 1984), as did East Germany. Only Yugoslavia had a looser censorship system that allowed the press some latitude in carrying out a journalistic function (Robinson 1977, Schopflin 1983).

Censorship in Romania created three informational worlds:

1. An official, overt informational world that was intended to manipulate, obfuscate and dissimulate for regime-defined purposes.

2. A covert, debilitating informational world on the interpersonal level, consisting of rumors developed on the basis of partial or false information

in the absence of an independent, credible indigenous mass communication system.

3. An informational world tied to the foreign, Western mass communication system to be discussed in chapter 2.

Manipulation, Pseudojournalism and Metareality

Romania's controlled media had strictly defined politico-ideological, agitation, educational or indoctrination, and mobilizations duties. It was a product "not unlike shoes and whose output is measured by 'good results'" (Gross 1990c). The media's very existence was justified by the intended results and their functions, which were to be unfailingly tied to their mission of fulfilling "the general policy of the Romanian Communist Party, in the construction of multilaterally developed socialist society and in the building of communism ... " (Preamble to the 1974/77 Press Law). Therefore, a definition of journalism and its practice was limited to

a. feeding the personality cult surrounding President Ceausescu and his family;

b. revealing and explaining party-state policies;

c. carrying out politico-ideological education or indoctrination, propaganda and agitation;

d. mobilizing for regime-defined economic, social, cultural and political goals; and

e. defending against and pre-empting foreign attacks on conditions in Romania or on the nation's or regime's policies.

The ideological function of mass media and their journalists, the need to "present things as they should be, not as they are," as Coman (1994) writes, led to a highly selective gatekeeping function intimately and exclusively tied to the values espoused by the Communist Party, its leader(s) and the goals they wished to achieve. Therefore, print and broadcast journalism per se were eliminated. In their stead Romanians received a diet of predigested, inauthentic, repetitive, highly limited information meant to persuade, assuage, encourage, warn, distract and dissimulate. The ignoring of events and ideas, their distortion or their invention was a daily occurrence (Lendvai 1981, 68–70; Gross, 1990c, d).

The only authentic pieces of information found in the pages of newspapers were the obituaries and sports reports or occasionally, if and when it suited the regime's policies, some foreign news reports. The latter, too, with only few exceptions, were mostly inauthentic, manipulative and dissimulating in nature (Gross, 1990c, d) or simply ignored major issues and happenings.

For instance, despite close politico-diplomatic ties and ideological affinities to China, Romania's mass media did not inform their publics in the aftermath of Mao's death of the "gang of four," the trial and conviction of Mao's widow, Deng Xiaoping's reforms, or the student protests that brought down Hu Yaobang. Such reports would have endangered the notion of a Ceausescu dynasty, of the pre-eminent Communist Party and media themes of "unity," "continuity," "modernization" (without change) and the infallibility of communist leaders or their policies.

One other major example of the convenient disregard of major international topics was the lack of coverage accorded to the fall 1987 suspension by the U.S. Congress of Romania's most favored nation (MFN) status. It was not until February 1988 that *Scinteia,* the party's mouthpiece, published an article in which it explained that the reinstitution of MFN would not be sought by Romania because the quid pro quo of observing the Jackson-Vanick amendment would constitute an inadmissible involvement in Romanian affairs (Gross 1990d).

Victor Ionescu, responsible for foreign news at Romanian Television before and after the revolution, recounts that after glasnost was instituted in the Soviet Union, that country no longer made it into the foreign news presented to Romanians.[8] Neither did Poland and Hungary, where major changes also began to take shape, and eventually Czechoslovakia, Bulgaria and the German Democratic Republic disappeared from Romania's foreign news reports. For Romanian Television, as for the rest of the country's mass media, the 1989 Tienanmen Square massacre of Chinese students never happened.

The dissimulation inherent in and practiced by the mass media was reciprocated by the population out of necessity, becoming "the effective (and ethically as well as politically debilitating) bridge between the domineering official and the societal supplicant ... " (Jowitt 1992). Some, such as dissident professor Mihai Botez, who was appointed Romanian ambassador to the United Nations in 1993 and ambassador to the United States in 1994, also suggest (1992) that the information chaos which existed in Romania created the perfect conditions for the growth of corruption that seeped into every facet of Romanian life. It should not be forgotten, however, that corruption was thriving even in precommunist days.

By the end of the 1980s the pages of Romania's print media as well as its television broadcasts were filled with official Communist Party documents and exhortations, Ceausescu's speeches and other domestic or international activities, political commentaries and propaganda. They included letters and poems dedicated to "the great leader" and mobilization attempts for politico-ideological goals and their celebrations. The cult of personality, the importance of ideology and political relevancy, all dressed in nationalistic garb, were the essentials of Romanian journalism. They were at the core of the Orwellian institutionalized lie, of the metareality created by the bureaucrats and pseudojournalists who were dominating the Romanian mass media.

There were some exceptions among Romania's media. Those exceptions were accidental, coming about as a result of individuals' manipulation of the system and its minions or sanctioned by the regime as a way of allowing some depressurization among certain quarters of the population. Also, some student publications constituted exceptions, such as Bucharest's *Viata Studenteasca* (which published the forbidden poems of Ana Blandiana) and *ING* (published by the Polytechnic), Iasi's *Dialog* and Cluj's *Echinox*.

Yet journalism in Romania, such as it was, was to be carried out only "within the functions and methods strictly defined by the party and ideology," as Buzek wrote back in 1964 (62) about totalitarian media systems. Schramm's (1956) communist press theory was perfected in Romania by the further narrowing of journalism's definition. It was then augmented to reflect the need to sustain a personality cult that outmatched that of Mao in China and Kim Il Sung in North Korea. In the aftermath of Ceausescu's downfall in 1989, Romanian editors and journalists acknowledged[9] that mass media's criteria of newsworthiness were exactly as Lendvai described in 1981 (87):

> anything related in any way to the life and activities of Nicolae Ceausescu, head of state and Secretary General of the Romanian Communist party, generally referred to as "the most beloved son of our nation," and, on festive occasions, as "the most genuine popular leader to emerge in the entire history of the Romanian people" or "the most remarkable statesman of our modern history."

For the overworked, underfed, cold, humiliated, manipulated Romanians, the gap between their life and their experiences and the pseudo- and metareality presented to them by their mass media grew to such proportions that they no longer sought out information on the pages of their newspapers, in their television news programs or even in their radio news programs (Coman 1993). The manipulation of information, the act of dissimulation which was passed off as "reporting of news," destroyed the very notion of truth or at least the ability to construct such truth on the basis of neutral, multifaceted, verifiable information. Yet, Kolakowski (1983, 127) was wrong when he suggested that "This is the great cognitive triumph of totalitarianism. By managing to abrogate the very idea of truth, it can no longer be accused of lying." Romanians, depending on their level of education and interest, either completely or partially, consciously or unconsciously, were cognizant that their news media were not giving them a view of reality, of the real happenings inside and outside the country. One of myriad political jokes in Ceausescu's Romania encapsulates the population's opinion of its own press (as well as supplying a commentary on the endemic shortage of basic hygiene-related items):

> —What do you think about *Scinteia*?
> —It's an excellent newspaper.
> —And *Romania Libera*?
> —Very good, too.
> —What about *Lumea*?
> —Oh, that one isn't any good. Its paper is too thick. It clogs the toilet.

The communist mass media, having lost whatever (little) credibility they had managed to acquire since 1947 (Merrill 1983, 86) and their roles limited to the perceived needs of their manipulators, could not bridge the chasm between themselves and their audiences. Therefore, they failed to be informers and surveyors of the society in which they functioned and even failed to fulfill the roles assigned them by the party and state. In the end, "they did not serve their audience or their manipulators; they did not mirror Romanian society, nor mold it in a manner intended by their manipulators." (Gross 1995).

Orwellian Newspeak

Czeslaw Milosz (1981) writes that totalitarian power can be maintained only through the control of language. Together with the attempted destruction of historical memory (Kolakowski 1983, Havel 1989), the institution of totalitarian language constituted the means by which the communist regime imposed its control, destroyed the old culture and attempted to install the new socialist culture and mold the new socialist citizen.

Language in Romania became the communist wooden language Francois Thom suggested had such devastating effects on culture, society and the very interactions between individuals and between the controlling regime and its subjects. Thom's (1989, 123) observations in her study of Orwellian newspeak in Soviet society and her conclusions are highly apropos to the situation created in Romania:

> Newspeak is complementary to economic planning. Deprived of economic initiative, society becomes deprived also of the power of speech. It can move neither into the practical world of economics nor into the symbolic worlds of linguistic creation. But it can freeze that society and force it to live in slow motion and to vegetate in extremely primitive forms. Each individual starts, as it were, from nothing and has to master language with-

out the benefit of the experience of others and without the power to transmit what he has learned. Each individual attempt remains isolated and society at large remains stagnant, because the movement of ideas, like the movement of goods, is blocked.

It was not just words such as *democracy, progress, justice, socialism, the people,* and *truth* that took on meanings of their own, devoid of reality. The value attached to other words, sentences and whole works took on the kind of unreal or duplicitous meanings that permeated all human relations. It was a new Romanian language that was forced on everyone, becoming the only language publicly spoken and written, a language that lost or never established its meaning as the ideology that created it lost or never established any meaning. Juliana Pilon (1992, 35), in discussing the introduction of this new, communist language, writes that "one became alienated from one's most immediate instrument of communication with one's innermost reality: language," in an experiment "never before attempted."

Critical examination of issues became impossible in this wooden language, with everyone being held "behind the bars" of the official syntax (Codrescu 1990, 99). The Romanian lost all possibility of individual expression, being forced to speak in the collectivizing newspeak, with its collectivizing meaning for collectivizing purposes. Each word in this contrived language, writes the Romanian-born exiled writer, professor, and National Public Radio commentator Codrescu (1990, 100), served "the function of obscuring vision, of cutting off the view, of dismissing the outside."

The success of imposing this wooden language upon journalists, writers and ultimately the entire population, has much to do with the self-censorship embarked on by the former two groups. The use of the prescribed language, part of the existing self-censorship and the abnegation of responsibility to the public, became at once a form of autoprotection and servitude.

This linguistic dictatorship was tied to an exclusive and all-inclusive ideology, which in turn was used to maintain a plain, ideologically devoid dictatorship and its dynastic aspirations. Havel (1989, 47) discusses this symbiotic relationship between ideology and language, writing that when ideology becomes more and more removed from reality, language becomes "a world of appearances, a mere ritual, a formalized language deprived of semantic contact with reality and transformed into a system of ritual signs that replace reality with pseudo-reality."

In McLuhanesque fashion, the medium became the message in Romania. Additionally, the new language, the Romanian newspeak, made "all other modes of thought impossible," as Orwell (1983, 246) articulates the problem, eliminating the possibility of a real public discourse on most subjects. Nicolae Manolescu (1991, 245), literary critic, professor, editor of *Ro-*

mania Literara and member of the new, post-Ceausescu parliament, defines the wooden language of communist days as a codified mode of expression, an ossified language, minimally transparent, "an ideal instrument through which the efficacy of an ideology is stolen, forcing its transformation into a body of dogmas, incapable of explaining real phenomena, and to foresee them: ultimately, to avert them."

In journalism, as in all other human endeavors in a communist society, the use of the wooden language signaled an abdication of the cognitive and the expressive. The thinking and feeling for everyone was accomplished by the leader(s) and the party. The people were simply relegated to the function of listening and, by implication, acquiescing to the leader(s)' vision of life, behavior, and so on (Wald, Sept. 28, 1990).

This wooden language, so harmful to "living in truth," was to survive the revolution and plague elements of the press and of public discourse in the immediate postrevolution period.[10]

The Underground Press and the Political Police

Ceausescu's regime "criminalized any form of opposition" (Tismaneanu 1992, 116). His dreaded Securitate made sure the message got through loud and clear. To make certain, at the very least, that opposition would not be allowed a public voice, the regime tightly controlled all means of public communications. It also controlled the private means of communications in an attempt to head off any organized opposition or noncontrolled information dissemination. For instance, the right to own a typewriter was strictly regulated beginning in 1977, and only individuals who obtained an authorization from the militia could acquire or keep their typewriters. Samples of writing from all typewriters were kept by the militia and had to accompany every request for authorization, which had to be annually renewed.

Dissidence was possible in Romania but expensive for those who embarked on that road. Imprisonment, house arrest, beatings, forced emigration or even death were the usual paybacks for any form of opposition to the Ceausescu regime. Consequently, opposition was limited, indirect and, as far as the intellectuals were concerned, couched in terms of defending Romanian culture, as K. Verdery so well describes the situation in her 1991 work, *National Ideology Under Socialism.*

However, a limited number of intellectuals committed individual acts of dissidence or opposition to the regime and even against Marxism-Leninism.[11] Most retreated into publishing novels or disappeared altogether from the national dialogue, combining a mental evasion with cynicism and double-talk. Several strikes by groups of workers, most notably in 1977 in the mining region of the Jiu Valley and in 1987 in Brasov, signaled to the regime and to the world that the population was, at the very least, dissatisfied with the regime's policies. Yet, on the whole, few Romanians had the stomach to take on the all-powerful organs of the Securitate and endure the wrath of the regime (Shafir 1985, Skilling 1989, Tismaneanu 1992). In the 1970s many Romanians, most of them intellectuals, managed to join those already in the diaspora. It is significant that there were no major anti-communist revolts in Romania, as occurred once or more in East Germany, Hungary, Poland and Czechoslovakia since the institution of communism in those nations in the 1940s. Stories of long-standing, organized dissident movements and clandestine labor unions (Randal, Jan. 9, 1990) are not verified.

Furthermore, by a combination of dissimulation, co-optation, control, repression, and appeals to nationalism, existing Romanian institutions such as the churches, the universities, the unions, and so forth were neutralized and eliminated as potential supporters of a dissident movement. There were other reasons for the lack of a major dissident movement and for the absence of institutions that could support such a movement in Romania, as Shafir (1985), Verdery (1991) and others have suggested. Whatever the explanations may be, valid or invalid, the result of the all-pervasive control and surveillance (particularly of the intelligentsia) was the total absence of an indigenous oppositional or alternative media. Unlike in other parts of the communist world where "Dissident journalists, usually operating illegally, have published—and have occasionally broadcast—versions of reality at odds with the official Communist version" (Mills, 1983, 182), in Romania this kind of free-lance journalism was generally nonexistent.

According to Skilling (1989) and Shafir (1985), the Hungarian minority in Romania was far more inclined, able and successful in establishing an underground press than the Romanian majority was. From 1981 to 1983, ten issues of *Ellenpotok* were circulated; from 1983 to 1986, the *Hungarian Press of Transylvania* "recorded not only the plight of the Hungarian minorities, but also the ills of Romanian society in general, and reported a number of strikes throughout the country" (Skilling 1989, 195).

These publications had no Romanian-language counterparts. Despite claims by journalists after the revolution of 1989 that they knew what was happening in the country and had contacts with those few who openly identified themselves in opposition to the regime or to communism,[12] no Romanian underground press was established. Dissident Radu Filipescu's leaflets stuffed into people's mailboxes did not constitute an underground press per se.[13] Neither did the one-page "newspaper" passed out on street corners in Bucharest about a year before the revolution, begun in Timisoara, brought down the Ceausescu regime. It was produced by Petre Mihai Bacanu, now the editor in chief of *Romania Libera,* along with Stefan Niculescu-Maier, Anton Uncu, Mihai Creanga and Alexander Chiroiu. Their "publication" was simply (but significantly) a denunciation of Ceausescu's regime, an act that resulted in their arrest on Jan. 24, 1989, and several months of solitary confinement in prison. Bacanu was freed last, on Dec. 22, 1989, and went straight to the editorial offices of *Romania Libera,* his old employer, where he was elected by the staff to lead the newspaper.[14]

The absence of an underground press meant that Romanian journalists could not and did not develop an approach and style separate from the one imposed upon them by the communist regime. More importantly, they did not develop a mentality that jettisoned the weight given to their active role as proselytizers and political fighters, rather than being mere reporters. Nor did they have the opportunity to practice a language devoid of the "wooden" quality nurtured by the communist system. If they did so on their own they did not put such an independent style or more authentic language into practice, unlike their counterparts in Poland, Hungary and Czechoslovakia. This inability to develop a journalism separate from Marxist-Leninist–inspired journalism had four major consequences:

1. There was no indigenous media that could be of help to any attempts at an organized dissident movement (even if such a movement were to have been only short-lived). No Romanian media were able to contribute to informing the people of what was developing and happening in the country as it was inevitably being drawn into a revolt, if not a revolution. And no Romanian media were available to articulate for their audiences a cohesive, practical and theoretical argument against communism, give voice to individual and collective suffering and anger and frame a dialogue regarding a democratic, postcommunist society;

2. As a result, the newly freed Romanian mass media in December 1989 served mainly as outlets for releasing pent-up feelings, for national and individual catharsis and for the circulation of rumors. In their first months of liberty, mass media became a gigantic psychiatrist's couch where Romanians could for the first time vent anger against their oppressors and tell their stories of suffering and humiliation, of shattered hopes and dreams and of future aspirations. The media, in great measure occupied with exercising their newfound freedom and providing an outlet for the suddenly freed multitude of individual voices, failed to serve as a forum for constructive discussions of contemporary problems and solutions and as an avenue of credibly informing audiences of developments;

3. Once the tyrant fled and the communist system crumbled, journalists were able to immediately move away from adhering to the communist codes and laws imposed upon their work, but not from the language and old journalistic methods and concepts.[15] Instead of reporting, an activism akin to that of communist journalism became the dominant journalistic mode, this

time for divergent ideologies and politics. There were few if any that stepped into the immediate post-December 22 era with much credibility because, as Bacanu described the situation,[16] "The same people (journalists) who scurried around to find nice things to say about the old regime and its leadership turned around in one day and found negative epithets with which to describe them."

4. Romanian audiences were not used to an indigenous media other than the communist ones. They were unaccustomed to making demands on media and to being discerning consumers. As Prime Minister Teodor Stolojan pointed out in 1992, the Romanians had to learn "how to react through and because of the press."[17] According to many in the Romanian press, it was difficult for audiences to trust the journalists who for 43 years had had to deceive them.[18]

December 1989 did not mark the end of an era, only the beginnings of a new one being built on the still-living organism of the old one, an organism that is partly systemic and in greater measure attitudinal or cultural. In Brzezinski's (1993, 58–59) words, this organism or system "not only stifled initiative and innovation but could not assimilate the need inherent in the postindustrial society for decentralized mass communications and for the spontaneous interaction of freely flowing information and multiple centers of decision making."

CHAPTER 2

Mass Media in Revolution

 Without information being disseminated about the beginning of a revolt, it may be very difficult to mobilize forces to sustain it and turn it into a full-fledged revolution. In a nation under an extreme totalitarian regime that managed to co-opt or cow an entire population, information about a revolt is particularly essential to individuals who have to or wish to decide whether to join the revolt or not, or to remain in the streets to fight the battles necessary to topple the ancien régime. Rumors of resistance turned into the small revolt that began in Timisoara on Dec. 15, 1989, yet they were insufficient to bring people out in the streets of other cities to nurture the revolt. People needed a signal or verification that "the event" had really begun, that it was sustainable, that people had the courage and that all the rumors about it were true or nearly true. The mass media were the only institutions that directly or indirectly provided them with verification of the rumors, if not the veracity of the details.

In Romania, information became an essential ingredient of the reawakening and re-empowering, or the psychological realignment, of the people between December 15 and December 22, the day the Ceausescus fled Bucharest, and between December 22 and Jan. 1, 1990, by which time the army and, allegedly, elements of the Securitate stopped battling in the streets of Bucharest.[1] This chapter examines the role and effects of the indigenous Romanian mass media and that of the foreign mass media during (a) the Timisoara revolt and its spread to other cities, most important among them

Bucharest, and (b) what is now being called a revolution by some, a hijacked revolt by others and a preplanned coup d'état by yet others.[2]

The Final Days of the Communist Media

The tightly controlled Romanian news media failed, as was their enforced habit, to apprise their audiences of what was going on in and outside the country during the last few months, weeks, and days of the Ceausescu regime. Needless to say, the revolt that began on December 15 in the multiethnic, westernmost city of Timisoara did not receive coverage from Romanian newspapers, radio or television. The news of a local dissident minister, the Rev. Laszlo Tokes of the Reformed Church, who was to be evicted from the church building for not complying with an order transferring him to another city, spread by word of mouth and by Hungarian radio and television[3] all over Timisoara and its surrounding area. According to people in Timisoara, Tokes' story of dissidence was known in Romania thanks to reports by Radio Free Europe's Romanian Service and those of Hungarian radio (Milin 1990), as well as from Hungarian television (Boyle, Dec. 26, 1989). It brought several hundred people to the church, and by the evening of December 15 about 1,000 people clashed with the police. The next day, December 16, the crowd grew. What had been a vigil turned into an anti-communist demonstration that began moving toward the center of the city. Clashes between police and demonstrators occurred in parts of Timisoara, and by nightfall the revolt had spread all over the 12-centuries-old city. On December 17, a day now remembered as Bloody Sunday, the clashes, the crowds and the provocations, allegedly on the part of the Securitate, increased. The city was occupied by army and Securitate troops. By that evening the indiscriminate shooting began, and the first victims of the revolution left their bloody marks on Timisoara's streets (Milin 1990; Bohlen, Dec. 20, 1989, and Dec. 23, 1989). Sporadic fighting continued for days. Brute force failed to stop the uprising, as did the efforts by Prime Minister Constantin Dascalescu and Emil Bobu, a high-ranking Communist Party official close to the Ceausescus, as well as other top governmental and military officials who came to Timisoara.

The Romanian mass media were silent. For better or worse, interpersonal communication, the extensive rumor mill in the country, took care of spreading the news. The foreign media proved instrumental as information and verification facilitators, albeit accurate in general but not in the particulars of the unfolding events. Yet, in their inimitable way, Romanian media and communications policies sent signals that something was going on, thereby confirming the essence of the myriad rumors and other unconfirmed information that were circulating among the country's 23 million citizens by December 16. For those who did not hear the rumors, the changes in the operations of Timisoara's communications facilities and, indirectly, the indigenous mass media alerted them to their existence and drove those people to seek them out and get informed through whatever means available.

For example, by December 18 the main post office in Timisoara was closed by the authorities, and all telephone links to the outside were broken off. It was a clear sign that something serious was happening in the city. The media, too, indirectly and unwittingly transmitted the news that something was going on and ultimately showed the fear and confusion of a dictator who was losing control and running out of time. Romanians from all walks of life said in the aftermath of the revolution that they began paying increasing attention to the communist media, reading between the lines for signs that confirmed the rumors of a revolt that the regime was hard-pressed to contain.[4] This time they were not disappointed by the communist media:

• December 17. Romanian Radio, hinting for the first time that something was going on but not referring directly to Timisoara, read for its listeners an official communiqué from the Executive Political Committee of the Communist Party's Central Committee (after an emergency meeting held to discuss the events in Timisoara). The communiqué admonished Romanians to "reject with great determination" the offensive by "reactionary, imperialist circles against socialism, aiming at destabilizing socialism and weakening its stand."

• December 18. The Communist Party's main mouthpiece, *Scinteia,* called for the "consistent promotion of the rule of (communist) law" and for "spirit and letter of the law to be applied in every field and every circumstance" (Ratesh 1991, 36). The regime had reason to be concerned. The uprising had spread to the cities of Arad, Brasov, Cluj, Sibiu and Tirgu Mures.

• December 20. Having just returned from a state visit to Iran, Ceausescu went on national television to blame the Timisoara "disturbances" on foreign intelligence services, primarily the Hungarian one, and calling the demonstrators a "gang of hooligans," "fascists" and "terrorists." (Bohlen, Dec. 21, 1989). He also thanked the army for doing its duty to the nation and to socialism. It was the first time Romanian media presented their national audience with material directly referring to happenings in Timisoara.

• December 21. A hastily organized pro-regime pep rally in Bucharest's palace square was televised live. A few minutes into Ceausescu's speech a commotion ensued. Shouts of "Down with Ceausescu!" and "Timisoara!" were heard. The broadcast was interrupted, only to be resumed three minutes later, and there on the television screen millions of Romanians saw the pandemonium grow. For the first time, Ceausescu, a small, insignificant figure on the balcony of the Central Committee building, was looking increasingly confused and frightened, desperately trying to save the situation and himself before finally retreating. It was too late, for as Tismaneanu (1992, 233) writes, correctly identifying the meaning of the moment, "power had already slipped from the balcony of the Central Committee building to the street." No one has yet discovered who counseled Ceausescu to organize and televise the rally.

Ratesh (1991, 39), who for years was the head of Radio Free Europe's Romanian service in Munich, Germany, and is a well-informed observer of the Romanian scene, writes that "the television viewers could sense that something unusual was occurring in the square but did not know for sure what had happened." It was yet another signal, the most powerful for being a visual one transmitted by an all-pervasive, communist-controlled medium, that Ceausescu was losing control. Events in Timisoara proved to be the portent of a major change. Romanians from all walks of life testified after the revolution that the image of a scared, fleeing Ceausescu told them the time had really come for a change, that it was possible, that it was time to display fortitude, that this was their big opportunity. In Timisoara, the newly constituted Romanian Democratic Front called for free elections, press freedoms, human rights, the immediate opening of borders and other eliminations of restrictions.

• December 22. Romanian Radio announced in the morning a presidential decree instituting a state of emergency. This was, indeed, news written between the lines of the announcement. While not providing the details of the fast-unfolding events all over the country, the news that a major revolt was unleashed and that the regime was panicking and ready to react violently to protect itself (it had already done so in Timisoara) was out. It made no difference. Groups of protesters were already in the streets of Bucharest, and by noon on the same day the Ceausescus left Bucharest by helicopter, only to be captured and executed after a summary trial on December 25.

Before the Ceausescus fled, both radio and television announced that Minister of Defense General Vasile Milea[5] had committed suicide. The army suspected that Milea was executed for not following Ceausescu's orders. The immediate effect on the army was to unite its efforts with that of what was already, unmistakably, a national uprising. Romanian broadcasting was finally—unwittingly—influencing events.

Other stories of communist mass media contributions to the revolution that surfaced after the bloody fighting stopped around Jan. 1, 1990, are unverifiable. For instance, a *Washington Post* story (Randal, Jan. 9, 1990) suggested that a 19th-century patriotic song ("Lion Cubs") was deliberately aired on December 21 on Romanian Radio by one or more station employees as a (prearranged) signal to an alleged 13-year-old clandestine free trade-union movement to trigger a nationwide uprising. *Scinteia Tineretului* on December 21 published a column that seemingly made no sense at all but which is said to have contained secret calls to start the revolution. No editor or reporter of the newspaper acknowledged any awareness of how the column appeared in the paper.[6] Some Romanian Television (RTV) personnel claim that the resumption of the broadcast of Ceausescu's speech on December 21 was deliberately engineered to show viewers that the revolt was really on, that it had spread and that the Ceausescus were finished.[7] It is a plausible claim that, however, implies a lapse in the Securitate's control at RTV (why were these individuals not arrested by the evening of December 21?) or even cooperation on the part of the Securitate people responsible for overseeing television operations. The latter scenario is given credibility by an unverifiable allegation that a preplanned coup by military leaders, disgruntled Communist Party members and some elements of the Securitate was behind "the revolution."[8]

There is no evidence that Romania's communist media in any way consciously, purposely, accurately, completely or even partially informed their audience of the events leading up to December 15. They did not disseminate information about immediately succeeding events or present the sentiments, thoughts and wishes of the people they purportedly served. Yet in a nation where people were accustomed to reading between the lines of mass media messages and were attuned to the nuanced meanings conveyed by the language used, the communist media did unwittingly disseminate information to a desperate, frustrated people whose patience and endurance had run out by 1989.

Television Revolution (?)

After Ceausescu's television performance on December 21, the revolt was taken up in earnest in Bucharest. Minutes before the Ceausescus were airborne in their desperate attempt to escape on December 22, some of Bucharest's citizens, together with the army, took over the Central Committee building in the middle of the capital and the Romanian Television headquarters at 191 Calea Dorobanti. Radio Free Europe's correspondent, Ratesh (1991, 48), sees the occupation of the television station as "one of the deftest moves by the group of dissidents and politicians poised to fill the power vacuum." Others (Shinar and Stoiciu 1992) suggest that it was a premeditated takeover, fitting into an overall strategy worked out before December 1989 as part of a larger plot by disgruntled Communist Party officials, some intellectuals, members of the military, and part of the Securitate. The latter scenario suggests a conspiratorial use of television by the future national leaders from December 22 onward, with or without the television personnel's knowledge. Whether the occupation of television was premeditated or a spontaneous event, the importance assigned to this medium was incontestably averred.

Fighting for control over the television station ensued on December 22 between the army and "terrorists," or Securitate personnel supporting the Ceausescu regime. Here again the conspiracy theory gains support from the fact that despite heavy fighting around the television station's headquarters, no serious damage was done to it nor its power supply cut off. Its broadcast tower at Palatul Telefoanelor was also not disabled. To do so, as Verdery and Kligman (1992, 121) conclude, "would have been not only easy—especially for a Securitate renowned for its commando training—but also a major setback for the persons holding the (National Salvation) Front in power through their presence there."

Whatever the truth surrounding the revolution and the use of television may be, Romanians were glued to their television sets (the great majority of people were not out in the streets demonstrating and taking part in the fight alongside the army). They saw a sight on December 22 that they could only have dreamed about even 24 hours earlier. Dissident Mircea Dinescu, accompanied by well-known actor Ion Caramitru, film director Sergiu Nicolaescu, an army officer who became an impromptu spokesman for the army, television employees and other Bucharest citizens appeared on the screen at 11:50 a.m. They announced the occupation of the television station and (prematurely) the victory of the revolution. Romanian Television became Televiziunea Romana Libera, or Free Romanian Television. In a strange development that provides yet another argument for the conspiracy theorists, people were urged to come to defend the television building which was already being defended by the military.

The television building was becoming the unofficial headquarters of the provisional leadership of the National Salvation Front (NSF), which was being formed by two former high-ranking communist officials, Ion Iliescu and Silviu Brucan, together with university professor Petre Roman, army generals and a number of dissidents including Doina Cornea, Ana Blandeana, Radu Filipescu and Mircea Dinescu.[9] By 10:30 p.m., Iliescu announced the formation of the leadership group, free elections by April 1990, freedom of thought and expression and the abrogation of the most unpopular of Ceausescu's laws (Amelunxen and Ujica 1990, 11–22; Bohlen, Dec. 28, 1989).

If seeing is believing, Romanians were finally getting the message that a major change was taking place, and television was not about to let them doubt it. That same evening, December 22, the capture of the dictator's son, Nicu Ceausescu, allegedly a monster in his own right, was announced, and he was paraded in front of the cameras. Anything that heightened the population's hatred for the Ceausescus was offered to a stunned audience: the gold objects in the dictator's palace, a Securitate torture room in Timisoara, and the steak-fed dogs owned by the ruling family. News of battles between the army and civilians on the one side and Securitate forces on the other side in other cities were broadcast, as was an unsubstantiated warning that the Securitate might have poisoned the water supply. Were these presentations strictly journalistic revelations or manipulation, deflecting attention from the new old guard taking over and directing it toward the now easy targets, the Ceausescus?

Petre Popescu, one of Romania's "star" anchormen, took to the air in Studio 4 and made the not-so-startling yet meaningful announcement that "For 25 years we (at Romanian Television) have lied" and promised that "From now on we will tell the truth." He invited the audience: "Whoever wishes can come to us and speak freely." And for the next two weeks they came, in small and large groups, individuals, young and old, males and females from all walks of life. It was, as explained by television's Victor Ionescu,[10] who later became for a brief period head of the RTV News Department, a "wonderful kind of anarchy." It was the kind of "anarchy," he said, that energized and vitalized a television operation that under Ceausescu and his communist regime was more like a controlled radio station with still photographs.

Guarded by army troops with tanks and armored personnel carriers, under sniper attack by Securitate forces, Free Romanian Television became the "symbol of revolution" (Kifner, Dec. 25, 1989). It also became a veritable experiment in community broadcasting. Everyone who had anything to say was given airtime. The array of people who paraded in front of the television cameras during the first two weeks after that fateful day, December 22, was stunning. Peasants, priests, doctors, engineers, students, homemakers, military personnel, factory workers, former prisoners in the communist gulag, all were given their few seconds of fame or at the very least brief, first and last ever national exposure. Never before and not since have the broadcast media been ruled by the politics of inclusion and been truly democratized media.

The silent majority were, for at least a short period, the most vociferous, prolific storytellers. Television and radio, along with the print media (see the next section), became the valves that allowed for blowing off steam and, later, vehicles for individual and collective or national catharsis. People told viewers what they had witnessed or heard as the fighting erupted in Bucharest, what they had suffered under the Ceausescu regime and under preceding communist regimes, about how the communists took power in 1947 and the repression that followed. Anti-Ceausescu and anti-communist sentiments were openly voiced on national television. Christmas was celebrated, and portions of church services were telecast for the first time. Long accustomed to having everything rationed, Romanians sarcastically spoke of taking "their ration of freedom" that Christmas. A certain, rare national unity was echoed through the mass media and, while these messages were politicized, there was little politicking (Gross, 1991a, b). New Year's Day came and went without Ceausescu's usual address to the nation. Romanians said, in a not-unusual double entendre, that "this year, for New Year's, no one will speak *to* us."

Romanians changed from a mostly vicarious mass of revolutionaries into television viewers when the capture of the Ceausescus was announced on television on December 23, according to testimony given by Mihai Sora (Amelunxen and Ujica 1990, 57). Sora is one of Romania's pre-eminent intellectuals who briefly served as minister of culture in the post-Ceausescu Petre Roman government. The highlight of television broadcasts came on December 26, one day after Nicolae and Elena Ceausescu were executed. At 11 a.m. a 10-minute newscast recounted the military trial of the Ceausescus, and at 3 p.m. a 15-minute broadcast showed for the first time the face of the executed dictator. The video of parts of the trial were shown for the first time at 12:30 a.m. on December 27, and video of the executed Elena and Nicolae Ceausescu was shown for the first time at 1 a.m. The brief footage of their bodies lying slumped by a wall was incorporated a few months later in a 90-minute film of their trial and execution. The film shows the firing-squad execution, but "French forensic experts have concluded that a film released by Romania's interim government showing the firing-squad executions ... was faked, furthering suspicions here that the two probably were victims of a coup carried out under cover of a popular revolution" (Schemo, April 30, 1990).

Jonathan Alter (Jan. 8, 1990), in a *Time* magazine analysis of television's role in 1989's successful East-Central European and attempted Chinese revolutions, made the point that "The sad truth of the TV age is that if there's no video, it didn't really happen." For Romanians, the video of the Ceausescus' trial and of their bullet-ridden, contorted corpses was yet another psychological turning point. It finally made believers of them: the hated dictator, his wife and his regime were gone and could not return to torture them again; at least that era was over. The video was shown over and over again for weeks, as if to drive home the point that the Ceausescu era was truly over. It was powerful, emotional imagery for a people who for so many years had wishfully fed on rumors that Ceausescu had cancer or some other terminal illness and would soon die, only to keep suffering under his heel year after year.

Aside from the details of the Ceausescus' capture, trial and execution, the focus of news reports between December 22 and December 27 was the fighting between the army and elements of the Securitate, the battle that was raging around the television station itself, the dead who were the newest heroes enshrined in Romania's long historical memory, and the first actions of the provisional National Salvation Front government. The daily scenes of the dead, in the streets and in the morgues, and of grieving relatives and strangers created a particularly powerful and poignant image of sacrifice and courage, of anger and pride, of the futility of death and the utility of its symbolism to a reawakened nation. A *New York Times* reporter (Kifner, Dec. 28, 1989), among many others who have noted the importance television broadcasts played in the revolution (Young, Jan. 3, 1990; Wilkie, Dec. 28, 1989; Talbott, Jan. 8, 1990; Longworth, Jan. 7, 1990), writes,

> In a sense it was like watching live coverage of the storming of the Bastille or the battle of Yorktown, interspersed with debates from the Constitutional Congress. But in this case the focus of violence was the television studio itself. Sovereignty, it seemed, was reduced to the ability to convey what was happening outside the studio door.

Television as the "motor of the revolution," as television personnel characterized it,[11] may be overstating the role of the medium. Certainly, it was a television revolution as much as the Vietnam conflict was the world's first television war, by virtue of at least a weeklong, round-the-clock blow-by-blow report of what supposedly was going on at the "battle front" and in the newly reshaped political arena. But Romanian television personnel are not the only ones to see television as having been intrinsic to the revolution's making. Silviu Brucan—the former communist official who turned against Ceausescu and his regime, a history professor who became the gray eminence of the National Salvation Front upon its formation in December 1989 and ultimately one of its most astute and cynical critics after his resignation on Feb. 4, 1990—writes in his memoirs, *Generatia Irosita* (1992, 217):

> The whole nation was glued to the television screen: it was a unique occasion and they were prepared to do whatever it was necessary to profit from it. Truly, television was the revolution's decisive factor. Every one of its important acts was directly seen on the small screen, from the popular

explosion in Piata Palatului, to the trial and execution of the Ceausescus. The most passionate call addressed to the people to rise and participate in the revolution resounded on the small screen, and the people responded in thousands and tens of thousand and came in the defense of the revolution. It was the first revolution in history made by and on television.

On the other hand, Ratesh (1991, 47), offering an argument on the other extreme, writes that by the time Free Romanian Television went on the air on Dec. 22, 1989, the "uprising itself was for all intents and purposes over." While he is correct in equating the end of the uprising, revolt or revolution with Ceausescu's flight from Bucharest, the revolution (i.e., the street fighting, struggle for power, change and the end of communism) continued and was vividly presented on Romanian television in the subsequent four weeks, as Ratesh himself describes in his book. Furthermore, the revolution was also a personal, psychological metamorphosis for each Romanian, constituting millions of lesser or greater personal revolutionary acts aided by the pictures presented on the television screen, as Amelunxen and Ujica (1990) illustrate.

Free Romanian Television in the first weeks after December 22, by giving voice to a wide diversity of opinions and views as to what occurred before and during the communist era to all groups and individuals who were preparing to form political parties and other civic and professional organizations, played a significant role in the initial emergence of (an infant) civil society and politics. It was also central in the overt reintroduction of many cultural symbols, including religion and Romanian history, the latter distorted and hidden by the communists to serve their purposes between 1947 and 1989. In an incipient, unscripted, new socializing role, it began recruiting new participants into social, political, economic and cultural life.

However, television was not a purveyor of accurate and verifiable information. It "fed directly on the street, on rumors, and on revolutionary pathos," as Shinar and Stoiciu (1992) correctly observe. It was not a news organization, but a platform for propaganda a la Lenin. It did not practice journalism in the strictest sense of the word, and its staff admitted that much, explaining that to do so was impossible and uncalled for at a time when everyone was testing his and her newly freed voice.[12] The argument was made that the trauma and emotion of those days called merely for an open microphone and an uncapped lens. Gabanyi (1990, 9) accurately points out, "Television remained the most important weapon of the new leadership in the fight for the hearts and minds of the population. Dark images, images of happiness were precisely targeted ... not just seldomly also manipulated."

Television also simply did not have the staff with the type of preparation and experience to professionally survey the myriad happenings in a society in the midst of great social, political and cultural convulsions. The newly named head of Romanian Television, writer Aurel Dragos Munteanu, told U.S. anchorman Ted Koppel on an ABC *Nightline* program in April 1990 that professionalism was lacking, that television's journalists were more accustomed to making propaganda than gathering and disseminating news. Still, information- and entertainment-starved viewers, after years of three-hour-per-night television broadcasts, could feast their eyes, ears and senses on 24-hour television transmissions that bombarded them with an abundance of views, images and (seldom accurate and complete) information.

Romania's television revolution and revolution in television also saw the birth of the first-ever independent local television station. In the "First Free Romanian City," as the 400,000 plus citizens of Timisoara called their city, electronics engineer Imre Gnandt, together with friends, acquaintances and strangers who volunteered to partake in the new venture, launched Free Timisoara Television. Using their own equipment and VHS tapes donated by Yugoslavian television stations just over the southwestern border of the country, Gnandt and his band began to tape the fighting in Timisoara, the opening of mass graves allegedly filled with the victims of the dreaded Securitate and the wounded and dead in the city's hospitals. By December 24, one day before the Ceausescus' execution, after commandeering a mobile television van belonging to what was already Free Romanian Television and taking over one of its local relay stations, Gnandt and his crew went on the air (Gross, 1990a).

The new station was an instant hit in Timisoara and its immediate surroundings, despite its late (1–3 a.m.) two-hour broadcasts.[13] Without an anchor or moderator, the station broadcast technically poor but vivid visuals of scenes from around the city and interviews with all manner of individuals during its first couple weeks of operation. The station's success did not surprise Gnandt, who equated its popular support with the amateur status of the staff. He claimed,[14] with sufficient justification, that amateurs "are the only ones who do not use the old vocabulary and are not tainted by their past association with official television and radio." This first independent local television was only the first of 16 to make its debut in the next three years (see chapter 4).

Romanian Radio's contribution to the revolution ran parallel to that of television. From December 22 onward it reported on events in Bucharest and other cities, doing countless "man on the street" interviews. It also attempted to bring as much accuracy to its news reports as was possible in the frantic and chaotic world in which its journalists operated. It was radio that on December 23 broadcast the call from the head of the Securitate (Gen. Iulian Vlad) for his troops to stop fighting—a call that remained unheeded.[15]

At least two of the six regional stations of Romanian Radio, closed since 1985, were reopened on Dec. 22, 1989, when their former employees, from management to technical personnel, simply showed up at the stations and went on the air. They were not paid by anyone for their services for weeks to come. Until February 1990 these stations had no legal status, operating essentially as pirate stations with the tacit approval and technical go-ahead from Romanian Radio. They added to the cacophony of sounds and information permeating Romanian society and were a significant beginning to independent radio considering that each station claimed to have an audience of as high as 1.5 million.[16] These stations also provided a local or regional approach to their news reports. Their transmissions in those first few post–December 22 weeks were limited to early morning (6–8 a.m.) and late afternoon to evening schedules (4–12 p.m.), with slightly more extensive broadcasting hours on Saturdays and fewer hours on Sundays.

Immediate Post-Ceausescu Print Media and a Search for a New Role

On the morning of Dec. 22, 1989, the Romanian Communist Party's newspaper, *Scinteia* (The Spark), appeared as usual. However, by 9 a.m. on December 22 the staff of the newspaper had already decided to put out a new edition, a "real newspaper" informing people of what was happening in the country.[17] There was some panic among the staff that such a bold step was to be taken because the Securitate's men were still in the building. By 6 p.m. that day, only hours after the Ceausescus flew out of Bucharest, the new, one-page newspaper hit the streets. It was now called, *Scinteia Poporului* (The People's Spark). Its headlines tell the story: "Glory to the free nation, to its heroic people," "The dictatorship has fallen, the people are free," "The victory of truth," "Ardent gratitude to the Romanian army." In a box on its front page *Scinteia Poporului* announced, using the same approach and language utilized by the communists, "Our newspaper appears today in a special edition, as an expression of new, real patriotism, as a people's newspaper."

There was no news in this newspaper with the exception of the brief international reports about foreign reactions to Romanian events. But that was hardly important on this day. Instead the symbolism of the name change and of the headlines was what mattered to the readers and to the newspaper's staff. The medium was once again the message. Two days later the newspaper, now independent of the disbanded Communist Party, once again changed its name to *Adevarul* (The Truth) so as to signal an irrevocable break with its past, according to the editors.[18]

The change of publications' names (e.g., *Drapelul Rosu* [Red Flag] to *Renasterea Banateana* [The Banat's Rebirth], *Drum Nou* [The New Way] to *Gazeta Transilvaniei* [Transylvanian Gazette], *Scinteia Tineretului* [Young People's Spark] to *Tineretul Liber* [Free Youth], and so on), status (from Communist Party–controlled to independent), editorial policy (from Marxist-Leninist values to independent communication outlets) and content was repeated in communities both far from and near the capital city. In the majority of cases the changes were mostly symbolic: the names were changed, independence was proclaimed and the content was decidedly anti-Ceausescu, but journalistic substance, practice and personnel remained the same.

While the editors of the renamed *Scinteia*[19] opined that the "press is well prepared to carry on given the quality of the people it has working on it," the editor of *Libertatea*[20] saw a more realistic and obvious task ahead when he said, "We have to relearn how to become journalists." Petre Mihai Bacanu,[21] the editor in chief of *Romania Libera,* summed up the basic nature of the change in Romanian journalism in the first few days and weeks after December 22 when he explained that those who sang the Ceausescus' praises just hours before they fled Bucharest "turned around in a matter of hours and found every possible abusive, contemptuous word to describe the very recent past and its architects." Liviu Man (1993), the editor in chief of the weekly *NU,* established in Cluj in 1990, supports Bacanu's view of the changes in those first moments of press freedom and elaborates on them:

> Newspapers that had recently extolled Ceausescu and dutifully obeyed the orders of Ceausescu and the Securitate now suddenly became pro-revolution and anti-Ceausescu, although they remained just as stalwartly pro-communist. The same men who had accused people from Timisoara and Cluj of being hooligans and "street Arabians" or "tools of a foreign agency (either the CIA or the KGB) now came out praising the revolutionaries suffering 60,000 deaths during the December events. ... These newspapers now reported eagerly on the fabulous fortune amassed by the dictator's family and about the hundreds of terrorists who defended Ceausescu up to his death. Today, it is still impossible to find out who these "defenders" were.

Man's characterization of the Romanian press remaining "stalwartly pro-communist" was in many cases an exaggeration and in some instances outwardly false. Bacanu's *Romania Libera,* a major national daily, is a case in point. Along with others in the country, it also put out a special issue on December 22, hand-distributed like all other publications. Its staff had elected Bacanu as its editor in chief only hours after his release from prison. The newspaper was, from its inception as an independent paper on December 22, as stalwartly, single-mindedly anti-communist as *Scinteia* was pro-communist before that fateful day. Ironically, Bacanu[22] related how those of his journalists who were zealous supporters of the Ceausescu regime were not fired but simply "marginalized," while *Adevarul* (the renamed *Scinteia*) fired 12 of its staff who were deemed hard-core Ceausescu cheerleaders.

The fact remained that all of Romania's old journalists required a radical professional readjustment and re-education or retraining to be effective gatherers and disseminators of news and credible symbols and agents of democratization. George Serban,[23] who together with a group of other activists founded the newspaper *Timisoara* in early 1990 in the city where the revolution began, expressed the view of most if not all new journalists who entered the profession after December 22 and that of many readers when he said that "all journalists and editors are tainted. They can't even do the job."

For all intents and purposes, the old communist press—all the cheerleading, myth-making, lying, dissimulating, one-track communist publications—disappeared on December 22. Truth, as Bacanu saw it rather optimistically in mid-January 1990, "is a new sacred word." Yet truth was onerous to obtain in the chaos of post–December 1989 Romania and was difficult for journalists to identify and transmit to the reading public, let alone to define as the presentation of complete, accurate, verifiable information.

Tircob,[24] *Libertatea*'s editor in chief in the immediate postrevolution period, complained that "journalists come with all sorts of stories, exaggerations, there a few facts, and verification." He added, "We are in a situation where we have to run retractions and corrections every day." And in Timisoara, Serban[25] confirmed that "rumors are the order of the day in the majority of publications."

Everyone wanted to contribute to the newly liberated press, setting the stage for the media explosion in 1990 and the quadrupling of the number of working journalists, creating a situation of "positive chaos" in which everyone had a "gusto for speaking out" in the print and broadcast media.[26] Editors and journalists repeatedly emphasized that their newfound freedom meant that they could carry out a journalism in which "everyone will be criticized," every political party, every idea will receive scrutiny. It was a philosophy which was to carry Romanian journalism away from reporting and toward subjective, polemical, argumentative presentation of select happenings, ideas, sources and their words.

The sudden cutting of the umbilical cord binding Romanian mass media to the Romanian Communist Party and Nicolae and Elena Ceausescu left the former adrift without any particular initial focus except opposition to the

Ceausescus, the recounting of years of oppression, the rulers' opulent lifestyles, their inflated egos and their crimes. The ongoing fighting or, in its immediate aftermath, its recounting and the championing of a clear accounting of what and how the revolt or revolution happened were at the core of almost every daily's and weekly's issue. The main press ingredients became the newly installed government, its machinations, its decrees and the finger-pointing over who was or was not a collaborator of the old regime and to what extent.

An accounting of the dead and the identification of the Securitate personnel who participated in the fighting became an obsession for the press that was to continue beyond the first few postrevolutionary weeks into the first, second, third and fourth years. Religion was reintroduced in the pages of the press, and pictures of nude women began appearing in some publications. Excerpts from classic anti-totalitarian and democratic, free-market ideology literature, banned under the Ceausescu regime, were printed daily (or weekly) by newspapers (e.g., writings by George Orwell, Hannah Arendt, Jean-Francois Revel, Alexander Solzhenitsyn, Raymond Aaron, Thomas Jefferson and John Stuart Mill). Whether intentionally or not, this fare began a process of reconnecting Romanians to the larger world community and indirectly, incompletely educating them in the concepts (but not necessarily the practices) of democracy.

The contents of all Romanian publications, from the literary magazines to the newspapers, while differing in the quality of writing and the extent of subjectivity and polemicism, were similar: they dealt less with news than with the various opinions and subjective analysis on the events of the day or of the past. The press, more than radio or television, became an avenue for journalists, the majority of whom joined the newly independent press after December 22, to express their views and analyze myriad topics, mostly from a personal perspective. What was passed off as journalism was the overintellectualized or anger-filled self-expression of people who were finally able to have their say, able to get into a profession that used to be closed to all but the politically correct or those who were willing to toe the line.

As Bacanu[27] and other journalists and newspaper readers saw it, despite the fact that the Romanian press had no one "pulling their ears" and "putting a fist in our mouths," it was not the kind of press needed in the transition period which began in December 1989. At best, as Bacanu[28] described the situation, everything was reported "in vague terms," and the great majority of the working journalists in the immediate post-December period "conformed to the old ways, writing essays and analysis pieces instead of reporting on events." The press gave voice to what the Romanian people were against but did not clearly begin outlining what they were or should be for. In those first few days and weeks of freedom, the press used the word *democracy* ad nauseam but without also offering readers a clear definition or a practical description of the shape such a democracy should take and the role that should be played by the citizen. The press trumpeted the value of freedom without its attendant responsibilities, and the journalists and their work exemplified this freedom and the lack of responsibility in exercising it.

The absence of professionalism and responsibility and the continuing presence of the old-guard journalists did not diminish the ravenous interest in the press on the part of a public hungry for ideas, views and information of any kind. In Bucharest, as in other Romanian cities, the longest lines each morning were in front of newspaper sellers. Romanians bought several publications each day, forcing the increase in circulation of existing newspapers to unheard of levels before or since.

National dailies such as *Adevarul* sold 2 million copies a day, *Romania Libera* 1.2 million, and *Tineretul Liber* 500,000; local papers experienced a similar circulation boom. (Before the communist regime was toppled, the largest-circulation papers were down to 250,000 issues per day.) The cost of an issue was 50 bani or less, and newspapers such as *Adevarul* made a net profit of 100,000 lei per day, a huge sum in those last days of 1989 and first days of 1990 (by comparison, a Romanian-made Dacia car cost 80,000 lei).

The higher circulation of the existing dailies and weeklies, soon to be joined by hundreds of other new publications, strained the capacities of the few printing facilities in the country, all still owned by the state. Their antiquated equipment—"We are still in the Gutenberg era," said Bacanu[29]—was hard-pressed to keep up with the demand for a huge jump in the number of issues for all publications. So was the distribution system, also still controlled by the state, which was unable to get newspapers to the many villages in the Romanian countryside. The absence of modern printing facilities and an effective system of distribution, not to mention the continued control or ownership of these as well as of paper-making facilities by the state, were to present nagging problems for the press in the first six years after the revolution.

The major role of the old-new press in the first post–Dec. 22, 1989, days was, as mentioned earlier, one of allowing for individuals and the nation to blow off steam accumulated over years of frustration, pain and unexpressed hatred in a society of enforced silence. It set the stage for the beginning of a period of catharsis, one which still had not run its course by the end of the first four years of freedom. The press also had a powerful symbolic role: it was the first institution to introduce an overabundance of choices; it established a marketplace of ideas and views, and therefore it began the re-education of people as free consumers. The plethora of views expressed in the press and the lack of professionalism also set the stage for a continuous, heated debate over the media's role in the transition, their functions and their very professionalism. The press's role as recruiter to a reforming civil society (and therefore as resocializing agent) by virtue of its presentation of the newly established political, civic and professional organizations was also important and paralleled that of television in those first days of freedom.

The new Romanian press was also a tangible, saveable proof of the change that was taking place. The first post–December 22, 1989, newspapers became heirlooms for many Romanians. The press's gigantic circulation levels in those first two to four weeks, together with its and the nation's new-found freedoms, the ensuing social and political dialogues, created an atmosphere in which many journalists, would-be journalists and businesspeople, intellectuals and newly formed professional, civic, and political organizations began plans for launching new publications. The establishment of new political parties and the re-establishment of the precommunist-era traditional parties added to that impetus.

Foreign Mass Media as Spark and Fuel for the Revolution

Writing about the role foreign broadcasts played in the Romanian revolution, in undermining the informational gulag built by the regime, *Washington Post* reporter Blaine Harden (Dec. 29, 1989) explains, "Romania's conspicuous silence for most of the past year was not the dismal quiet of hopelessness. Rather, it was the stillness of people paying attention."

Since the 1970s, as the regime's repression grew, as life became increasingly miserable, and as indigenous media lost all credibility, creating an insurmountable chasm between themselves and their audiences, Romanians paid increasing attention to Western, Soviet and other East-Central European radio and television broadcasts. They became "information seekers, eager to seek out media giving expression to their views and experiences," because they lacked the opportunity to become communicators in their own right, just as Jakubowicz (1989) theorizes about the Poles' behavior while living under their communist regime. In what was to become the glasnost spirit of the 1980s, Romanians granted themselves the informational openness denied them by the Ceausescu dictatorship.

Radio

In 1971–72, 51 percent of Romanians listened to broadcasts of Radio Free Europe (RFE), 22 percent to the British Broadcasting Company (BBC), 18 percent to the Voice of America (VOA), and 14 percent to Radio Paris (Paulu 1974, 429). A decade later, RFE's audience was 64 percent of Romania's population (McIntosh 1986), and VOA's audience had climbed to 20 percent (Mainland 1986). One year before the revolution, an East European Area Audience and Opinion Research survey showed that 63 percent of Romanians followed RFE broadcasts, 31 percent listened to VOA, 25 percent tuned in to the BBC, and 16 percent to the Deutsche Welle. It is not unreasonable to speculate that these audiences increased in 1989 as Poland, Hungary, Czechoslovakia, and East Germany underwent their "velvet" but noisy revolutions. Romanians paid careful attention to these developments.

No data are available to indicate the extent of listenership to other Western radio which some Romanians said they followed, most notably Italian and Austrian, particularly in the western part of the country. Nor are there any data on how many Romanians regularly listened to radio broadcasts from Yugoslavia, Hungary, Bulgaria and even the Soviet Union by the late 1980s.

By all accounts, tuning to foreign broadcast became a daily, eagerly anticipated ritual, and polls taken in the aftermath of the revolution bear out individual testimony. For instance, U.S. Information Agency (June 14, 1990) surveys in Romania found that 71 percent of the population regularly listened to foreign radio broadcasts. The information obtained served as the principal focus for discussions with family and close friends for the next day or even week. The broadcasts also were instrumental in providing not only information but also a psychological boost to an imprisoned people. Because people listened to different foreign radio broadcasts, or more than one foreign radio station, the discussions often centered on comparing notes on what they heard. Nicolae Manolescu, the writer, professor and new editor in chief of the leading literary journal *Romania Literara,* summed up the importance of foreign radio for Romanians in an April 17, 1990, interview aired on the Voice of America's Romanian broadcast:

> What did these radios mean to us until the events of last December? The metaphor of the reed comes to mind. It was as if we were living under water and we needed reed pipes to breathe. The reeds were the radios. Without them, the entire people surely would have suffocated.
>
> Practically everyone listened to the radios. At a certain time of day, in the evening during broadcast hours, or when something especially important was being aired, such as General Pacepa's book [Ion Pacepa was the chief of Romania's CIA, the Departamentul de Informatii Externe, until his

defection to the United States in 1978] on RFE, we saw that auto traffic in Bucharest simply stopped. No one was in the streets ...

And the next day, on streetcars and buses and in offices everyone talked about nothing other than what they had heard the night before.

The consumption of foreign media, mainly radio, was part of the information diet of educated, urbanized Romanians throughout the 42 years of communist rule. In the first 18 years under communism, foreign media were consumed out of a habit nurtured in precommunist days, as a resistance to or in defiance of communist rule and as a counterbalance to the indigenous new communist media. For a brief period between 1965 and 1975, foreign media became relatively more accessible, and the monitoring of foreign broadcasts continued out of habit. Because Romania's situation held some promise in those years (Shafir 1985, Fischer-Galati 1970), Romanians (relatively) decreased their search for alternatives to their own media. After 1975, consumption of foreign media was forbidden, but as the chasm between Romanian audiences and their media became unbridgeable and the politico-economic situation worsened, foreign media became central to their lives.

The information transmitted by foreign news broadcasts was particularly important in the years after Mikhail Gorbachev took the reins of power in the Soviet Union, allowed for the evolution of glasnost, and signaled that the Brezhnev doctrine no longer ruled relations with other East-Central European communist states. The changes that were slowly emerging in the Soviet Union and in the rest of East-Central Europe's communist world were transmitted to attentive Romanians. They were alerted to the fact that change was possible, that the world had evolved to a new era, that the "old guard Communist governments collapsed before the will of the voters and demonstrators" (Harden, Dec. 29, 1989).

Just as important, credible news about happenings inside Romania was transmitted to an assiduously listening public, a public whose own media failed in their journalistic tasks. The words of Romanian dissidents in Romania and in the diaspora were broadcast throughout the period of communist control. In March 1989, for instance, the BBC and Radio Free Europe broadcast an open letter signed by old party members (Gheorghe Apostol, Alexandru Birladeanu, Silviu Brucan, Corneliu Manescu, Constantin Pirvulescu, and Grigore Raceanu) calling on Ceausescu to reform the system. News from Western nations and Western reactions to what was happening in East-Central Europe, including Romania, were also regular features of foreign news broadcasts. The messages carried by the foreign news reports (Gross 1995)

increased and sped up an already begun psychological readjustment slowly gaining momentum among Romanians by 1989: many lost their fear of the regime and its security organs, and were willing to brave bullets and tanks in the streets of their cities to topple the regime. Furthermore, it reinforced in the mind of audiences the illegitimacy of the Romanian regime and the society it created, providing alternative images accepted as legitimate, and therefore, credible. It proved that what is important to audiences is not only "what" is being disseminated but, in some cases even more importantly, "who" the communicators are.

The importance of foreign radio broadcasts was cumulative over the years, having a sociopolitical, cultural and psychological impact on listeners (Viviano, April 22, 1991a, b). It assured Romanians that they were not alone, or forgotten, that one could talk about *"them"* (the dictator and his spouse) in a different way than how they were presented on Romanian radio and television. The foreign broadcasts' importance and impact increased "in significance and in scope in tandem with the worsening socio-political, economic, and cultural situation within the country, and the regime's complete loss of legitimacy" (Gross 1995).

In December 1989 foreign radio was to play a decisive role in informing Romanians of developments in Timisoara and, equally important, letting them know that the rest of the world knew what was happening. In early December, Hungarian radio following events in Romania broadcast Tokes struggle with the authorities. These broadcasts were carefully monitored by the Hungarian minority in Romania, but also by many Hungarian-speaking Romanians. The call to come defend the reverend against the eviction threat and the events which unfolded beginning December 15 were broadcast by Hungarian radio and television, alerting listeners and viewers to what was occurring in Timisoara.[30]

The BBC was the first among Western radio stations to broadcast news of the Timisoara events on the afternoon of December 17. By the evening of that day, RFE broadcast its first news of the Timisoara events, which was obtained secondhand from Hungarian television. RFE's senior correspondent, Ratesh (1991, 35), describes his station's second broadcast that same night:

> One hour later, ... quoting Hungarian and Western, RFE informed its Romanian listeners that the vigil at the Reformed Church had turned into an anti-Ceausescu demonstration. No other details were given. At that time the information was scant and uncertain, coming mostly from travelers who managed to cross the border from Romania into Hungary and Yugoslavia. Their stories seemed quite incredible at the time and were viewed with a good deal of skepticism. Because of the explosive nature of the news, it was treated with great caution. Nevertheless, RFE's Romanian broadcast, which usually goes off the air at 1:00 a.m., stayed on all night with a program of live uninterrupted music and news. Although there was

little new information during that night, the sheer fact of an all-night broadcast gave listeners a sense of urgency and a hint that something of consequence was happening.

RFE Romanian Service's Nicolae Stroescu even claims that RFE broadcasts into Romania "at the very least accelerated the army's decision to join with the people" (Lunin, June/July 1990). By December 17 and 18, nearly all major Western news broadcasters were informing their audiences about events in Romania, as best they could, given but a small handful of foreign correspondents in Romania, all of them restricted in their travels. It was not until a few days later that some French, Italian, Yugoslav and American correspondents finally made it to Timisoara to report the ongoing street battles. Four of them were wounded covering the fighting ("Two American and two European journalists shot and wounded," Dec. 25, 1989).

Thus, foreign radio broadcasts were instrumental in alerting Romanians of events in their own country and focusing their attention, first on the small events surrounding a dissident's struggle and then on the string of explosions it triggered. Inaccurate and overblown in many instances, foreign news broadcasts in those first days of revolt nevertheless not only incited their listeners, but gave them food for thought, for decision making. The exaggerated figures of 5,000, 6,000, 7,000 dead in Timisoara on Bloody Sunday, December 17, incensed people to such a degree that they convinced themselves that every sacrifice was worth overthrowing the communist regime. These inaccurate, secondhand newscasts of massacres of thousands pushed them over the line psychologically. They no longer feared death, and therefore they no longer feared the regime and its killers.[31] Johanna Neuman's (June 1991, 17) view of the media's roles in the East-Central European revolution of 1989 applies as much to Romania as to the other communist nations in the region.

> There was an agenda-setting role in their mass coverage, a maestro's baton-twirl [sic] to their news judgment. The pent-up demands of East Europeans for freedom were the heart of the revolution, but the media got the blood pumping—first by raising expectations of life in the West and then by spreading the news that the Soviets were not going to cut off circulation. Without the media, Eastern Europe might still have rebelled. But this particular revolution could not have occurred without the media.

Television

For Romanian audiences, taken with the visual medium as much as the rest of the developed world, Western and East-Central European television broadcasts became as important as foreign radio broadcasts by the 1980s. This was particularly true for urban audiences and those in the countryside adjacent to borders with Hungary, Yugoslavia, Bulgaria and the Soviet Union. The UNESCO *Statistical Yearbook* (1988) reports 175 television receivers per 1,000 inhabitants. There is no authoritative accounting of how many privately owned satellite receiving dishes, outlawed by the regime, were operational in Romania. Unconfirmed reports told of around 500 to 750 dishes, 200 of which were reportedly operational in Timisoara, Cluj and the rest of the Banat region.

One story, some say fictitious, tells of a visit to the Timisoara region by Ceausescu and his asking what the satellite dishes were for, and being told that they were solar collectors. When Ceausescu learned the real function of the dishes, so the story goes, he ordered them dismantled, but only a fraction of them were taken down. In the city of Oradea an engineer by the name of Adrian Hepes reportedly put up a satellite receiving dish and via a small cable system transmitted foreign broadcasts to 800 apartments in the city, charging each a subscription fee. Whether the Securitate turned a blind eye to this operation or was bribed, no one can tell, but the upshot of this veritable information coup was that viewers were exposed to a number of foreign television broadcasts, including England's Sky News.

The satellite receiving dishes were important but not absolutely necessary for Romanians to be able to view foreign television. The dishes made it possible to receive a wider array of programs, including Sky News and CNN. But even those who did not have satellite dishes, depending on their geographical locations within the country, increasingly since the late 1970s were able to watch Russian, Bulgarian, Hungarian and Yugoslav programs (mostly sports and musical events and movies). Romanians in the northwestern and southwestern regions were able to regularly view Hungarian and Yugoslav television transmission, and to a lesser degree Czechoslovak television. Bulgarian television programs were received by Romanians in the southeastern part of the country, including Bucharest. In the eastern part of the nation that bordered on the Soviet Union, its predominantly Romanian-populated Moldavian Republic, viewers watched Soviet television programs by the end of the 1980s in what Questor (1990, 131) calls "a bizarre reversal of liberalizing impact," because of the "far richer and freer rendition of the news, news which played a major role in the dictator's violent downfall." The impact of Soviet television news programs on the "dictator's violent downfall" is highly exaggerated when one considers that in the northeastern cities of Romania close to what was then still the Soviet Union, the anti-Ceausescu revolution was highly limited.

Whose television played a major role in the revolution is hardly important. Hungarian television first, and then Yugoslav, Soviet and Bulgarian television (not necessarily in that order) broadcast news of events in Timisoara. What is important is that foreign television, along with foreign radio, did play an unquestionably important role in Romania in the revolt or revolution and during the months and years before. This role was testimony to the failure of Romania's media and to the urgent need for information that pushed a significant portion of the population to turn to outside sources. Only anecdotal evidence is available regarding the size of the audience that daily followed foreign television broadcasts. Yet, gauged by the knowledge Romanians displayed of happenings in the Western and fast-changing East-Central European world, their knowledge of Romanian dissidents in the diaspora, their works and their words, and new Western films, lifestyles and products, the audience was sizable. It is convincing evidence that points to a regular, major Romanian audience for foreign television and radio broadcasts.

The Romanians' television world was significantly enlarged by the presence of between 800,000 and 1 million videocassette recorders (VCRs).[32] Radu Cosarca (1993) a former RTV deputy chief editor and beginning in 1992 member of the National Audio-Visual Council, claims that unofficial statistics indicate that in the 1980s Romania had more VCRs per thousand inhabitants than any other European country. There is no way to ascertain the truth of his claim. Most certainly, only the high cost of a VCR unit (about 10 times the average monthly salary) prevented the faster spread of this new technology in Romania, whose private importation was allowed (Pompey, Dec. 17, 1987, 32). The buying, trading and loaning of VCR tapes of movies from the Western world became a major enterprise in the country during the 1980s. The viewing of the many (new) Western films on tape became a regular social event for families and friends and a forum for sociopolitical as well as cultural debates in the privacy of the home. In Cosarca's (1993) words, "The 45 years of socialism forbade—with small and rare exceptions—any form of revolt. The only accessible salvation was intellectual resistance through culture. ... [N]othing prevented the Romanian citizen from creating an oasis of spiritual liberty at home."

The private showing of videocassettes also became a way of making money for people who charged five to 15 times the price of a movie ticket (Pompey, Dec. 17, 1987, 32). In the final months before the revolution, the taping of television news reports in the rest of East-Central Europe and its sharing with friends, neighbors and others also became an important element in the spread of information that ultimately led to the Romanian revolt (Rosenstiel, Jan. 18, 1990, p. A-10).

Both foreign television, inclusive of VCR tapes, and radio provided Romanians with a window to the outside world through which information and entertainment provided them with images of themselves and others.

News, because of its "capacity to create meaning independent of the specific events to which the stories refer" (Dahlgren 1981, 102–3), as much as entertainment, served as an agent of information and socialization. Thanks to these foreign programs, Romanians were privy to advances in technology, differing and changing cultures, lifestyles, mores, philosophies, music and social and political upheavals. Western entertainment, particularly music and films, provided them with a boost, "drawing them daily into another world, happy or sad, funny or serious, away from their own" (Gross 1995). Neuman (June 1991, 25) is again accurate when she states,

> Television and movies did not, by themselves, topple Stalinist regimes, anymore than Western books or music or art had rid the world of dictatorship in earlier attempts at thought control. But they did provide glimpses of a society where creature comforts were common, where expression was open, where the link between a free people and a free press was assumed and even where bad taste was given mass license to broadcast.

The very existence of foreign broadcasts, particularly those in the Romanian language, also signaled that the rest of the world had not forgotten Romania or the Romanians. Together with the news of changes occurring all around them by 1989, Romanians derived emotional and psychological support from foreign broadcasts. The broadcasts gave them hope.

Urbanites, in particular, learned Serbian, Hungarian, Bulgarian and Russian from watching television and with the express purpose of understanding foreign newscasts and entertainment programs. It illustrated their strong need for information, even if only as background noise, other than that of their own mass media's. Learning other languages in order to access foreign media was a process of retooling, of adaptability, which indicated "a rejection in toto of a state/government/party-forced information and communication unidimensionality and isolation" (Gross 1995).

Foreign news and entertainment broadcasts were perceived by Romanians as highly legitimate and credible. They reached a people living on the brink of starvation and in total frustration. Because of that, foreign media functioned as major contributors to communist Romania's sociopolitical disintegration. For instance, foreign news broadcasts of conditions in Romania and events in that country matched the reality of the Romanian's daily life, and the foreign media's presentations of the Western world matched the vision of life Romanians wanted to experience. Therefore, foreign news and entertainment broadcasts aided the "concretization, augmentation, and enlargement of the negative relationship between citizens and the regime, and the final disintegration of that relationship" (Gross 1995).

CHAPTER 3

Media on a Noncommunist Footing

The growth of mass media outlets in Romania since December 1989 has been nothing short of spectacular. The suddenly unencumbered print media were the first to explode, followed by radio and, finally, television. This spectacular expansion occurred for sociopolitical, economic and even psychological reasons. It was accompanied by a number of still-unresolved problems associated with the degree and speed with which it happened.

The Press

Nourished by the absence of any official restraints, the Romanian press tripled in size by 1991, from 495 publications prior to the December 1989 revolution (National Statistical Commission 1992). Constant turnover and the absence of a nationwide, all-encompassing registration process make it difficult to ascertain the exact number of publications available to the reading public in the first six post-Ceausescu years.

In 1990, the Romanian PTT, the principal distributor of publications to all subscribers showed 589 periodicals being distributed in Romania (Ministerul Postelor si Telecomunicatiilor 1990). The unofficial count of publications by fall 1990 was more than 1,500.[1] The National Library's catalog (Gheorghiu 1991) showed 1,440 periodicals in 1991, a figure supported by Rompres (the national news agency) research showing 1,468 titles being distributed (1,379 in Romanian and 89 in other languages); the National Statistical Commission (NSC) in 1992 reported 1,545 dailies, weeklies and other publications. By 1994, the exact number of publications was still not easy to determine. It was widely estimated that around 1,800 publications were in existence. Ion Raus, executive secretary of the Romanian Association of Press Editors, claims there were more than 3,000 publications in Romania, inclusive of all those that appear more than twice per year (Caluschi, Sept. 26, 1994).

The revolving door of Romania's print media allows for continuous exits and entries for all manner of publications. For instance, a new daily newspaper with national circulation, *Ultimul Cuvint* (The Last Word),was introduced in Bucharest with great expense, fanfare and hope in January 1994, only to be laid to rest in April. Almost immediately a new daily sprang up, *Ziua* (The Day), with an initial circulation of about 80,000 that then fell to under 35,000 within weeks. Locally, too, new publications continue to be introduced.

Between December 1989 and 1995, the press was divided into three sometimes overlapping categories: the national press, the regional press, and the local press. The nature of this press ranged from the purely party and general-circulation periodicals to the more specialized intellectual, literary, religious, pornographic, sports, and other special interest-oriented publications.

The decentralization of Romania's press system (i.e., the increase of publication of newspapers outside of Bucharest) occurred almost instantly in December 1989. Gheorghiu (1991, 32) reports that 41.58 percent of publications were edited or published in Bucharest and 58.42 percent in other cities. Furthermore, she pointed out that of the dailies, 23 percent were published in Bucharest and 76 percent in other cities. She adds (33),

> The central/local balance manifest stronger variations with respect to the content and message of the existing newspapers. The score turns in favor of the local press in the case of the socio political papers (294:99). Among them, the most discriminating class is formed by the political parties' newspapers, of which about ⅘ are published outside Bucharest (80), and only ⅕(19) in the capital. Similar distortions appear in the case of the independent journals, where three quarters are local newspapers and one quarter is represented by the central press.

By 1995, the party press at the national and the local or regional levels had shrunk from a high of around 100 titles to about 50. No verifiable data were available by the end of 1995 regarding the central-local balance in newspaper publishing.

Aside from being the first institution to liberate itself from communist rule and to symbolize a new freedom, the Romanian press was also the first to signal a return to a market economy. For instance, the R Company, publisher of *Romania Libera,* received license number 001 in February 1990, the first private business to be officially recognized in postcommunist Romania. Ownership of publications ranged from individual ownership (e.g., Ion Ratiu and his *Cotidianul*) and private publishing houses, some of which have become miniature media empires controlling publications, radio and television stations (e.g., Expres Trust, Romania Libera, Nord Est Publishing), to publications owned by political parties, unions, associations, churches, and the state (at various levels).

Their circulation skyrocketed after Dec. 22, 1989, or was high when first introduced, only to plummet by 1995. For instance, two of the leading dailies, *Romania Libera* and *Adevarul,* published 1.2 million and 2 million issues, respectively, in January 1990. By the end of 1995, their daily circulations were down to 85,000 and 110,000, respectively. *Evenimentul Zilei,* a tabloid of the *National Enquirer* type, was introduced in fall 1992 and was an instant success. In two months it reached a daily circulation of 750,000. Yet by fall 1995 its circulation was down to 130,000 per day. Other dailies that fancied themselves to be national in reach had daily circulations in 1995 that ranged from around 7,000 to 30,000 (e.g., *Tineretul Liber,* 15,000; *Cotidianul,* 7,000; *Libertatea,* 30,000). Regional and local newspapers did not fare any better. For example, Timisoara's *Renasterea Banateana,* Constanta's *Telegraf,* Iasi's *Monitorul de Iasi,* Brasov's *Gazeta de Transilvania* and other local newspapers in the larger cities and towns claimed a circulation of 20,000 to 70,000 in 1995. More likely, their circulation was 15,000 to 20,000. Small-town newspapers (e.g., those in Vaslui, Ialomita and Lugoj) claimed circulations of between 5,000 and 6,000. The many national weeklies boast of circulations that had stabilized at between 20,000 and 150,000 in 1995 (e.g., *VIP,* 200,000; *Academia Catavencu,* 30,000; *Romania Mare,* 20,000). Major weeklies such as *Tinerama* and *Expres* ceased publication by 1995.

The economic problems besetting these publications are legion: the price of newsprint, printing costs, distribution costs, high taxes and the general inflation which has played havoc with the cost of equipment, building, personnel, and so on. In the immediate aftermath of the revolution, newsprint and printing costs were still partly or wholly subsidized by the state. According to Coman (1993),

These suitable prices of paper, energy, transports, manual labor, linked with the huge quantity of copies made the selling of written press one of the most blooming affairs. It turned into a kind of El Dorado, receiving all kinds of people who rushed toward this field, hungry of a quick profit.

Indeed, small fortunes were made in 1990. Alin Teodorescu, in 1994 in charge of the Institute for Marketing and Polls (Institutul de Marketing si Sondaj, or IMAS) in an interview in the intellectual weekly *22* (Armeanu, Feb. 25–March 3, 1993) described the ease with which anyone could get into publishing in the first few postrevolution months:

> Whoever had a few thousand lei could put out a newspaper: buy 100 kg. of paper which cost nothing at that time. *22* (a weekly published by the Group for Social Dialogue in Bucharest) started with 5 lei and some credit. *Expres* (national weekly published in Bucharest) started with a few hundred lei and the rest credit.

Yet, by the end of 1990 the liberalization of prices, the inflationary and (partly) artificial price hikes for newsprint and printing at the state-owned publication house, and tax increases somewhat dampened the opportunities for a quick buck. In spring 1990, a ton of newsprint cost 14,000 lei ($1 = 90 lei), in fall 1990, 32,000 lei; by 1991, the price was 50,000–70,000 lei. The cost of paper promised to continue to increase (Mediafax, Aug. 5, 1994), and indeed it did. Unless those newspapers were able to purchase newsprint from abroad, they had to decrease their circulation by almost 50 percent by 1991.[2] The trend continued. In summer 1995, the government-owned SC Letea SA Bacau, the sole newsprint producer in the country, raised its prices by 23.3 percent (Leca, June 1995). In December 1995, newsprint prices increased again, this time by 25 percent. Because of a shortage of newsprint, one that was artificially created, according to many,[3] the government allocations affected particularly those publications considered in opposition.

Making matters worse, the leu was made convertible on the world market in 1991. Thus began a process of repeated devaluation of the leu, contributing to the continued increase of newsprint prices. By 1992, the cost had more than doubled over the previous year to around 120,000 lei; by spring 1994, it had skyrocketed to 1,100,000 lei; and by the end of 1995, it was a whopping 2,600,000 lei ($1 = 2,500 lei). Independent newspapers threatened to strike in 1991 unless the government provided subsidies for newsprint purchases.[4] None were forthcoming. Yet, newspaper publishers and editors met with President Ion Iliescu three years later, in March 1994, and received his commitment to tackle the problems of paper prices, distribution and transportation (*Telegrama* no. 10, March 22, 1994). In April

1994, editors and publishers of *Adevarul, Romania Libera, Evenimentul Zilei, Ora, Libertatea, Curierul National* and *Curierul Romanesc* petitioned Prime Minister Vacaroiu to exempt the press from taxes for newsprint and advertising, a 60 percent reduction in tariffs paid for transporting newspapers and the elimination of the last increase in tariffs. (*Telegrama* no. 28, April 15, 1994). Despite these efforts, the availability and price of newsprint will continue to be a problem for newspapers.

The monopoly of printing facilities enjoyed by the state also assured its ability to attempt to control the print media by raising production costs. Two printing houses in Bucharest, Libertatea and Presa Libera (formerly Casa Scinteii) controlled all publishing, particularly after the June 1990 riots by miners who destroyed printing equipment belonging to a handful of other publications considered in opposition. Outside of Bucharest the same monopoly persisted, so that in Timisoara, for instance, 30 publications were printed by the same state publishing house. Romanian printing houses, with equipment from the 1950s and 1960s, are slow and produce poor-quality printing. "We are close to the Gutenberg era," admitted Petre Mihai Bacanu of *Romania Libera* in January 1990.[5] The state monopoly was not to be broken until 1992–93, when Ion Ratiu installed his own new press at *Cotidianul, Romania Libera* put a new printing facility into operation and a number of publications outside Bucharest followed suit (in Timisoara, Brasov, Constanta and other cities and towns).

Printing costs began increasing in August 1990, when an 80 percent increase was announced by state-controlled printing houses, followed in September by a demand that the press pay in advance of printing (*Article 19*, 306), which sometimes amounted to 30 percent of the value of each issue. (Ruston, September 1990, 5). Printing costs have continued to go up since then. Adding to the cost of publishing was a July 1990 law which forced newspapers to pay quarterly income taxes on their income *in advance, based on estimates of future income calculated by the state.*

Distribution, too, was still mainly in the hands of state agencies (Rodiped), although by 1991 individual newspapers or groups of newspapers began forming their own limited distribution systems. Ruston (September 1990, 6) reports that "the service takes 30% of the profit made from sales and, as from August 1990, demands 10% of the issue's value in advance."

To illustrate the increase in costs, a brief look at *Tineretul Liber* in January 1990 and June 1991 provides a microcosm of the problems encountered by the independent press.[6] In January 1990 the newspaper had a circulation of 500,000 and paid 7,000 lei per ton of paper, 580,000 lei for printing, 800,000 lei in salaries to its 100 employees and 270,000 lei in taxes. It had 71,000 lei in other expenses (including telephone, transportation and other materials) and paid 3,720,000 lei for distribution (30 percent of its sales of

12,400,000 lei, to which was added another 100,000 lei in advertising revenues). In June 1991, the newspaper's circulation was down to 180,000. It paid 50,000 lei per ton of paper, 976,000 lei for printing, 2,500,000 lei in salaries to 125 employees, and 900,000 in taxes. It had 247,000 lei in other expenses and paid 5,440,000 lei in distribution costs (32 percent of income from sales). In spring 1994, the cost of printing and newsprint for 50,000 copies of a newspaper was up to 6,000,000 lei ($3,572 at the exchange rate of $1 = 1,680 lei in May–June 1994); for 100,000 copies, 10,400,000 lei ($6,190). Average salaries for 100 employees had gone up to 10,000,000 lei ($5,952) or higher and some newspapers were paying as much as 36 percent of their sales income toward distribution.[7] The overall cost of publishing has risen faster than the average 200–300 percent annual inflation rate that persisted until 1995, when it fell to 27.8 percent.

There is also a great deal of inefficiency built into the press system. Staffs are sometimes enormous for the size of the publications, adding to the expense of publishing. *Romania Libera, Evenimentul Zilei* and *Adevarul,* the three largest national-circulation publications, each publishing between 8 and 16 pages daily, had editorial staffs of 200, 500 and 90, respectively, until 1995. The size of the staffs is a function of nepotism, friendships, bragging rights and a lack of experience in running modern-day newspapers. In Romania, Garnham's (1990, 110) argument that the "pursuit of political freedom may override the search for economic efficiency" has been averred. By mid-1994, moves to restructure newspaper staffs and reduce the number of employees were hoped to prove successful in increasing productivity and lowering costs by 1995. Limited success was recorded by the end of 1995.

The aggregate affect of this continuing upward spiral in the price of producing and distributing a publication has been a continuous inflation in its price. While newspapers charged 1 or 2 lei per issue in January 1990, by 1995 the price of a daily was up to 300–400 lei and that of a weekly up to 400–600 lei, at a time when the average monthly income of a Romanian worker was 120,000–180,000 lei.

The smaller-circulation newspapers rely almost exclusively on subscription and street sales for their income. Even the country's largest-circulation daily newspaper in spring 1994, the eight-page *Evenimentul Zilei,* had a total of only one page worth of advertisements, inclusive classifieds, or just 12.5 percent of each day's issue. The 16-page *Romania Libera,* with the second-largest circulation in the country, published roughly four to six pages of advertising per issue, or 25 to 37 percent of its newspaper. A full-page ad in *Evenimentul Zilei* cost 5,040,000 lei ($3,000 at the May–June 1994 exchange rate) in spring 1994; at *Romania Libera* the cost of one page was 4,116,000 lei ($2,450). Around 40 percent of *Romania Libera*'s income in spring 1994 was derived from subscriptions and street sales and around 60 percent from advertising; *Evenimentul Zilei* earned only around 20 percent of its income from advertising; *Adevarul,* the third-largest-circulation daily, received roughly 15 percent of its income from advertising. The rest of the Romanian press's income from advertising is estimated to range from 1 to 15 percent of total revenues.

The primary reason for Romanian publications' minimal reliance on advertisements as their main revenues stems first and foremost from the not-yet-completed privatization of the Romanian economy and its low level of development. Second, the low circulation numbers of the many newspapers also contributed and still contribute to the disinterest of would-be advertisers. Third, there is as yet not a market mentality which values advertising as a reliable, significant tool of aggressive selling. Fourth, on the one hand, in the first postrevolution years the increase in the availability of products and the hunger of the population for all manner of articles made it unnecessary for sellers to advertise in order to move their wares; on the other hand, increased inflation, and salaries that have not kept up with it, coupled with unemployment have made the many imported products far too expensive for most people and therefore considerably lessened the perceived need to significantly advertise these products.

Yet, the aggregate number of publications and their circulation and readership are still impressive. Alin Teodorescu[8] in 1992 estimated that 8 million Romanians (35 percent of the population) purchase one or more newspapers each day. Considering that these newspapers are passed along to at least one other reader in the household (mother, father, brother, sister, son, daughter) or a neighbor, nearly 70 percent of the population is daily exposed to the press.

And it has been an extremely diverse press. This pluralism has persisted, albeit tenuously, despite every publication wanting a bigger slice of the readership pie. A March 1994 national survey by IMAS revealed that 39.8 percent of those polled read *Evenimentul Zilei,* 36.9 percent a local newspaper, 16.4 percent *Adevarul,* 15.7 percent *Romania Libera,* 5.6 percent *Gazeta Sporturilor* and 3.9 percent *Sportul Romanesc.* Other publications read by between 2.4 and 0.2 percent of those polled are (in descending order): *Tineretul Liber, Ora, Curierul National, Romaniai Magyar Szo* (a Hungarian publication), *Cotidianul, Ultimul Cuvint* (which died in April 1994), *Cronica Romana, Vremea, Jurnalul National, Dimineata, Azi, Meridian* and *Vocea Romaniei.*

A French group, Mediametrie, surveyed the Bucharest media scene in the May 6–26, 1994 period, replicating a study it carried out in the same period in 1993, and found only slight changes (Un Sondaj Occidental, Aug. 3, 1994). By December 1995, readership had dropped drastically, according to a poll conducted by the Center for Urban and Regional Sociology (December 1995).

TABLE 3.1.   Newspaper Audience Size in Bucharest (in percentage)

	Dec. 1995	May 1994	May 1993
Evenimentul Zilei	24	71.8	82.3
Romania Libera	11	50.2	34.0
Tineretul Liber	2	26.3	21.6
Gazeta Sporturilor	6	25.0	28.4
Adevarul	13	21.2	23.2
Jurnalul National	4	20.1	N.D.
Libertatea	N.D.	19.7	24.0
Sportul Romanesc	4	17.5	20.8
Curierul National	2	14.8	11.5
Cotidianul	7	14.7	12.6
Ora	N.D.	11.8	10.5

N.D. = no data.

In part, economics has led Romania's general-circulation press to become more sensationalist in its approach to news coverage and more enter-
tainment-oriented. In the 1990–95 period, economic threats, combined with
sociocultural and political threats, have been directed more or less successfully at the "special" press: pornographic, party, intellectual and literary or
artistic publications.

By the end of 1994, the local press was also hard-pressed by competition from major national newspapers that sought to establish localized versions of their publications. This competition directly threatened the future of
the local press, because it has fewer resources to compete with its major national counterparts.

The political party press fell from around 100 daily and weekly party
or party-affiliated newspapers to fewer than 50 by spring 1994.[9] Most of
them disappeared because of economic reasons or because of a shrinking
readership. In a strange twist, the independent, nationalistic newspaper *Romania Mare* gave birth to its own party on June 20, 1991, bearing the same
name.

Pornographic publications, which quickly appeared in the wake of
Ceausescu's fall, had run out of steam by 1993 and their numbers were drastically reduced. *Bordel, Sexpress, Club Sex Caprice,* and *Pink House* either
disappeared altogether or their circulations fell to a few thousand. Only *Pa-
siunea* (formerly *Prostitutia*) was still on newsstands in 1993 (Comanescu,
Aug. 13–19, 1993). However, by 1995 the number of pornographic publications once again increased.

The most threatened of the long-standing press are the literary, art-re-
lated, and intellectual publications. Poet Mircea Dinescu presciently saw the
threat to the cultural publications back in 1990 and dubbed it the Romanian
culture's "second (period) of darkness" (Dinescu, Nov. 16, 1990). Without
the full government subsidies enjoyed during the communist period, they
must hustle for funds, newsprint, time on printing machines and for readers.

Cristea noted back in 1991 (Oct. 25–Nov. 1, 1991) that "in principle there is no one for whom the crisis of the cultural publications provokes even a minute's-worth of a nightmare. No protection exists, and there is no exit [from this crisis]."

Despite dire predictions, the most important of the cultural publications were still published on a regular basis in 1995: *Romania literara* (Bucharest), *Orizont* (Timisoara), *Convorbiri literare* (Iasi) and *Equinox* (Cluj). Others like *Secolul XX* had temporarily disappeared and yet others were published only intermittently, whenever funds were obtained from some source or another. Even new publications were being introduced, such as the monthly *Premiera,* published by Romanian Express and Romaniafilm (S., Calin, May 4, 1994). The cost per issue, 1,200 lei, was about four times the cost of a weekly and six times that of a daily.

Publications with a distinctively intellectual leaning, such as the weekly *22* of the Group for Social Dialogue (which sold around 50,000 copies each week in 1990), were down to 5,000 to 9,000 copies sold nation-wide in 1995. The Civil Society's monthly, *Sfera Politicii,* which publishes longer treatises, essays and other scholarly ruminations, also sold fewer than 5,000 copies.

Smaller circulation and fewer choices in the cultural and intellectual area aside, the Romanian press is still diverse and rich in numbers. Daily and weekly newspapers account for 45 percent (around 700) of all publications in Romania. Altogether, the plethora of mass media belies Schramm's (1972, 34) notion that "the size of communication activity—the development of mass media and their audiences ... the stretching out of communications chains" reflects economic development in transitional society. Also, the relatively high total media consumption was and still is not in step with the low consumption patterns suggested by Lerner (1958) for societies in the process of transition or development. In part, the press's situation in Romania can be explained by its relatively high literacy rate of around 80 percent, a long cultural tradition, and readers who were for 42 years starved from a communication or information perspective by the policies of the communist regime.

Unlike in Hungary, and to a lesser extent in Poland and the Czech Republic, the international media moguls did not see fit in 1990–94 to pursue the purchase of Romanian newspapers or invest in them. Murdoch, Springer Verlag, Maxwell, and Berlusconi have stayed out of Romania. A relatively limited amount of foreign money seeped into the Romanian mass media market via Romanian expatriates returning with foreign capital (e.g., Dragan and Givelakian).

One other feature of the press system in Romania that was demonopolized after December 1989 is the news agency field. The largest agency, Rompres, is the renamed Agerpres that was the main gatekeeper of news for the Romanian press during the communist period. Reorganization of Ager-pres began on Dec. 27, 1989, and was followed by a Jan. 8, 1990 decree establishing its new name (Rompres) and duties. It is still a government, or quasi-government agency, employing roughly 270 journalists and translators, covering every judet or county in the country. It has foreign correspondents stationed in Brussels, Washington, D.C., and Paris, and it has collaborative agreements with the major world news services, according to Rompres's new head, Neagu Udroiu.[10] Rompres provides daily national and international news items to Romanian press and broadcasting outlets throughout the country and puts out 20 publications on various subjects.

The major change since December 1989 was the establishment of independent news agencies that provide national and international news to the newly configured Romanian news media system. They sprang up essentially to provide a counterbalance to Rompres, which is still not trusted by many editors, and because it promised to be a money-making endeavor. The most significant of these news agencies include AR Press, R Press and MediaFax. Other smaller news services include Vest Press, North East Press and Telegrama, which is being developed as an international news service distributed by electronic mail (E-mail).

Broadcasting

The introduction of independent broadcasting followed shortly on the heels of the press's sudden divorce from its communist masters in December 1989. What distinguished broadcasting from the press in the immediate post-Ceausescu months was that the former was monopolized on the national level by Romanian Radio and Romanian Television, while the latter instantly demonopolized. The new private stations, whose numbers had increased spectacularly by 1995, catered to a strictly local or regional audience.

With the new freedom and the birth of independent broadcasting came the establishment of associations and societies whose main purpose was to represent the new radio, television and cable stations. Romania now has, among other similar groupings,

1. Romanian Society for Cable Television (Societatea Romana de Televiziune prin Cablu)
2. Union of Radio Broadcast Creators (Uniunea Creatorilor de Emisiuni Radiofonice)

3. Romanian Association of Audio-Visual Communication (Asociatia Romana de Comunicatii Audiovizuale)

4. Association of Local Private Television Stations (Uniunea Nationala a Televiziunilor Locale Particulare din Romania, or UNTELPRO)

Radio

The story of Romanian radio, which began in 1925, took major turns with the communist takeover in 1947 and the communists' subsequent overthrow in December 1989. The communists' use of radio for propaganda purposes was sealed by their control over the medium. Still, there was a modicum of freedom left to radio that was not available to print or television.[11] For economic reasons, as well as to increase and further centralize control, communist-controlled Romanian Radio closed its six regional studios in 1985. One story told by Bogdan Herzog,[12] the director of the Timisoara station, has it that when the regional stations were closed, their tape and record libraries were taken to Bucharest and interred in a prison.

Romanian Radio

Late on December 22, 1989, Romanian Radio (RR) freed itself from its communist shackles, and at least three of its regional stations (Timisoara, Iasi, Constanta) returned to active service, albeit with skeletal staffs.

In Timisoara, the head of RR's Timisoara Radio studio, Herzog,[13] related how he and at least 30 other radio reporters and technicians, as well as some citizens, resumed broadcasting. Without permission from Bucharest, they took it upon themselves to cover events in the city in around-the-clock broadcasts on the renamed Free Timisoara station. In Iasi, Grigore Ilisei[14] of the Iasi Radio, along with a handful of others, did the same as their colleagues in Timisoara.

RR has reorganized since December 1989. As of Jan. 2, 1990, the new leadership had reformulated it main objectives. RR, according to a speech given by the new director general, Eugen Preda, at a seminar held in Prague, the Czech Republic, in December 1992 (Preda, Dec. 17–18, 1992):

1. was to do away with the [then] state of chaos,
2. was to remake RR so that it may be listened to even when no tragic or dramatic events are occurring, and
3. was to move to new headquarters and re-equip its studios.

Furthermore, because Preda (1993) recognized that in "a moment in which there are radical structural transformations, the general tension is accentuated by the fact that the social actors fail to assume clear roles," RR assumed new roles. He defined these new roles as:

1. A national public radio station, "which presumes a change from a status of subordinate to the power to that of a partner to the citizen."

2. A voice, "which fights for the implementation of certain new moral principles in society."

3. A "partner to political forces in the process of renovating the legislative process (through contributions to the editing of laws specific to the audio-visual field and through special consulting ... to Parliament)."

With the enactment of the new Public Radio and Television Law (see the Television section later in this chapter), Romanian Radio became separated from Romanian Television and an autonomous public service. It now broadcasts on five programs: Romania-Actualitati (news and feature reports); Romania-Cultural (cultural, artistic programs); Romania-Tineret-Stereo (programs for youth and children); Antena Bucurestilor (local Bucharest news and features); Antena Satelor (news and features directed at the countryside). RR also has a National Minorities program in German and Hungarian, Radio Romania International with four simultaneous, daily broadcasts on medium and shortwave in 14 languages. It operates six regional stations: Cluj, Timisoara, Iasi, Tirgu Mures, Craiova, and Constanta.

In 1993–94 RR had about 1,800 employees, including technical and administrative personnel, as well as journalists, translators and others. Between 300 and 400 of RR's employees came on board after December 1989 and are in their 20s and 30s. RR's budget, after the enactment of the Public Radio and Television Law, is to come from a variety of sources (see the Television section of this chapter).

By 1994, the leadership of RR had considerably improved the physical and technical endowment of this now-public broadcasting service. New equipment to replace the vintage 1950s Siemens equipment was slowly being installed, and RR's studios began looking more like modern broadcast facilities rather than a museum.[15] A new building was assigned to RR by a government decision (No. 571/992), on Stirbei Voda Street in Bucharest—ironically, the former National Museum.

RR's success or failure is entirely in the hands of its leadership and personnel—it has no competition on the national level. It has plenty of local competition. Its news program listenership in Bucharest has been rising, as surveys taken in May 1993 and May 1994 by a French institute, Mediametrie (Un Sondaj Occidental, Aug. 3, 1994) illustrate. However, its cultural program lost some of its already limited audience, partly because of competition for independent radio. By the end of 1995, according to the Center for Urban and Regional Sociology (December 1995), listenership went up again.

TABLE **3.2.**   **Romanian Radio Programs' Audience Share** (in percentage)

	Dec. 1995	May 1994	May 1993
Romania Actualitati	64.0	52.4	58.8
Romania Cultural	6.0	3.8	4.3

Independent Radio

In the aftermath of the Ceausescus' demise, independent radio made its appearance in a number of cities. Makeshift, one- or two-room radio studios cropped up in several cities, aided in part by equipment donated by American, French, English or Belgian organizations.[16] Some managed to get a temporary license and frequency from Romanian PTT, while others piggybacked on regional RR frequencies. None had its own transmitter.

Independent stations such as Nova 22, which began broadcasting on Feb. 4, 1990, Radio Contact, on the air since Feb. 25, 1990, and Radio Fun, on the air since Jan. 11, 1990, encountered a slew of problems. These included the lack of adequate financing, equipment, trained personnel and studio space.

Initially, no license fees were charged to noncommercial stations. However, many were in fact commercial or partly so.[17] Since 1993, local radio has had to pay taxes or fees in accordance with the NAVC's Ordinance No. 9 of Aug. 4, 1993 (*NAVC Buletin* no. 4–5, 1993, 12–13):

TABLE 3.3. **Radio Station Taxes** (initial 1993 rates)

NAVC taxes	
Sign-up fee for license competition	80,000 lei
Initial license tax	320,000 lei
Authorization tax	20,000 lei
Annual license tax	160,000 lei
Ministry of Communication taxes	
Initial technical notice fee/tax	80,000 lei
Technical authorization tax	200,000 lei
Total initial cost for new radio station:	860,000 lei
(at 1993 exchange rates:	$537.50)

Transmission fees were high and on an upward spiral from 1990 to 1995. For instance, the Herzog-led[18] radio in Timisoara paid 800 lei per transmission hour in 1991. In Brasov, a small station run by Adrian Ureche[19] was paying out 140,000 lei per month in transmission costs. By 1994, the PTT charged broadcasters a per-minute and per-kilometer fee: between 0 and 100 kilometer radius, each minute cost 750 lei plus 5 lei per kilometer; for greater than 100 kilometer radius, each minute cost 750 lei plus 2.5 lei per kilometer.

In 1991, independent Radio Contact had six full-time staff and 30 volunteers, none with any prior experience in radio, working in a space of 16 square meters.[20] Ninety percent of its income was derived from commercials and 10 percent from "donations."

At independent Radio Delta, five full-timers (two of whom had prior broadcasting experience) and 40 part-timers worked in two rooms. Half the station's income came from production contracts and the other half from (unidentified) nongovernmental allocations.

By 1993–94, the personnel situation had not markedly improved for independent radio and the financial situation, while ameliorated, had not kept up with rising costs of producing programs, acquiring new equipment, raising salaries to keep in step with inflation, and other expenses of transmitting. At Uniplus Radio, Dan Klinger[21] reported in 1993 that only four employees were responsible for reporting and producing four minutes of news programs for every hour of the day. Uniplus was running five to eight commercials each hour, earning 75 percent of its income from commercials. Managers of independent radio stations are quick to divulge the size of their expenditures but keep secret the amount of income and its sources.

Independent radio in every corner of Romania still concerns itself mainly with local or regional news, entertainment and the retransmission of programs received from the BBC, VOA, and other French, American, English or Italian stations. Talk radio was introduced in 1993 with a modicum of success. Max Banus,[22] owner of Radio Tinerama and the host of a new talk show, says that this format "gives people a chance to talk, especially old people. All of a sudden they have a voice and an audience." Despite growth, independent radio has rarely, and only marginally, been a subject in the many public discussions of Romanian media in their various aspects, in articles, in seminars, in colloquia and other forums.

The size of radio audiences was not authoritatively calculated, individual stations guessing the number of listeners by subscription numbers and informal telephone polls. A 1993 Gallup poll reported by Radio Romania (1993) showed a 25 percent audience share for independent radio. The French survey institute, Mediametrie shows a growth in independent radio listenership in the capital between May 1993 and May 1994 (Un Sondaj Occidental, Aug. 3, 1994):

TABLE **3.4.** **Radio Audience Shares in Bucharest** (in percentage)

	May 1994	May 1993
Contact	26.4	18.3
Pro FM	12.1	7.0
Uniplus	8.6	11.4
Fun Radio	5.0	0.4
Antena 1	4.3	N.D.
Radio Total	3.1	N.D.
Radio Tinerama	2.0	N.D.

N.D. = no data.

A national IRSOP poll by the end of 1994 (December 1994), showed listenership over a seven-day period divided among the following stations: Romanian Radio–News (62 percent); local public radio (28 percent); Romanian Radio–Cultural Program (16 percent); local private radio (12 percent) Romanian Radio–Youth Program (12 percent); Romanian Radio–

Village Program (8 percent); a foreign-language station (7 percent); a foreign station broadcasting in the Romanian language (4 percent).

By July 1995, 141 radio licenses had been issued to groups or individuals in 57 cities and towns (14 of them were annulled by the NAVC for various reasons). As 1995 came to a close, radio listenership changed slightly from 1994, according to a poll by the Center for Urban and Regional Sociology (December 1995): Romanian Radio–News (64 percent); local private radio (26 percent); local public radio (25 percent); Romanian Radio–Cultural Program (6 percent); Romanian Radio–Youth Program (6 percent); a foreign station broadcasting in the Romanian language (6 percent); a foreign-language station (5 percent); Romanian Radio–Village Program (4 percent).

Television

Romanian Television

The history of Romanian television began in 1956 with the establishment of the state television entity. It broadcast on a national channel, Channel 1, and a Bucharest-and-surroundings channel, Channel 2, which reached about 13 percent of the country. Until December 1989 Romanian Television was tightly controlled by the Communist Party. On Dec. 22, 1989, it became Free Romanian Television (see chapter 2).

Free Romanian Television's life span lasted less than two months. By February 1990, Romanian Television was once again a valuable and manipulated asset of the powers-that-be. Coverage of major events such as the miners' rampage through Bucharest in June 1990, the May 1990 elections, the anti-communist demonstrations in Bucharest's University Square and the ethnic conflicts in Tirgu Mures in March 1990, to name only a few, was deemed biased by the political forces in opposition to President Iliescu and the National Salvation Front. London's *Index on Censorship,* in a report on Sept. 25, 1990, said that "the role of state-run television during the election campaign and the violent events of June 1990, and since that time, reveals a persistent misuse of power." Dumitru Iuga, the leader of the Free Union of RTV, went on his first of many hunger strikes in December 1990 to try to force change in RTV's management and in the government and the presidency's influence over RTV and to raise salaries of television employees.[23]

In 1991, more controversy surrounded RTV. A semiweekly program featuring debates between representatives of opposition parties and representatives of government was canceled in February, and German- and Hungarian-language programs were cut in half. Throughout 1992, RTV continued to be lambasted by the independent press and by the political opposition for doing President Iliescu's and the government's bidding. There were more strikes at RTV. Controversy surrounding Channel 2 exploded regarding its rumored takeover by a joint Anglo-American company (C. Pavel, Dec. 22–25, 1992) and even the opening of a third RTV channel.

Not much had changed by 1993, except that the appointment of Paul Everac to replace Razvan Theodorescu at the helm of RTV made matters even worse. The union went on strike (Preisz, July 15, 1993), and RTV's leadership was reshuffled. Iuga and the union continued their calls for the severing of the economic umbilical cord to the government and state. Iuga's demands included[24] "neutrality for RTV, to be separated from all political forces, to have both professional and political autonomy." In a public news release in July 1993,[25] Iuga called for

1. The enactment of the new Public Radio and Television Law.

2. The immediate dismissal of General Director Paul Everac, through whom "RTV is in this moment ... subordinated to (the) ruling political structures of Romania."

3. Political and economic independence for RTV.

4. Removing the military guard around RTV, through whose presence the "Romanian government controls RTV with armed forces."

In the news release, Iuga reiterated what he had been saying for four years: "We must underline that political independence of RTV is a necessary condition for its existence. Otherwise we cannot talk about a real democratization of the social and political life in Romania, because the private TV stations do not represent a real competition for RTV."

Salaries were also an issue, and the union demanded a 78 percent increase. It did not get it. In January 1994, Everac was finally replaced by Dumitru Popa, who became the fourth director general since the December 1989 revolution. A former professor of journalism from the now-closed Communist Party university, the Stefan Gheorghiu Academy in Bucharest, Popa served as the head of the government's Information Department before Prime Minister Nicolae Vacaroiu appointed him to head the RTV.

The enactment of the new Public Radio and Television Law launched a new era, but the changes at RTV are yet to be measured, and its troubles seem to multiply. The Christian Broadcasting Network sued RTV over a film contract (Leahu, April 29, 1994), then more than 30 RTV editorial and technical staff left RTV in April 1994 for a new private television station, Tele 7 ABC. It was expected that altogether 200 RTV employees would leave for Tele 7 ABC (*Telegrama,* April 6, 1994). The battle over control of RTV, between the government and Iuga's union, continued into 1995, and so did Iuga's periodic hunger strikes ("PDSR's strife," April 1995).

RTV is a dinosaur, an anachronistic institution, steeped in mystery.

Clear, verifiable truths are hard to obtain. Iuga[26] said in 1993 that RTV employs 5,300 people, of whom 150 are engaged in television journalism, while RTV's administrative director reported around 2,600 employees. RTV's news operation had 14 bureaus scattered around the country but no permanent foreign ones. Its technological and physical endowment, although somewhat updated since 1990, dates back to the 1950s and 1960s. Its budget is derived from subscriber fees, state allocations, production contracts and commercials. The latter have become a common and growing staple since 1990. From January 1990 to June 1991, RTV reported a doubling in advertising revenues (i.e., from 17 million lei per month to 35 million lei per month), a reflection of an increase in the number of commercials as well as a 200 percent inflation rate. In 1993, RTV's Channel 1 broadcast a total of 67 minutes per day of commercials, at an average cost of $4,166 per minute (Maratu 1993). RTV's Channel 2 charged $2,433 per minute of commercial time. Overall income from commercials for both RTV channels was kept "confidential" in 1993–94.

As a public broadcasting service, RTV has certain benefits not extended to the new private stations. For instance, in August 1994 it was announced that RTV would be exempt from paying any taxes on any equipment it purchased abroad valued up to $3 million (*Telegrama*, Aug. 19, 1994). Additionally, it has a guaranteed income: subscription money.

Despite its long list of problems, RTV is the most pervasive of the Romanian mass media. It does not yet have competition on the national level. At the local level the competition was still growing, but RTV remains the most watched station, as attested by a 1994 French survey by Mediametrie in Bucharest (Un Sondaj Occidental, Aug. 3, 1994):

TABLE 3.5. **Television Audience Share in Bucharest** (in percentage)

	May 1994	May 1993
RTV 1	81.9	79.3
RTV 2	34.8	13.4
Antena 1	22.3	N.D.
Soti TV	14.8	8.1
MTV	9.6	0.1
RTL	5.6	0.1
Canale 5	4.1	N.D.
Sat 1	3.7	N.D.

N.D. = no data.

Not much had changed by the end of 1994 when an IRSOP (December 1994) poll conducted over a seven-day period showed 83 percent of the public watching RTV 1, 22 percent a foreign TV station, 19 percent RTV 2, 15 percent a neighboring country's TV station, 13 percent a local private station and 6 percent a local public station.

In April 1994, RTV announced plans to begin transmitting its programs via satellite (*Telegrama,* April 27, 1994), thus extending its reach even beyond Romania's borders. In May 1994, it signed an agreement with Music Television (MTV) to broadcast the latter's programs two hours per week. RTV had been broadcasting some American Worldnet programs, as well as other U.S. productions such as "Wild America," "Computer Chronicles," "Good Morning America," and the "George Michael Sports Machine." RTV's audience share remained high in 1995. Its Channel 1 attracted 87 percent of viewers; its Channel 2, 36 percent (Center for Urban and Regional Sociology, December 1995, 22).

SOTI Television

The establishment of an independent national television station, as a counterbalance to the RTV, was a central demand of the opposition forces in spring 1990. It was also a rallying cry of the anti-communist forces that occupied University Square in Bucharest in summer 1990. In September 1990, the Romanian Society for the Creation of an Independent National Television Company (Societatea Romana Pentru Infiintarea Unei Companii Nationale De Televiziune Independenta, or SOTI) was established in Bucharest.[27] Its initial organizers and supporters included some of the most well-known Romanian journalists, intellectuals, dissidents and civic leaders.[28]

A seven-person leadership committee conducted its first meeting in October 1990 at the headquarters of the intellectual weekly *22*. SOTI set up a bank account and called for donations which were to be turned into shares in the company. It also encouraged Romanians from all walks of life to subscribe to the new service in advance (see advertisement, "TALON-SOTI" and "TALON Post T.V. Continental" in *Romania Libera,* Dec. 14, 1990). Millions of lei were collected.[29]

SOTI received support from the Washington, D.C.–based International Media Fund (IMF) in the form of a $400,000 turnkey production studio in 1991, and additional financial help in subsequent years. In time, it also received aid from the Soros Foundation. A concerted effort was made by Romanian civic institutions, political parties, the U.S. Embassy and the IMF to encourage a reluctant Romanian Parliament and government to allow the appropriate authorities to grant SOTI a temporary license and RTV broadcast time on its frequencies. The authorities, including Prime Minister Petre Roman,[30] argued that no authorization for SOTI could be given before a new Audio-Visual Law was enacted.

Feeling the intense pressure from domestic and foreign quarters, on April 11, 1991, the Parliamentary Commission on Culture, Art and Mass Media gave its assent for RTV to allow SOTI to broadcast three hours of programs on Channel 2 beginning at 11 p.m.[31] It is significant to note again that Channel 2 is a local Bucharest-and-surroundings channel and not one with a national reach. The whole notion of an independent, national television was thus eliminated. In an accompanying letter, the president of the Senate, A. Birladeanu, stated that the commission only gave permission for two-hour broadcasts "after the end of the program" (RTV-Channel 2).[32] RTV balked at allowing SOTI any time on its frequencies. Domestic and international pressure increased.

The granting of authorization for SOTI broadcasts and access to RTV frequencies was clearly a political question, as a letter from Prime Minister Petre Roman (June 7, 1991) to Marvin Stone, president and chairman of the International Media Fund, suggested. While expressing commitment to establish independent local and national television stations, Prime Minister Roman stated, "The initiative of the SOTI group for a national independent television could be called rather politically alternative than independent, which is compatible with the principle of political pluralism, of course, but leaves the problem of representativity [sic] at a national level still open."

It was not until the end of August 1991 that RTV agreed to allow SOTI to "experiment" on Channel 2 with one-hour programs Mondays, Tuesdays, Wednesdays and Thursdays between 11 and 12 p.m.[33] The programs were to include no commercials, and thus effectively eliminated potential income for SOTI, which signed a one-year contract with RTV.

The powers-that-be had nothing to fear from SOTI as it lacked a truly professional technical, journalistic and managerial staff, organizational skills, money and everything else required to establish a bona fide television operation, particularly one that could provide RTV with serious competition (Tripcovici, April 22, 1991). Those journalists from RTV and newspapers, notably *Romania Libera,* who helped out initially were in the preprofessional phase, as were all their other colleagues. SOTI's collaborative relationship with the Group for Social Dialogue and the League of Students was short-lived, as was that with the existing local television stations in other cities.

This attempt at an independent television with a national reach became, if not a disaster, an addition to Romania's local broadcast media that was of relatively limited consequence. It disappointed the expectant public as much as it did the political opposition which anticipated it to act as a "Fifth Column" in Romania's political wars (Stanescu, Jan. 22, 1992). By December 1991, the infighting within SOTI grew and the first of the many executive directors (Radu Budeanu) was abruptly fired.[34] By January 1992 the infighting increased and split the leadership council, with some members being kicked out. Financial, staff and production problems mounted despite the diligent, professional work of IMF consultants sent to help the operation, and an eager staff of 10 to 15 youngsters. An attempt at creating a SOTI network with other local television stations succeeded but without the participation of SOTI Bucharest, which, for reasons never clearly explained, resisted cooperation.[35]

For better or worse, the public viewed SOTI as an alternative to RTV Channels 1 and 2, and it did manage an 8.1 percent share of the audience in 1993 and even an increase to a 14.8 percent audience share in 1994, trailing RTV1, RTV2 and the new Antena 1 ("Un Sondaj Occidental," Aug. 3, 1994). In 1993, finally able to run commercials, it charged an average of $373 for a commercial minute and claimed to run 72 minutes worth of commercials per day, Monday through Saturday, and 56 minutes on Sunday. (Maratu 1993).

By spring 1994, SOTI was no longer on the air. It lost its permission to share the frequency of RTV Channel 2. Its small production facility still churned out some programs that were once in a while seen on some local channel. SOTI was the right idea at the right time, but organized and managed in the worst possible way. Its preprofessionally produced programs provided somewhat of an alternative to RTV's. The return on the investment in SOTI by Romanians and foreign supporters is questionable at best; more realistically it belongs in the lost column.

Local and Regional Television and Networks

The first independent television station to take to the airwaves was Free Timisoara Television (Gross 1990a). By 1993, 16 local stations were transmitting a hodgepodge of programs ranging from local news and documentaries to foreign films and self-produced talk shows or interviews, from Worldnet to other U.S.-produced programs.[36]

None of these newly established stations had anything resembling a professional studio, producing their programs with a few odds and ends of equipment, much of it loaned by individuals. The mix of equipment was more or less the same at each station: a couple of TV monitors, one to three video cameras, a couple of video recorders, one or more cassette players, two to four lights, a sound mixer and some microphones.

Armed with temporary licenses, they obtained permission to transmit their programs on the RTV channels, after the latter had ended its programs, having no transmission equipment of their own. In Brasov, the local television station transmitted programs by taking a video camera with a tape of a locally produced program to the RTV's transmitting antenna, plugging it in and running the tape at their appointed hour.[37] It cost them 60,000 to 100,000 lei per month in transmission fees in 1992. In Bucharest, the Polytechnic used French-donated transmission equipment and broadcast 17 hours of French programs and seven hours of Romanian-language programs.

Despite their amateurishly produced programs and middle-of-the-night broadcasts, the new stations constituted the only television alternative to RTV. They reported audiences of 30,000 (Oradea) to 2 million (Timisoara).[38] Donations and a minimal amount of advertising revenue allowed them to continue functioning and fighting the RTV, the Ministry of Communication and, sometimes, local governments to stay on the air.

In 1992, attempts were made to form a network around SOTI-Bucharest. SOTI-Bucharest and the Group for Social Dialogue were in touch with all functioning independent television stations in the hope of forming a Federation of National Independent TV Stations. Ultimately, eight of 12 functioning local television stations joined in a quasi-formal SOTI network—ironically, without SOTI-Bucharest.[39] Members of this loose network cooperated by exchanging some news and other programs and providing mutual moral and political support. A new network, UNTELPRO, was eventually established in 1992 and in April 1993 was integrated into the Romanian Associations of Audio Visual Communication (Asociatia Romana de Comunicatii Audiovizuale, or ARCA), with a membership of approximately 40 stations.

By 1992, infighting in various local stations either ended their short-lived experiment or produced new, breakaway independent studios (e.g., Timisoara, Brasov) and multiplied the demand for frequencies, time on RTV channels, and already limited potential sources of financing. A year later, the newly established local television stations had either purchased additional equipment or had equipment donated by a number of foreign organizations, among them the U.S. groups such as the International Media Fund, the Soros Foundations and others. Some added dish receiving and transmitting antennas. Still, as Cosarca (1993) saw it, the problems of independent television were immense: from amateur personnel to programs, from lack of studio space to financial resources. Foreign investments have not poured into Romania's independent television field, and part of the problem was the limited seven-year license awarded stations, an insufficient number of years to recuperate what by necessity is a sizable investment.

By spring 1994, the NAVC had awarded 73 television licenses in Romania (*NAVC Buletin* no. 7, 1994). The cost of competing for a television license and paying annual fees was relatively small (see subsequent table Cost of Television Operation). By early 1995, most of these new stations were on the air, and by mid-1995, 77 license holders in 39 cities and towns were on the NAVC's books (though 21 were later annulled).

The absence of a national station offering competition to RTV was still sorely felt by the end of 1995. Some developments held out the promise of possible national television competition for RTV. The new Tele 7 ABC station went on the air in 1995 via satellite, reaching 40 percent of Romanian viewers, according to its own estimates. Also in 1995, the U.S.-based Central European Media Enterprises (CEME) announced its investment of $20 million in Pro-TV in a joint venture to challenge the dominance of RTV. The satellite-delivered program was expected to reach 55 percent of the Romanian market by the end of 1996 (*Telegrama,* Dec. 2, 1995).

Cable Television

Cable TV is one of the fastest-growing segments of Romanian media. In spring 1994, there were 351 TV cable license holders in the country (*NAVC Buletin* no. 7, 1994). Most of them are in the western part of the country, encompassing Banat and Transylvania. By mid-1995, there were 678 cable license holders in Romania (National Audio-Visual Council, Aug. 16, 1995).

Cable TV existed in a number of locales even before the 1989 revolution, as small, illegal operations serving one apartment building at a time and sometimes whole blocks. Subscribers of these VCR-driven, free-lance cable setups were able to view movies and porno films.[40]

In Timisoara, the city of the revolution, approximately 7,000 cable subscribers were reportedly found in 1993 in any one of the city's quarters. Four cable television broadcasters catered to the city's approximately 400,000 people. Signals were pulled down by dish antennas or through the fiber-optic cables slowly being installed all over the city (M. Ion, June 12, 1993). Cluj was also being wired for cable television transmission, supplementing satellite transmission by the two groups that operated in the city in 1993 (Lazar, May 4, 1993).

The majority of the new cable stations in 1993–94 retransmitted between six and 24 programs received by satellite from foreign sources. Their contracts with these sources were restrictive, reports Cosarca (1993). Romanian cable companies could not interfere in these programs, could not translate them and were to retransmit them at the time of receipt and in their entirety. He concludes (11),

> The role of an open window to the world (played) by these programs is not undebatable. The Romanian viewer's contact with the great televisions of this world, with the variety and the professional standards of these telecasts and with the editorial norms of ... respectable companies, cannot be anything but beneficial. However, the impact of these untranslated [from other languages] programs is minor.

Only a few, such as Channel 7 in Baia Mare, Tele 89 in Timisoara and SOTI-Constanta, produced and disseminated a substantial number of their own news programs, documentary features and other programs. The number of cable subscribers to any one company ranged in 1993 from none (e.g.,

Satline in Calarasi, INTERSAT in Bucharest) to a low of 500 to 700 (e.g., NOVEL in Slatina, TELESON in Sighisoara) and a high of 20,000 (e.g., INTERSAT in Arad, CRD in Baia Mare and Sibiu, and TVS in Oradea).[41] By early 1995, 1.7 million Romanian homes were accessing cable television, and the numbers are obviously growing.

Judging by the number of cable license holders, the ever-rising number of subscribers and the installation of fiber-optic cables in many Romanian cities, cable television will constitute a significant factor in Romania's media scene. Encouraging to cable operators, and diversifying the viewing options of Romanians, is the existence of an estimated 2.5 to 3 million satellite receiving dishes.

Media Laws

On November 21, 1991, the Romanian Parliament by a vote of 414 to 95 adopted a new post-Ceausescu constitution (Constitutia Romaniei, Nov. 21, 1991). Two of its 152 articles speak directly to matters affecting the mass media.

There is a modicum of built-in flexibility in interpreting Article 30, which deals with freedom of expression, and Article 31, which defines the right to information. This flexibility stems less from the ambiguity of the words outlining the articles than from the absence of definition to the restraints one could read into them. For example, Paragraph 1 of Article 30 says that "freedom to express thoughts, opinions or beliefs" in all manner of public communication is "inviolable." Paragraph 2 forbids "censorship of any kind." Paragraph 6 specifies that freedom of expression cannot prejudice the "dignity, honor, private life" of a person, leaving it to the Romanian Penal Code to define the nature of defamation. Furthermore, Paragraph 7 declares it unlawful to "defame the country and the nation, to incite war, national, racial, class or religious hate, to incite discrimination, territorial separatism or public violence, as well as obscene acts contrary to good morals."

The same "vagueness," as Middleton (1993, 406) puts it, is also a built-in feature of Article 31, which in Paragraph 1 guarantees, "The right of a person to have access to whatever information of public interest cannot be limited." Paragraph 3, however, specifies, "The right to information must not jeopardize measures to protect the young or national security." And Paragraph 4 states, "The public and private means of mass communication (information) are obligated to ensure that public opinion is accurately informed." As a sentiment, it is a noble one, but who decides whether public opinion is "accurately" informed, or what "national security" might mean? Indeed, what is the definition of *national security* or, even more pertinent to the mass media, *accuracy in information*? Furthermore, the word *obligated* sounds much like the communist approach to urging "social responsibility." Last but not least, Paragraph 5 specifies that public radio and television are "autonomous" and that they have to "guarantee" the right of access to "important" social and political groups. The last paragraph, Paragraph 8, adds to the flexibility of the constitutional guarantees of press freedom by establishing that "Offences committed by the press are to be established (defined) through law." What "offenses" could the press commit, except libel, invasion of privacy, copyright infringement and the like?

The flexibility of interpretation built into the Romanian constitution, or rather its vagueness, is not necessarily intrinsically dangerous to freedom of the press and of expression. What makes it palpably dangerous, as Middleton (1993, 405) accurately points out, is a justice ministry which is still politicized and "a judicial system lacking independence." In fact, such publications as *Romania Mare,* which clearly incites racial and religious hatred and discrimination, are free to continue publishing.

Still, the new constitution, adopted only about one month short of the two-year anniversary of the anti-Ceausescu revolution, is a radical departure from its earlier communist counterpart. And, despite the built-in flexibility in its interpretation, it is at least a qualified commitment in principle to freedom of the press and of expression. It served as a starting point for the enactment of the Audio-Visual Law, the Law of Public Radio and Television, and the still to be made changes in the Penal Code.

The Audio-Visual Law

It took Great Britain nine years to prepare and enact its present broadcasting law. Two and a half years from the day the Ceausescus were executed the new Audio-Visual Law had been drafted, enacted by the Romanian Parliament on May 19, 1992, signed by the Romanian president on May 20, 1992, and officially published in *Monitorul Oficial* on May 25, 1992. With its enactment, the stopgap measures referring to Romanian Radio and Television built into Law No. 136 in 1990 were abrogated. The Audio-Visual Law was the second broadcasting law to be enacted in postcommunist East-Central Europe, after the Czech one enacted in June 1991. Lacking any experience in the outlining of such legislation, the Romanian Parliament examined the French, U.S., Italian, German and English broadcasting laws before shaping its 45-articles-long Audio-Visual Law.

The new law generated instant controversy from the time it was first formulated and debated (Cosma, Jan. 25, 1991, Feb. 22, 1991, March 1, 1991, March 8, 1991) to the time it was enacted and put into effect and throughout its first years of applicability. First to raise the hackles of opposition forces was the establishment of the National Audio-Visual Council (NAVC), mandated by Article 11. The NAVC's makeup is outlined in Chapter 5 (Articles 25–34) of the Audio-Visual Law. The NAVC "exercises its duties under the control of the Parliament" (Article 34). Two of the 11 NAVC members (Article 25) are nominated by the president of the country, six by the Romanian Parliament (Senate, three, and Chamber of Deputies, three), and three by the government, and all serve four-year terms. The first NAVC, constituted on July 16, 1992, included seven members who were alleged by the opposition to be to some degree or another controlled by President Iliescu (Rasvan Theodorescu, Ecaterina Oproiu, Vasile Bihon, Titus Raveica, Alexandru Piru, Constantin Vaeni and Tudor Cheorghe), and four members who were independent (Radu Cosarca, Iolanda Staniloiu, Horea Murgu and Mircea Baciu).

But there is more to it than the alleged control President Iliescu may or may not have exerted on some members of the NAVC. The key weakness of the council, says Iolanda Staniloiu,[42] is the professional nature of the people appointed to apply the law and "the way they understand to interpret it." Only five of the first 11 members (Cosarca, Bihon, Staniloiu, Baciu, and Theodorescu) had any direct experience with radio or television, and two of the five (Baciu and Theodorescu) only since 1989. In 1993 the first "changing of the guard" occurred when Staniloiu, who received a Humphrey Fellowship to study in the United States in 1993, was replaced by Marin Traian. In 1994, Horia Murgu and Radu Cosarca were replaced by Romulus Vulpescu and Gheorgeta Adam.

There are five main problems, according to Staniloiu, Murgu and Cosarca, that are central to the function of the NAVC and its decisions.[43]

1. The number of NAVC members, they say, is "grotesquely big given the Council's goals and tasks at this incipient stage of democratic institution building, which requires speed, determination, commitment, pragmatism, etc. [A large Council] may work in an established democracy, but in today's Romania [it] is impractical, counter-productive, and counter-reformist," says Cosarca.

2. The politics-versus-professionalism issue in the appointment process is also counterproductive and counterreformist, they say. According to Cosarca and Staniloiu, "The appointment procedure is arbitrary, leading to political nepotism, corruption, and lack of any criteria based on professionalism and expertise in [the Audio-Visual] law's enforcement."

3. The law "is confusing," and the upshot of this confusion is that the

national public television and radio stations get automatic licenses and frequencies, contends Murgu.

4. Assertions made in the license applications are not always verifiable, according to Murgu and Staniloiu, "especially the financial aspects," and there are "no ways to follow up to see if licensees do what they are required to do."

5. The secret vote on the NAVC means that those whose requests for licenses are rejected never find out why they have been rejected. "The secret vote on the council has to be eliminated," argues Staniloiu.

Organizational, personnel, clarity and specificity problems aside, the Audio-Visual Law and the NAVC's existence have had the immediate effect of officially demonopolizing broadcasting in Romania, thus diversifying the source and content of television and radio transmissions. Licenses are issued on the basis of "a competition open to applicants who have first obtained technical approval from the Ministry of Communication," which also establishes the frequencies (Chapter 2, Article 12, Section 2). The criteria for granting licenses (Chapter 2, Article 12, Section 4) contain some vague and therefore controversial provisions:

> Criteria for granting a broadcast license must ensure pluralism of opinions, an equal treatment for all participants, quality and diversity of programs, fair competitive conditions for all participants, *promotion of the national A-V product and of the national culture, the independence and objectivity of programs broadcast by public judicial entities* (emphasis added).

NAVC's Mircea Baciu (March 1993, 6–8) reports that 140 radio and television stations and 100 private cable stations were given licenses and frequencies in 1992, adding that they "will assure, without a doubt, not only an adequate response to the interests of the communities to which they [the stations] address themselves, but also to pluralism of ideas and free competition."

By the end of 1995 the NAVC had granted 56 television licenses, 127 radio licenses and 678 cable television licenses. Radio licenses are issued for five years and television licenses for seven years. The Audio-Visual Law does not set a limit to the number of broadcasting stations a company can own. The frequencies available are established by the Ministry of Communication, which also advises the NAVC on the technical aspects involved in the licenses granted.

The Audio-Visual Law's main provisions include the denial of broadcasting licenses to "political parties or other political formations, nor to public authorities" (Article 6, Paragraph 4); "pluralism of opinions, equality of the participants' treatment, the quality and diversity of programs" in deciding who gets a license (Article 12, Paragraph 4); and the principle that "No public or private, natural or legal person shall be a direct or indirect majority investor or shareholder in more than one audio-visual communication company, and it shall not hold more than twenty per cent of the registered capital in other similar companies" (Article 6, Paragraph 1). Foreign capital can be utilized in Romanian broadcasting, inclusive of cable, but the ownership has to be Romanian (Article 5, Paragraphs 2 and 3; Article 7). The law also addresses "the Authorization of the Reception of Audio-Visual Programmes Transmitted via Satellite" (Chapter 2, Section 3, Articles 19 and 20) and "The Authorization of Audio-Visual Communications Distributed by Cable" (Chapter 3, Articles 21–24). However, the regulation of satellite and cable transmissions is still relatively limited.

Among the NAVC's tasks is the elaboration of criteria for broadcast commercials. This the council did, for example, in its July 22, 1993 Decision No. 105. It has also had to elaborate on the norms and procedures for judging license applications and their awarding. It is in this realm that the NAVC has added fuel to the already raging controversy surrounding the Audio-Visual Law and its applications. Three examples out of many:

1. In early 1993 MEDIAPRO received a broadcasting license to air CNN programs for over 20 hours per day in the city of Oradea, despite the NAVC's criterion that requires the inclusion of programs covering local issues.

2. Licenses were granted to stations with connections to the most extreme nationalistic groups and individuals (e.g., Europa Nova, owned by Iosif Constantin Dragan, an Iron Guardist who fled to Italy after World War II, a Ceausescu supporter and since 1989 the bankroller of a number of new media organizations).

3. Some broadcast stations which had held provisional licenses since 1990 and 1991 lost their licenses to new groups which did not have an established organization, little equipment, if any, and no trained personnel.

Adding to the controversy have been reports that during interviews with license applicants, fewer than the required nine members of the NAVC were present on a number of occasions. Additionally, despite the fact that the debates on the awarding of licenses are supposed to be public, some television stations were not allowed to tape them for their broadcasts (Radio Bucharest did record all the debates).

There is an overall, far wider-reaching negative side to the NAVC's work since 1992: the licensing process has only touched the local and regional broadcasting scene. Staniloiu[44] insists that "the biggest strategic mistake we could have made was to start the licensing process with the local stations. Thus we lost momentum for national privatization. The prospects are very gloomy now." There are three available national channels; two of them are public ones (RTV Channel 1 and Channel 2), and the third one "will be granted on political sympathies and favors," according to Staniloiu.[45]

Politics will continue to dominate Romanian broadcasting for the foreseeable future.

The Public Radio and Television Law

According to the Audio-Visual Law (Chapter 6, Article 41), Romanian Radio and Television "shall be reorganized by an organic law in separate, self-managed public services of radio and television broadcasting." On June 17, 1994, the Romanian Parliament enacted "The Law Concerning the Organization and Functioning of the Romanian Radio Society and of the Romanian Television Society" (*Monitorul Oficial*, June 18, 1994). President Ion Iliescu signed it into law on the same day.

According to the new law, Romanian Radio and Television was to be split into the Romanian Radio Society and the Romanian Television Society, both "autonomous public services of national interest" (Article 1). The new law repeats some of the constitutional provisions protecting the dignity of the individual and forbidding the incitement to discrimination, war, national, racial, social or religious hatred, and the like (Article 5). It also loftily calls for the two societies (Article 4) to

> make public, objectively and impartially, internal social, political and international facts, to assure correct information of citizens upon public and personal issues, to competently and firmly promote the values of the Romanian language, of authentic national and universal cultural and scientific creations, those of the national minorities, as well as democratic, civic, moral, and athletic values, to militate for national unity and the independence of the country, for cultivating human dignity, truth and justice.

Other salient provisions in the new, 54-articles-long law include the following:

1. Both public services have to reserve a portion of broadcasting time for the political parties represented in Parliament (commensurate with the number of representatives each party has) (Article 5).

2. At least 40 percent of radio and television programming has to be of Romanian origin or creation (Article 7).

3. Editorial autonomy and independence are guaranteed by law, and programs are protected from any interference from public authorities and from the influence of any party, sociopolitical party, syndicates or unions,

commercial and economic organisms or pressure groups (Article 8).

4. Public service radio and television are obligated to give priority to the free transmission of all communication and messages of public interest received from Parliament, the president of Romania, the Supreme Council of National Defense, or from the government (Article 9).

5. The public radio and television services are directed to outline statutes protecting the professional independence of their journalists (Article 10) and spell out the rights of employees in working for another broadcaster and contributing to publications as well as the employees' obligation to observe all the rules and regulations and ethical codes of the services (Articles 11, 12, 13).

6. Information must be transmitted with "fidelity," and commentaries must be made with honesty without any influence on the part of public authorities or other public or private persons. News and information (both text and images) must be verified, and their meaning cannot be deformed or manufactured. An individual who feels wronged by a broadcast has the right, within seven days of the offending broadcast, to demand that a correction or rectification be broadcast (Article 14).

The new law also outlines the objectives of public radio and television's activities (Chapter 2) and the organization and functioning of the two societies (Chapter 3). Each society is to have a 13-member administrative council voted by the Romanian Parliament (Articles 19 and 20). The president of the council will also be the director general of the society. Names of candidates for the administrative council are to be forwarded to Parliament as follows (Article 20):

1. Parliamentary groups (parties) can nominate candidates for eight of the council seats.

2. The president of Romania can nominate candidates for one of the council seats.

3. The government can nominate candidates for one of the council seats.

4. The professional personnel of each public service can nominate candidates for two of the council seats.

5. The parliamentary groups representing national minorities can nominate candidates for one of the council seats.

Both societies are under the control of Parliament (Article 2). The two administrative councils are obliged to report annually, or "whenever the Parliament decides," to Parliament (Article 52). Attempts were made to curb

Parliament's control over the two new broadcast entities and "continue total control over public television," as the head of the Free Union from RTVR, Dumitru Iuga, was quoted in *Romania Libera* (Preisz, May 16, 1994).

The financing of the two new public services is spelled out in Chapter 4. It consists of a mixture of state allocations, advertising, donations, sponsorship, license fees and income from other promotions, shows and radio or television concerts, the sale of films, television serials, records, editing of publications and "other sources."

How the new public services will change the nature and influence of news and information dissemination and how politics will affect the administrative councils will be judged with benefit of hindsight long after the new century begins.

The Penal Code

Romania's first Penal Code was adopted in 1936 and revised after the communist takeover in 1948, and again in 1968 and in 1973.

One of the first pronouncements made by the National Salvation Front interim government in December 1989 was that the body of communist laws was to be abrogated. By necessity and perhaps by design, some communist laws were kept on the books. Defamation laws included in the nation's Penal Code, intrinsically affecting the mass media, remained untouched until 1991 and then were changed only slightly to eliminate some of the more egregious communist-inspired elements (Law No. 61).

In spring 1994, after a prolonged public debate, the Romanian Senate approved the first major postcommunist revisions to the Penal Code. The Juridical Commission of the Chamber of Deputies followed suit in November 1994, proposing almost identical revisions. One feature of the proposed amendments that raised a red flag for journalists and the democratic opposition in Romania, as well as for foreign observers of the Romanian media scene, was that of special punishments to journalists for defamation, insults and injury against individuals—and specifically against government officials.

In December 1994 the Chamber of Deputies rejected its own Juridical Commission's proposed amendments and put the issue on the back burner. This action followed vehement, consistent protests by the democratic opposition, by professional journalism organizations and by the press beginning already in fall 1993 when Parliament first started its deliberations on the subject (e.g., Pavel and Turianu, Dec. 7, 1993, Jan. 13, 1994; Preisz, Nov. 12, 1993, Nov. 16, 1993; Costandache, Dec. 4, 1993). These protests took on an even more vehement and desperate meaning by October–December 1994 during the chamber's debate over the proposed amendments (AZR, Oct. 25,

1994; Burileanu, Nov. 15, 1994; David, Nov. 16, 1994; Stanescu, Dec. 5, 1994).

The Chamber of Deputies' and the Senate's almost identical versions of the Penal Code were veiled attempts to indirectly legislate journalistic ethics and professionalism. More important, they were and still are mechanisms for increasing the size and swing of the sword of Damocles hanging over journalists' heads. In fact, one journalist (Preisz, Nov. 16, 1993) writes, the suggested changes in the Penal Code are a "masked press law, a mean form of the independent press' 'political police.'" Pavel and Turianu (Dec. 7, 1993) call it a preamble to self-censorship. Addressing themselves specifically to proposed changes in Article 239 that deals with insults, libel and threats against a civil servant or public functionary, they said, they are "neither timely, nor efficient, nor corresponding to the juridical reasoning which are at the [Penal Code's] basis"(Jan. 13, 1994).

Former Prime Minister Petre Roman says[46] that the articles of the Penal Code addressing defamation and insults, as approved by the Senate and those changes proposed by the Juridical Commission of the Chamber of Deputies, meant "a return to the times of sad memories of the Ceausescu dictatorship."

The increased punishment that was specified for any infractions of the Penal Code articles through or by the mass media, even if enacted in a slightly milder form, would have made the code one of the most severe in Europe—both Western Europe and the former communist Eastern Europe—according to Bucharest's Helsinki Watch (Nov. 29, 1994). It characterized the punishments included in the new Penal Code Articles 205, 206, 236 and 239 as being "incompatible with civilized society." Additionally, it noted that the articles "accord disproportionate protection to public functionaries and politicians," and, "In regard to the exercise of the right to free expression, it is drastically limited through these modifications. They [the modifications] are obviously anti-constitutional and constitute a real attempt to intimidate the press and the critics of the activities of public authorities."

By mid-September 1995, the Chamber of Deputies revisited the issue and approved essentially the same amendments it had rejected almost one year before. Domestic and foreign pressure against the amendments was, again, severe and instant.

Robert Menard (Sept. 27–Oct. 3, 1995), director of the Paris-based Reporters Sans Frontieres, addressed an open letter to President Ion Iliescu asking that he not promulgate "articles 205, 206, and 239 of the Penal Code, for the sake of protecting the elementary rules of press freedom." He added, "Keeping in mind that last June 22 [1994] Romania filed a request to join the European Union, our organization reminds you that joining [this Union] presupposes the conformity of Romanian law to the European Convention on

Human Rights whose Article 10 guarantees freedom of expression."

On Sept. 28, 1995, 123 deputies signed a memorandum asking the Permanent Bureau of the Chamber and the Social Democratic Party of Romania (Partiolul Democrat Socialist Roman, or PDSR) to reconsider Articles 200, 205, 206, 236, 238 and 239 of the Penal Code. And after leading newspaper editors and the directors of Rompres and Romanian Television met with the president of the Chamber of Deputies, Adrian Nastase, on Oct. 14, 1995, its Permanent Bureau announced it would propose that the chamber reconsider amendments made to Articles 205 and 206.

On Oct. 24, 1995, the chamber voted to eliminate any special punishment against journalists or mass media in case of injury, defamation and insult. However, the chamber failed to approve the code when it came to a vote in November. So, back to the drafting board. It appeared unlikely the issue would be addressed again before the parliamentary and presidential election sometime in the second half of 1996.

There were essentially seven articles in this latest version of the Penal Code that directly and indirectly related to mass media and their journalists. They offered a glimpse of the mentalities that underlie their formulation and the nature of the dangers faced by media and their journalists if they are ever signed into law.

1. *Article 168* threatens a one- to five-year prison sentence for "communicating or disseminating, through whatever means, news, data or false information or falsified documents, if the facts included are of a nature [that] touches the security of the state or Romania's foreign relations." The introduction of the concept of "state security," as opposed to "national security," is troublesome because of its implication that anything published related to the structure and authority of the state could be subject to legal action. The same is suggested by the phrase "Romania's foreign relations."

The Bucharest branch of the Helsinki Watch (the Association for the Defense of Human Rights) commented (Helsinki Watch, Nov. 29, 1994) after the Chamber of Deputies' version of the Penal Code was made public in 1994 that the term *foreign relations* is so vague that it could "include anything, from the purchasing contract of one ton of cereals, negotiated by a governmental agency to the country's joining of the North Atlantic Pact." The formulation of the new Article 168 seems to be another catchall article meant to put a chill on any reporting that might identify state and government failure or culpability on the part of one or more of their officials.

2. *Article 205* of the Penal Code deals with damage through words, gestures or other means or exposure to ridicule, brought to the "honor or rep-

utation" of an individual. One cannot attribute a "defect, sickness or infirmity" to an individual or be "pointed out," even "if real." A guilty verdict under Article 205 can result in a prison sentence of one month to two years or a fine.

3. *Article 206* addresses "the affirmation or imputation in public of a [determined] fact concerning a person, which, if true, would expose that person to penal sanctions, administrative or disciplinary [sanctions] or public contempt." A guilty verdict under this article could bring punishment of three months to three years in prison or a fine.

4. *Article 207* addresses the "test of veracity" and is as obtuse as it is ambiguous: "The test of the veracity of what was affirmed or imputed is admissible if what was affirmed or imputed was committed in the protection of a legitimate interest. The act which was the subject of the test of veracity does not constitute an insult or defamation infraction." What exactly may constitute "legitimate interest" is not spelled out. In any case, it is a far cry from truth being an absolute defense in defamation cases.

5. *Article 236* calls for a prison sentence of three months to one year for "Any manifestation through which contempt is expressed for the emblems and symbols that are used by the authorities." The word *contempt* is not defined and could mean a wide array of actions, words and gestures.

Furthermore, a new paragraph was added to Article 236, threatening a prison sentence of six months to three years for anyone who hoists "the flag and symbols of other states or the intonation of their national hymns on Romanian territory under conditions other than those specified by law." This limitation to the freedom of expression, whether on private or public property, is a clear contradiction to Articles 26 and 30 of the new Romanian Constitution.

Andrei Cornea, writing in the weekly *22* (Oct. 4–10, 1995), suggests it was highly unlikely that someone singing the *La Marseilles* would be prosecuted under Article 236. However, he asserts, "ethnic Hungarians singing their own anthems risk being imprisoned."

The proposed new version of Article 236, in its very first paragraph, not only increases the penalty but also adds a chauvinistic, exclusionary note that appears to be directed at the co-inhabiting minorities: "Public defamation by any means of the country or of the *Romanian nation* [emphasis added] is punished by one to five years imprisonment."

Furthermore, the article may be interpreted to mean that any criticism of those who govern, of the powers-that-be, who represent the "Romanian nation," constitutes defamation of the country and nation.

6. *Article 238* provides protection for government officials, from the

president on down—more protection than ordinary citizens enjoy. It specifies a prison sentence of six months to five years for those found guilty of "Damage brought to the honour or threat proffered in public against one of the persons provided under Article 160 in relation to that person's activity and liable to bring offence to the authority ..." The "persons provided under Article 160" includes "any person discharging an important state activity or other important public activity ..." Once again, the wording of this article allows the mass media and their journalists to be brought to trial for almost anything they publish about a public official or that person's activity. Criticism of a public official's actions, statements, policies and so on may be actionable under Article 238, and therefore it directly impinges on freedom of the press and expression.

7. *Article 239*, as if to provide a double punch, follows in the conceptual and philosophical footsteps of Article 238 and strengthens its intent to curb criticism of public officials and civil servants. As with other articles of the Penal Code, Article 239 is designed to take away not only the watchdog's bite but also its bark.

Article 239 forbids "insults, libel or threats" to a civil servant or public functionary while he or she carries out a function, or *because* he or she carried out a function which involves the exercise of state authority. Anyone found guilty under this article is subject to imprisonment from three months to three years.

What might or might not constitute an insult or a threat is left open to wide interpretation. Equally significant is that "insults" are given equal weight by the law to "defamation." Additionally, the article may be interpreted to mean that any criticism of the president of the country or any other civil servant or public functionary constitutes an insult, a libel or a threat.

Also ominous and dangerous to journalists is the last article of the proposed new code that specifies if and when the insult, libel and threat are directed at a magistrate or a member of law enforcement or the military, an additional three years are added to the punishments specified.

A new Penal Code, if redrafted in 1996 or 1997 in the same spirit as the 1994–95 version, will offer disproportionate protection to civil servants, public functionaries and politicians. Additionally, the lack of definitions to the terms used and the absence of an independent judiciary mean that such a new code would be or remain a vehicle for intimidating the mass media as well as critics of government activities and of those who plan and carry out these activities.

The battle over press freedom and the journalists' rights and protection is hardly over and, as in the rest of the world, it continues daily.

Attempts at Enacting a Press Law and Access to Information Laws

As of December 1989, Romania's press functioned without having any law speak to its functioning, responsibilities or rights. Defamation provisions were included in the Penal Code (see previous section). The communist Press Law enacted in 1974, altered and augmented in 1977, was no longer respected, but neither was it explicitly abrogated. The enactment of the new 1992 constitution implicitly did so, but still in force is Article 95 of the old press law: "In case a complaint falls under criminal law, if the deed was committed through the press, the complaint is brought against the organ which caused the criminal action and the violation will be established by the courts."

From 1990 to 1994, several versions of a new press law have been proposed by Parliament, by the government and by Romanian journalists. All Parliament and government versions have been opposed by civil rights groups, the press itself, and all press organizations.

In 1990, the draft of the government's proposed press law, drafted by the Ministry of Justice, was labeled as yet another version of the communist press law of 1974 (Cosma, July 27, 1990). Expressing the sentiments of the majority of Romanian journalists, Alina Mungiu (Aug. 10, 1990) in an article whose title encompassed the distrust felt by media personnel regarding the ambiguity of the proposed new law— "Will all of us be equal in front of the Press Law?"—writes that the proposed law "constitutes the gravest attempt ... against freedom of the press." On Oct. 2, 1990, the government withdrew the bill.

In August 1990, in response to insistent calls for a press law, the Society of Romanian Journalists drafted a 12-article, quasi press law (Charter of Freedom of the Press). The government rejected it without it ever being publicly discussed.

Despite clear opposition to any press law on the part of the overwhelming majority of journalists, Prime Minister Petre Roman on Feb. 25, 1991, gave preliminary approval to a proposed 10-article law. The Romanian Parliament was to discuss and pass judgment on the proposed law. Those sections of the proposed law which were not dangerously vague were directly oppressive, seriously endangering freedom of the press. For example,

1. Article 5 of the proposed law said, "Defamation in the media of the President of Romania, the judicial bodies, the courts, the government, the army, or any other public authority is punishable by a prison term of two to five years or a fine of between 200,000 lei and 500,000 lei."

2. Article 1 ensured the "free and unlimited" expression of opinions and dissemination of information, but added that freedom of the press can be carried out only under conditions of "correctness, loyalty, and good faith." There was no indication as to the object of "loyalty," nor "correctness."

3. Article 3 specified the penalties for disseminating allegedly "false information." It failed to differentiate between intentional and unintentional libelous material.

4. Article 4 specified the punishment to media which sought to incite the army to deviate from its legal duties—those duties including the maintenance of public order.

On March 19, 1991, the government announced it was withdrawing the proposed law. But the Romanian government and Parliament's desire for a new press law did not die down. On Dec. 13, 1991, yet another press law draft was introduced in Parliament by Senator Ilie Platica-Vidovici. It was a drastic change from the previous press law drafts only by virtue of it length: it contained 49 articles (versus 10 in previous drafts). If anything, its enactment would have been even more detrimental to press freedom than the previous draft proposals. It got nowhere.

Talk of a press law and attempts at introducing one in Parliament ("In Camera Deputatilor," Dec. 17, 1992) have still not subsided and are not likely to subside. In March 1994, the new minister of justice, G. I. Ghiuzbaian, wrote in the ministry's publication, *Palatul Justitiei,* that he is in favor of a press law, whose existence would "perfect penal and civil legislation." Partly, attempts at enacting a new press law will not subside because it is an altogether European tradition to have a press law and because freedom of the press is considered by many politicians, government officials and individual Romanians, who have little understanding of a press's role in a democracy, as dangerous unless strictly controlled. Furthermore, the professional chaos, the "anything goes" mentality of many journalists and the personal, libelous attacks found in the press have convinced many that "rules are needed" for journalists, and the "dimensions and proportions of journalistic conduct" as well as the journalists' rights must be defined by law.[47] On the other hand, Romanian journalists on the whole are not convinced of the need for a press law, as Stefanescu writes (April 3–4, 1993*a*), "probably out of fear that it [the press law] cannot be anything but restrictive. All press law projects introduced to date in Parliament confirm this fear, almost annulling freedom of expression, the right to opinion and to information."

While journalists are vehemently opposed to a press law, they do see the need for laws that guarantee their ability to carry out their job. The need for laws protecting journalists is suggested by a number of instances in which they were attacked, beaten, arrested and threatened for simply being journalists and doing their work (e.g., Nicolaescu, July 26, 1993; Alexandru, Aug. 13-19, 1990; Preisz, July 26, 1993). One of the most famous and controversial cases arose during the 1992 presidential election campaign when the incumbent candidate, President Ion Iliescu, allegedly attacked a journalist in the city of Constanta, taking him by the lapels and yelling the now-famous words in Romania: "You animal." In another case in which two journalists working for *Jurnalul National* were threatened, Amnesty International was officially asked for protection (A.M. Press, May 14, 1994).

In May 1995, two Romanian Information Service officers were caught shadowing two Romanian journalists, Tana Ardeleanu from the daily *Ziua* and George Scutaru from the press agency Mediafax (Lucan, June 1995). Ardeleanu had written a series of articles alleging that President Ion Iliescu worked for the Soviet KGB. Scutaru had just returned from Moscow where he was investigating the same story. Working journalists in Romania were still without any legal protection by the end of 1995.

Additionally, while Article 31 of the postcommunist Romanian Constitution guarantees access to "any kind of public information," there is no law guaranteeing journalists access to information. Middleton (1993, 23) aptly observes, "Although access to information is recognized in Romanian law as a fundamental right, the constitutional articles establishing the right of access also establish wide latitude for arbitrary denial of access." He is referring to the contradictions and vagueness built into the constitution which, (1) while guaranteeing access, also demand that media present only "correct" information to their audience, and (2) while stating that parliamentary sessions are open (public), gives wide leeway to the legislative body in deciding if and when it wants closed sessions.

Since 1990, journalists have been complaining that they are barred from many parliamentary hearings and legislative sessions and that there are no procedures for gaining access to records and meetings (see Chapter 4). In 1992, an attempt was made by a group of 75 young broadcast, print and news agency journalists to have the Romanian Parliament enact a three-article law guaranteeing access to information ("Proiect de lege initiat de reporterii revistei Expres," April 24–27, 1992). The proposal was a combination American Freedom of Information Act and Open Meetings Laws (Sunshine Laws):

Article 1.   Journalists have a right to ask for information of public interest from all central state and local administrative institutions, and they have an obligation to provide the solicited documentation within 10 days from the date of the request (for information).

Exempt are data which refer to state security, the organization and equipment of the army, as well as that information which by its publication would injure the economic interests of the state.

Article 2.   Representatives of the press have access to all meetings of organs of the central state (national) and local administrations, with the exception of cases in which the matters referred to in Article 1, Paragraph 2 are under discussion.

Meetings of a majority of the members of the leadership councils of the units mentioned (central—national—and local state administrations) outside of their headquarters and without the participation of press representatives is forbidden.

Article 3.   Disrespecting the obligations outlined in the preceding articles constitutes a violation.

The mass media have a right to complain [file a complaint] to judicial bodies which, ascertaining that a violation [has taken place] can fine [the violator] 100,000 to 500,000 lei. The fines will be levied against the persons who have violated the provisions of the present law.

The proposal received scant support despite arguments such as those of NSF parliamentarian Vasile Scortan, who said the proposed law is "Short, pertinent. With this law the press will enter [a state of] normality." He added, melodramatically, "Without legal access information (the press) will be forced to steal. Or to invent." ("Fara legea accesului la informatie, presa va fi obligata sa fure," May 5–11, 1992). The proposal for such a law, representing the young generation's first coalition, was rejected. The *Expres*'s Rasvan Popescu (May 19–25, 1992) writes that the proposed law of access to information is "too beautiful not to become reality one day."

The journalists' struggle to gain access to all parliamentary debates and commissions, to have agendas be circulated before parliamentary debates on issues and to have draft laws and vote counts be made public continues. In 1993 yet another declaration, signed by nongovernmental, sociopolitical organizations, unions and newspapers, once again demanded "transparency in the legislative process" ("Declaratia in favoarea transparentei procesului legislative," April 3–4, 1993). Summarizing why there is a need for a law guaranteeing access to information, Manuela Stefanescu (April 3–4, 1993b) states, "A law concerning the free access to information for all Romanian citizens is more than just necessary, it will mean the concrete applications of the Constitutional provisions and will align Romanian legislation with international standards."

The legal protection of journalists and guaranteed access to information constitute the very essence of freedom of the press. In Romania today, press freedom is absolute, but it is the freedom of the wild. Journalists can write anything they want, whether true or false, defamatory or laudatory. They can rant and rave. The profession, society and clear, strict defamation laws can in time correct this situation. Laws giving legal status to journalists, protecting them and assuring them access to governmental information of public interest, are necessary to transfer the profession's freedom from that of a dangerous jungle to the civilized, ordered freedom demanded by democracy.

CHAPTER 4

Journalists and Journalism

 There is a telling difference between Western journalists and journalism and their East-Central European counterparts, the contexts from which they come and in which they operate, their professional attitudes and perceived roles. Understandably, that difference is far more marked when the U.S. model is used as a reference, because at least historically, philosophically and culturally, East-Central European journalism is European. Still, even Western European journalism and news media differ sharply from their East-Central European counterparts today.

American and Western European journalists and journalism are also different from one another (Kepplinger and Kocher 1990). Yet, they do share basic characteristics that are lacking in East-Central Europe, as the ones Jakubowicz (1992) notes are missing in the Polish media: "the basic skills of objective news reporting and analysis or the ability to unravel fully and completely for their audience the immensely complex process unfolding on the political scene."

In the West there are continuous debates whether fair, neutral, objective reporting is possible or even desirable (McQuail, 1992, 183–95). To varying degrees, in the context of their individual cultural traditions, the Western European and American media (journalism and journalists) manage to do so. At the very least, the partisan press coexists alongside the market-guided press.

On the other hand, East-Central European journalism and journalists generally did not seek to meet such standards in the first postcommunist years. While some progress has been made in professionalizing the field, to date the region's journalism is not of a caliber consonant with that of its Western neighbors (Horvat 1991, Jakubowicz 1992, Goban-Klas 1994). Their partisanship and inclinations to propagandize and their lack of professional standards and ethics are leftover traits from the precommunist era,[1] refined and hardened by the communist experience, its exigencies and teachings. It is also a characteristic of transitional societies (Passin 1972) whose futures, as in this case, are uncertain.

In postrevolution Romania, the media explosion that so drastically changed the communication and information landscape is distinguished by (1) the concomitant increase in the number of journalists, (2) a tendency to wittingly and unwittingly use past journalism models as a guide to journalistic evolution, and (3) a struggle to find new journalistic models, more Western in their professional orientation (while culture-specific in presentation) and better-suited to the task of influencing democracy's growth by virtue of its products, as well as to find a methodology and ethic that symbolizes a democracy and a democratic media.

The Journalists

Establishing the number of journalists who worked full or part time in Romania by 1993–94 is a nearly impossible task. The memberships of the major journalistic organizations and unions that provide a professional "home" for broadcast or print media journalists are overlapping and thus provide an inaccurate reading of the number of journalists working in Romania's bloated media field. Furthermore, there are journalists, particularly in the local media, who do not hold membership in the national unions and associations. Finally, there are many others in the local and national media who continuously enter and exit the still-growing and constantly changing journalistic field without being counted.

The four largest associations and unions serving print journalists had a combined membership of around 4,815 in 1993–94. The Association of Romanian Journalists (Asociatia Ziaristilor Romani) claimed 1,015 members, among them Romanian journalists stationed abroad; the Society of Romanian Journalists (Societatea Ziaristilor din Romania), 1,500; the Union of Professional Journalists (Uniunea Ziaristilor Profesionisti), 2,000; and the Association of Hungarian Journalists in Romania (Asociatia Ziaristilor Magyar din Romania), 300. New journalists or media organizations spring up every year. This proliferation, characteristic of a wide spectrum of other organizations (including political parties), is symptomatic of a lack of satisfaction with the activities or leadership of existing ones and a search for more proactive, professionally satisfying ones. The majority of the 150 journalists working for Romanian Television and the 100 journalists working for Romanian Radio were members of the Free Union of RTV (1,400 members) in 1993–94. There are 20 other smaller unions that are still vying to become the official standard-bearers for television and radio personnel.[2]

The number of working full- and part-time journalists, print and broadcast, is estimated at about 20,000. A report in *Expres* magazine (no. 22, 1992) set the number of working print journalists in 1991 at 10,000 and broadcast journalists at 4,384. Whatever the exact figure had grown to by 1995, the number of working journalists constituted a significant increase from the 3,000 to 6,000 journalists and contributing journalists who labored in the communist-controlled media in the pre–December 1989 era.[3]

The rapid growth in the number of journalists also meant a wholesale change in the makeup of the corps. At the end of December 1989 and beginning with January 1990, more than 90 percent of those working as journalists were leftovers of the communist era. By 1995 a dramatic switch had taken place with more than 90 percent of journalists being new to the field and young, their median age in the mid- to late 20s.

Monitorul de Iasi, in the northeastern city of Iasi, close to the border with the Republic of Moldova, is one example of media staffed by young people new to the journalistic business. The editor of the daily was 23 years old in 1993 and directed an editorial staff whose median age was also in the early 20s. At the other end of the country, in the city that launched the revolution, Timisoara, the newspaper that bears the city's name was likewise started in the immediate aftermath of Ceausescu's overthrow by a group of young men and women in their 20s and early 30s. One of the two top national weeklies, the Bucharest-based *Tinerama,* was led in its initial phase by a 26-year-old editor in chief who oversaw a staff with a median age of 24. There is no profession in Romania that is as dominated by the young as is postrevolution journalism.

A great number of the new journalists came to the profession with engineering backgrounds. This situation is testimony to the Stalinist mania for industrialization and the overloading of the engineering field, the relative prestige and money enjoyed by engineers in the communist days and the overbearing politico-ideological considerations that kept intelligent, capable, interested young men and women out of journalism. Iolanda Staniloiu, an engineer by training, went into television work in 1990, was later engaged as Prime Minister Theodore Stolojan's spokeswoman, served on the National Audio-Visual Council from 1992 to 1993, and now heads the Center for Independent Journalism in Bucharest. Engineer Razvan Popescu began his journalistic career with the national weekly *Expres* shortly after its founding in 1990 and in 1993 became the BBC's correspondent in Bucharest. Harald Zimmerman, another engineer by training, was one of the founding members of the newspaper *Timisoara* and then became a correspondent for *Expres*. Dan Vardie, also an engineer by training, became the editor of the Bucharest-based *Tineretul Liber*. Cristinel Popa,yet another engineer, became secretary general of Romanian Radio. All the engineers-turned-journalists mentioned here as examples were in their late 20s or in their 30s when history provided them with the opportunity to change professions. A list of working journalists could quickly grow to a few thousand similar entries.

Many of those who first joined the ranks of Romania's postrevolution journalists' corps in December 1989 and during 1990, people like Popescu, Zimmerman, Radu Eugeniu Stan, Bogdan Teodeorescu, Lia Trandafir, Dragos Seuleanu, Lilian Zamfiroiu, Harald Horia Birbea, and Silviu Alupei, wrote for student newspapers during their university days. Others entered the journalistic profession directly out of high school or while still university students: Daniel Klinger, an engineering student, launched the new, successful Uniplus Radio; Cezar Caluschi, also a university student, took charge of advertising for *Monitorul de Iasi*. Some double as part-time journalism students. Andrea Esca, an anchorwoman at the independent, local SOTI Television in Bucharest (before it was taken off the air in April 1994), turned 21 in 1993 and was attending the private Atheneum University as a journalism student.[4] She joined Pro-TV in 1995.

Then there are the many intellectuals who, after years of public silence, joined daily and weekly newspapers or even launched new intellectual publications devoted to commentaries and analysis or satire. Novelist Gabriela Adamesteanu became the editor of *22,* an intellectual weekly established in December 1989 and first edited by Stelian Tanase, a writer of romance novels. Sociologist George Onut launched a new TV station in Brasov. Psychologist Mircea Toma became a driving force behind the successful satirical weekly *Academia Catavencu*. George Serban, a former philosophy professor at the Timisoara Polytechnic, became editor in chief of the daily *Timisoara*. Dan Pavel, a graduate of the Faculty of Philosophy and History at the University of Bucharest, was the political editor and later deputy editor in chief of *22*. A long list of other intellectuals with backgrounds in the humanities and social science work full time for or contribute on a regular basis to the many publications.

But there is no cohesiveness in this post–December 1989 generation of journalists. There are great differences in general and professional education and training and in mentalities. These differences have had an impact on the manner in which journalism was practiced in the first four to six postrevolution years and in the twists and turns professional careers took in the 1989–95 years. Some have used their initial entry into journalism as a steppingstone to related careers in government and public relations (e.g., Iolanda Staniloiu, Radu Cosarca, Virginia Gheorghiu) or employment with the better-paying, more prestigious foreign media (e.g., Petru Clej, Gilda Lazar, Razvan Popescu).

Journalists today, whether working for radio, television, newspapers, magazines or news agencies, are self-taught and received their professional education on the job. Some of this autodidacticism is carried out by uncritiqued trial and error. In other instances, journalists are helped by colleagues whose professional experience is also limited or questionable given their professional upbringing or its absence during the communist period. Rompres, the dominant news agency, organized courses for its journalists together with the British Reuters news agency. Romanian Radio and Romanian Television personnel completed training courses and internships in a number of Western European countries and in the United States. Hundreds of print media journalists have also attempted to adopt Western methods and techniques learned with varying degrees of success since 1990 in courses and internships completed in Belgium, Germany, France, Italy, Great Britain and the United States.[5]

The majority of these new journalists have run into stiff resistance from editors, most of whom are older and were schooled during the communist regime. Despite these editors' protestations to the contrary, they do not fully understand the role of media in a democratic society and the need for a journalism that can fulfill that role. And they fail to understand the need for universal standards of reporting and writing and an enforced professional ethic, according to the testimony of many young journalists who have received firsthand exposure to Western journalistic practices, mentalities, philosophies and ethics. Ironically, the old guard, which includes journalists, politicians, government officials and, in post-Ceausescu days, businessmen, blames the young journalists for a lack of professionalism in the media. The latter point the finger at the former for the professional deficiencies of Romanian journalism. Both groups are equally guilty of lacking professionalism. Many younger journalists also constitute a conservative force. At the very least, a Western-style journalism, one of information, demands hard work. Generally, a Romanian-style journalism, one of opinion and sensationalism and incomplete information, is far more convenient and more in keeping with both communist and precommunist tradition.

Cotidianul Editor Doina Basca's view, shared by many other editors and journalists, that the "young ones attempting to learn journalism, are not learning it from the old guard," is only partly supportable.[6] Many of the editors at the established, largest-circulation dailies and weeklies, certainly at Romanian Television and Radio, are part of the old guard, sometimes called the "press section" after the infamous censorship section of the Communist Party's Central Committee. The old guard also includes those who consider themselves "in opposition" to the Democratic National Salvation government and President Ion Iliescu or claim to have been anti-communist (e.g., Octavian Paler, Vartan Arachelian and others). After all, Romania's senior media leaders are almost all products of the communist era: from Romanian Radio's Eugen Preda, a capable and dedicated old professional, to the younger Petre Mihai Bacanu (*Romania Libera*), who was imprisoned for anti-Ceausescu activities; from Romanian Television's whole leadership and its news editors to the editors of *Adevarul* (formerly the Communist Party's *Scinteia*); from Ion Cristoiu of the infamous and successful *Evenimentul Zilei* to Cornel Nistorescu of *Expres,* Sorin Rosca Stanescu of *Ziua* and Neagu Udroiu of Rompres, along with many others in the established local or regional press and radio. Additionally, part of the old guard, as exemplified by Ceausescu sycophants such as Cornel Tudor Vadim and Adrian Paunescu, are in charge of the extremist, xenophobic, chauvinistic, nationalistic publications such as *Romania Mare, Politica, Si Totusi Iubirea* and *Europa.*

Broadcast and print journalists acquired an estimated 60 percent of their professional knowledge on the job, the rest from books, domestic and foreign journalistic examples and discussions with colleagues.[7] Since 1990, the journalists' on-the-job education has been affected more often than not by the media's individual political battles on behalf of a particular politico-ideological idea or the increasingly bitter competition for commercial survival. Many journalists agree that since 1991 the struggle for commercial survival and success brought about either a demand for sensationalism or a blandness that is accompanied by a lack of journalistic initiative. For example, the tabloid *Evenimentul Zilei* has sensationalized the death penalty, rape and other crime issues. *Curierul National, Meridianul, Ultimul Cuvint* and *Monitorul,* newspapers that began their public life with some journalistic promise, degenerated into a journalism that avoids important issues and, most journalists and readers will testify, are written in a style meant to cure insomnia. More significantly, the embracing of sensationalism as an evolution from opinion journalism did nothing to break the nonprofessionalism or preprofessionalism pattern of Romanian journalism.

Tia Serbanescu,[8] who wrote for *Romania Libera* and then *22* until 1993, when she became one of the editors of *Cotidianul,* and who is one of the sharpest critics of the media, asks a rhetorical question that is apropos to the direction professional education and the new Romanian journalism are taking: "Is there freedom when the press exists only for economic reasons/gain or personal political interests?" In a similar vein, the head of the Free Union of RTV, Dumitru Iuga,[9] decries the fact that Romanian journalism and journalists serve the media's owners when they should serve "their real masters, their audiences, and the democratic ideal." Only a handful of journalists have significantly evolved professionally since the press was freed in December 1989, struggling against sensationalism, partisanship, blandness and the owners' and editors' interests and proclivities. Cumulatively, these factors interfered with the adoption of professional standards consonant with those in Western democracies.

The problem of determining what is to be learned is primarily defined by a crisis of professional identity, thanks to the uncertain, uneven role journalism has played in Romanian society since December 1989, and the media and journalists' questionable influence and power (see chapter 5). The education of journalism and journalists, as well as their credibility, is in large measure dependent on an ability to recognize shortcomings, as a French journalism instructor teaching at the University of Bucharest's School of Journalism wrote (Capelle, Jan. 7–13, 1993). Until 1992–93, most journalists were reluctant to openly discuss the very notion that Romanian journalism or its journalists harbored significant professional deficiencies. They fell "into a trap thinking they are important," according to Dorel Sandor,[10] a former aide to Prime Minister Stolojan. Sandor heads his own think tank in Bucharest that, among other subjects, concerns itself with the role and efficacy of the Romanian media in the new society. This egocentrism has greatly contributed to the crisis of professionalization, noted by Romanian media critics beginning in 1990 and finally and overtly recognized by some journalists by the third and fourth postrevolution years.[11]

The lack of contemporary or even positive historical role models, of a clear definition of journalism's and the journalists' roles in the new Romania, as well as the accompanying absence of universally agreed-upon professional criteria by which to judge journalistic products, places the country's young journalists in a perpetual ethical crisis. It is a crisis whose advent was noted already in 1990, only months after Ceausescu's forced "abdication" changed the media scene (Mihailescu, July 27, 1990).

They are also in a continual financial crisis, most of them receiving low pay (particularly in the local and provincial media) and thus moving from one publication to another to try to improve their income. Worse yet, the need to augment incomes by working for more than one publication or crossing over to broadcasting affects the process of professionalization. On the one hand, the articles written for dailies sound the same as those written for weeklies, radio news copy is the same as that for television, news agency releases the same as articles in monthly publications. On the other hand, writing for a publication attempting to be "serious" news and opinion while at the same time contributing (under a pseudonym) to a tabloid or even a porno magazine does not allow for the development of a professional journalistic style. The continuous musical chairs played by print journalists is a somewhat less frequent occurrence in the broadcast field. But that may change with the beginning of a significant expansion in broadcasting after the issuance of new licenses and frequencies in 1993 and additional ones in 1994 and 1995. Indeed, by April 1994 broadcast personnel began to play the same game as print journalists when 30 RTV employees, journalists, editors and technical personnel left for the new commercial, national television network, Tele7 ABC.

The few highly paid journalists were earning 200,000 to 250,000 lei per month (about $200 to $250) by fall 1993, with the majority earning an average of 75,000 to 125,000 lei. At that time, one kilogram (2.2 pounds) of beef cost 3,500 lei; bread was 120 lei per loaf, a still subsidized price; a movie ticket cost 150 to 500 lei, depending on which theater one attended; a pair of average-quality, indigenously produced men's shoes cost 18,000 to 20,000 lei; a Romanian-made Dacia car's sticker price was 3 million lei; and a one-bedroom apartment's purchase price in Bucharest ranged between 6 million and 30 million lei, depending on the neighborhood.

The concern for their weekly and monthly financial survival, many have testified, also affects their work. Furthermore, the general lack of technical endowments at their newspapers, magazines, radio and television stations—the shortage of cars to quickly get to news scenes, the absence of computers, the inadequate number of audio and video recorders, and so on—is frustrating and also contributes to their lower level of professionalism.

The establishment of new journalism schools and programs (Gross and King 1993, Freedom Forum 1994) meant that by 1994–95, young journalists with a modicum of professional education began entering the field. They encountered some of the same problems faced by their slightly older colleagues who began work after December 1989, particularly those who worked hard to professionalize themselves. It will be up to these two groups to significantly contribute to changing journalism, its role, professional criteria, effectiveness and credibility in Romania. Yet, the process will not evolve without major conflicts between these two groups. Those who are already working in the field may very well belittle the quality and efficacy of existing journalism education programs, and the newly graduated may dismiss the value of the experience gained by the more experienced young journalists during their working time.

Furthermore, the establishment of such independent groups as the Club of Economic Reporters (inaugurated in summer 1993) and the Club of Young Politicians (with which young political reporters are associated), the launching of the UNIPROF program for journalists interested in being theater critics and the establishment of journalism awards patterned after Pulitzer Prizes are steps toward the slow professionalization of Romanian journalism.

Forward to the Past or
Back to the Future

From December 1989 onward, Romanian journalism struggled for a direction, personality and identity tied to a professionalism worthy of its status as a European nation, to its professed desire to aid the establishment of a democracy and to its specific national-cultural character. The expectation that professionalism was to be quickly established in the aftermath of 45 years of communism, and in the absence of an indigenous historical model viable in a democratic society, was overly optimistic on the part of Romanians and of Western institutions and nations that began aid programs for Romania. However, the argument made by journalists, such as Lia Trandafir, formerly with the weekly *Tinerama* and since 1995 a spokeswoman for the Democratic Convention, among others, that there is yet "no Romanian journalism" to be found in the various media's editorial rooms, is only partially supportable.

A "Romanian journalism" was operational in these first five post-Ceausescu years. It can be defined as an odd mixture of precommunist and communist journalism, the former being at the basis of "Romanian journalism." While this precommunist journalism is not known by the young journalists, it simply constitutes a natural phase, and a parallel one to post-Ceausescu journalism: that quasi-amateur phase or preprofessional phase that precedes the journey toward professionalization.

One of Romania's greatest savants, Mircea Eliade (1987, p. 80), wrote in 1937 that only the journalist "can avail himself in Romania of the prerogative of not knowing anything, to harangue about important unimportant things in the name of the country, of not having any principles, or better yet, of having too many; and, finally, to preach morality from the pulpit of immorality." The description fits the great majority, if not all, of the post-1989 Romanian journalists as much as it did the journalists of precommunist and communist days (in the latter case, in the context of the Marxist-Leninist press theory which served as its foundation). Eliade's characterization was still valid by the end of the fourth and fifth post-Ceausescu years. In 1993, however, a handful of young journalists began slowly and tentatively applying autodidactic lessons absorbed through the monitoring of Western European and American press, the concepts and techniques learned in the various training sessions they attended in Western countries and the slow-maturing process in progress.

The Marxist-Leninist legacy weighed heavily on journalists, journalism and its audiences in the first three post-Ceausescu years—this despite denials by many young journalists that they, directly or indirectly, learned anything in that period and are emulating its journalistic techniques. And, therefore, the 1989 demise of the Ceausescu regime in the eyes of many Romanian and foreign observers ("New Press Challenge in Poland," April 14, 1990)

> failed utterly to establish a free press. There is a free press in the sense that there is a complete abolition of censorship in Romania. But news organizations don't know what the free press really means because they were used to propaganda for more than forty years. They don't know how to do anything but propaganda. They can do nothing but express opinions.

Communism or Marxism-Leninism, first and foremost, reinforced, refined, focused, and worsened the most negative aspects of precommunist Romanian journalism: its partisanship and polemical nature in which dissimulation and rumormongering, personal and vituperative attacks, opinionated and judgmental writing were meant to convince and reinforce rather than inform. This kind of journalism was present in the communist and precommunist days and was intrinsic in the first post-1989 years, to varying and incrementally decreasing degrees by the end of 1993. Without a doubt, in the latter two cases, it was present in a far more fragmented way, offering a great deal of diversity compared to the communist years. Its practice, historically and in the post-Ceausescu days, is based on the notion that journalism is a combat weapon in the ongoing sociopolitical warfare in a society with a multitude of varied political parties, sociocultural views, ethnic groups, a yet-to-be-established sociopolitical modus vivendi and sundry passions.

One of the great luminaries of Romanian journalism and literature, Mihai Eminescu, whose prolific 19th-century journalistic writings are held up in the 1990s as an example to be followed by young journalists, is nevertheless recognized even by some of his contemporary admirers as having practiced a journalism with (Cretia, Aug. 3, 1990) "too vehement a tone, disproportionate personal attacks, excessive forms of political aversions (inclusive of his unquestionable xenophobia), his hyperbolism which resembles at once that of the great prophets of the Old Testament and that of the unmatched Dante."

This type of traditional journalist and journalism was primarily a natural outgrowth of Romania's battle in the 1700s and 1800s to gain freedom from foreign subjugation and to unify its provinces in an internationally recognized or sanctioned national state. It was also an intrinsically European type of journalism practiced in a less-than-democratic Europe. In Romania its roots were to be found in the French journalism of that period which it emulated both in spirit and in form up until the communist takeover in 1947 (in the province of Transylvania, the Austrian and German influence carried equal weight). Specifically, it was a journalism of personal expression and not information, of national and political consciousness building, of romantic ideals, a daily theater, literary and poetical in presentation.

Many contemporary Romanian journalists and observers of the press judge the press of the 1920s as being of high caliber and its journalists as positive role models for the post-1989 journalism corps. This judgment exists despite the fact that few if any have read the press of that period. Indeed, in the aftermath of the 1989 revolution, broadcast and particularly print journalism have now returned, as the literary critic Nicolae Manolescu (1991, 155) asserts, "to the tradition of the national press, which was from its birth in the last century an important factor in the formation of our modern institutions and a guarantee of their maintenance."

This tradition, which regards journalism as an exercise in commentary and polemics on the issues of the day and passionate combat against political, intellectual and personal opponents, only secondarily regards it as the presentation of verified, balanced, accurate information. It again took over journalism with a vengeance in the first three post-1989 years. It remained a major characteristic of mass media in 1993 despite the beginning of a slow change, in particular among some young journalists, and in the nature of the press. By 1993, the party press had been decimated. The partisan press suffered the consequences of its partisanship with reduced circulations or outright death, and a sensationalist as well as a somewhat more neutral and more information-oriented press was born.

Manolescu,[12] among other public figures, was deeply bothered in 1992 by the "lack of distinction between information and commentaries" and the competition between newspapers that takes the form of "a competition of opinions." The now-retired Richelieu of Romanian politics, Silviu Brucan,[13] likewise bemoans the "intolerance in the press and of the press vis-à-vis other opinions" than the ones the individual newspapers supported. Not without his own political biases and reasons for his view of the press, Nicolae Ulieru,[14] the official spokesman of the Serviciul Roman de Informatii, or SRI (the Romanian Information Service), née the dreaded Securitate, concluded with sufficient justification in 1993, "In Romania there does not exist real independent publications." He simply meant that each newspaper has a definite political leaning which affects its reporting as much as its editorial stands. Many politicians, too, view the media as manipulative, as former Prime Minister Petre Roman observes,[15] "raising a question and giving the answer without giving information." Some journalists and editors agree that the media, while free, are not necessarily independent from political and commercial interests. And Roxana Iordache,[16] of *Romania Libera,* echoing to some extent the SRI's Ulieru, describes the "news media" as missing the "news" part.

Indeed, national newspapers such as *Adevarul* have attempted a certain amount of depoliticization of their approach to journalism and have paid the price by becoming bland but also more informative in a selective way, on selective and nonpartisan topics. By the end of 1993, many of the national as well as some local and regional newspapers began separating what they labeled news and news feature articles from commentaries, editorials, and other opinion columns. All subjectivity and commentary did not entirely disappear from the news articles themselves, even in the most positive examples of a move to professionalization, yet, for instance, in much of the economic reporting and in the publications devoted to business and economics, the "news" is dominant and the commentaries have been in great measure excised. At *Tineretul Liber,* Dan Vardie, who was appointed editor in 1993, claimed his newspaper was "keeping an equal distance from all political parties."[17]

The same changes could be observed by 1993 among some local and regional newspapers. In Iasi, for instance, Andy Lazescu, publisher of *Monitorul de Iasi,* recognized in mid-1993 that "success is tied to a divorce from certain interests either political or commercial."[18] Most important, a small group of young journalists have taken on the mantle of independence and an increasing degree of professionalism.

There are three identifiable camps among the 1990–95 corps of journalists: (1) those who tend to lean toward "traditional" journalism, (2) those who say they lean away from it while still practicing it to a greater or lesser degree, and (3) those few who have slowly begun a course of professionalization without abandoning the culture-specific style meant to attract Romanian audiences. It is at once a division between the older and younger journalists, between a rightist (conservative nationalist) and leftist (Marxist nationalist) mentality versus a more democratic one and between those who see journalism as a profession and those who view it as an art form to be employed in the service of a cause or simply a way of earning money. Each group will point the finger at the other, accusing each other of a lack of professionalism.

At a colloquium held in Costinesti in Summer 1992,[19] editor Ion Cristoiu of *Evenimentul Zilei* spoke for those journalists who believe in a return to tradition and a "Balkan" approach to journalism. Mindful perhaps that Romanian society is, indeed, still a very traditional one—with palpable class distinctions, a wide chasm between intellectuals and the rest of the population and only a small middle class—he said that the "Romanian press is adapted to the character of the Romanians." He argued that "'Coloring' information is necessary in this transitional society" because the revolution has not been consummated, and the return to "Caragiale"[20] and to a Balkan tradition is a return to normalcy for Romanian journalism. These arguments are defensive ones, protective of the post-Ceausescu journalism against the threat of professionalization.

Those who do not see themselves returning to "traditional" journalism do not, however, practice a form of journalism far removed from the politically motivated "coloring" and selection of information and from a subjectivity with political or sensationalist overtones. Many postrevolution journalists who practice this type of journalism, and editors who allow it (while some recognize its negative essence), will admit to Harald Zimmerman's[21] conclusion in 1992 that "Romanian journalism is still too amateurish, overly tied to the emotions and personal feeling of individual journalists to the topics they cover, instead of being more detached and professional."

Observers of the journalism scene, such as Adamesteanu (March 22, 1991, pp.4, 5 and March 29, 1991) and Pora (June 5–11, 1992), while recognizing severe deficiencies in Romanian journalism, consider the accusations of dilettantism, the presence of an excess of commentaries, and anemic reporting to be clichés cultivated mostly by foreign journalists. These foreign journalists, they argue, lack an understanding of the underlying reasons for the type of journalism practiced since December 1989.

Leading Romanian critics of media in the post-Ceausescu society, such as Adamesteanu, Serbanescu, Alina Mungiu, Stefana Steriade, Andrei Cornea, Mihai Coman and others, together with some journalists and editors admit that the press often does offer more opinions than information. They admit that the press is full of libel and personal attacks and lacks at least a degree of professionalism. In the first three post-revolution years, they mostly pointed to the press supportive of the government and the president and that of the leftist and rightist parties. By 1993 they were also critical of the scandal press, as exemplified by *Evenimentul Zilei, VIP, Scandal, Infractorul, Dracula* and *Delict,* and even the partisan opposition press whose standard-bearer is Bacanu's *Romania Libera,* having come around to the need for a more professional press in a more Western mode. Also by 1993 they praised the progress made by individual journalists working for the national and local or regional press whose reporting has unearthed a long list of corruption among government officials and state employees. They also praised the specialized publications such as the weekly financial newspaper, *Capital,* whose reporting provided a contribution to the general knowledge on the state of the economy, individual industries, privatization, the new stock market, investments and other related matters.

Still, in 1993 Adamesteanu (April 8–14, 1993) points to the difficulty in judging when Romanians are faced with "disinformation" and when with a "banal de-professionalization." Her conclusions are predicated on a view of a press that "manipulates with a precise objective inaccurate information" while the rest allows such manipulation and inaccuracies because of "indifference" or in order to "provoke scandal that attracts readers." George Carpat-Foche of *Cotidianul* sums up the press' problems when he writes (Aug. 6, 1993),

> The extraordinary vivacity of our press is due, in the first place, to the return to tradition. The newspapers count themselves among the few institutions that succeeded, in the present regime of "continuity," to return through a "restoration" to their pre-war ways. But just from that reinsertion comes, in great measure, the amateurishness and the obstacles in the way of the press' professionalization.

Even Romanian Radio, generally considered more professional and less "traditional" in its journalism by audiences and journalists working in all media, began its post-1989 era, as Doru Ionescu admits,[22] being "subjective." Yet, it had to change and quickly because it was and is in direct competition with Romanian-language foreign radio broadcasts that reach every corner of the country (e.g., the BBC, Radio Free Europe, Voice of America), as well as with a number of independent radio stations quickly established after the Ceausescus fled Bucharest on Dec. 22, 1989. Since 1990, Romanian Radio has striven to provide a more objective selection and presentation of news items, claimed its new director, Eugen Preda, during a roundtable discussion at the Black Sea University's Center for Political Studies and Comparative Analysis in 1993 (Preda, July 15, 1993).

While generally the claims of increased objectivity and professionalism are not contested, not everyone agrees with that positive characterization of the new Romanian Radio. Some accuse it of being far too selective in its news items when these involve the government, which it subtly favors (D. Popescu, July 15, 1993). A report by the Association for Free and Accurate Information Through Radio and Television, analyzed in a 1993 commentary in *Cotidianul* ("Legea Audiovizualului," Feb. 3, 1993), includes praise for Romanian Radio for having improved the quality of and accuracy in all its programs. Yet it also criticizes the station for selecting news and commentaries in many cases from news agencies with "a singular orientation," such as Rompres, ITAR-TASS (Russian) and Bulgarian agencies, which leads in some situations to "one-sided information" being broadcast. It is an unjustified criticism given that both Rompres and Bulgarian agencies have agreements with the major Western news agencies that supply them with the international news they pass on. As far as local radio is concerned, there is general agreement that given its infancy, radio reporters are in a learning process and that, on the whole, it practices a generally respectable level of journalism (Ghibutiu, Feb. 22, 1993).

At Rompres, not universally looked upon by journalists as an objective, professional news service because of perceived biased gatekeeping, its director, Neagu Udroiu, said in 1993[23] that his agency's journalism is quite objective because "every attempt to be subjective or partisan comes back to haunt us. We are, therefore, very attentive to that." He stressed that the agency is not involved in politics or that it "acts in accordance with one particular political belief." Regarding the agency's gatekeeping function in foreign news dissemination, he claims that it is as professional as any independent news broker, offering this example: "If there is a foreign article negative to [President] Iliescu, I feel obliged to give it to our subscribers."

Romanian Television news, the only television news program with a national reach to date, in particular is seen by print, radio and even its own journalists as a partisan instrument of the newly entrenched power. For example, in August 1993 Jeana Gheorghiu, an RTV anchorwoman, left her post, stating that her resignation represented "an act of conscience through which [I] distance myself from the reintroduction in RTV of careerism, nonprofessionalism, as well as against putting this institution in the service of the present political power" (Burileanu, Aug. 3, 1993).

It was not a surprising statement given the person at the helm of RTV from early 1993 to February 1994. Paul Everac, yet another Ceausescu sycophant, an individual with no background in journalism or television who is reported to have made the statement that he never watches television, managed to infuriate just about everyone during his tenure at RTV. Dumitru Iuga,[24] head of the Free Union of RTV, claimed in 1993 that Everac "follows orders. His role is to name [to leadership positions] people devoted to the political party in power." Commenting on the findings of a 1993 study of RTV, Campeanu (July 29–Aug. 4, 1993) stated that RTV, in comparison to the "monolog" of Ceausescu's days, is now a "space for a social dialogue." Yet, he added, "without preventing the expression of other positions, Romanian Television of today provides a net and constant advantage to the positions of the power [the government]."

The charge that Romanian Television is a direct or indirect mouthpiece of the government did not, of course, crop up in 1993. As Berindei et al. have shown (1991), television (as well as elements of the press) was used by the government to orchestrate its attack on anti–National Salvation Front (NSF) demonstrators in 1990 and 1991, the University Square's "Neo-Communist-Free Zone," the rampage of miners through Bucharest and the ransacking of many headquarters of newspapers in opposition to the NSF government.[25] It is no irony that one of the main demands of the anti-NSF, anti-Iliescu alliance since 1990 was for permission to be granted for an independent national television station.

Print journalists, government officials, and media observers are in general agreement that television is unprofessional and that it has not been informing but disinforming its audience since its heyday as Free Romanian Television in the immediate aftermath of the December 1989 revolution (Vighi, Feb. 25–March 3, 1993; Mungiu, June 1–7, 1993; Antonesei, Jan. 21–27, 1993; Bucurescu, Oct. 1, 1992). Far from improving, it continued to be as it was described in 1991 (Adamesteanu, April 26, 1991): its news program was "interminable," with information that was disorganized, with national and international news mixed together, with long speeches transmitted unedited, with disinformation and censured information offered its publics on top of the "sour commentaries" of its anchormen and anchorwomen.

With the appointment of Everac to head RTV, it had become even more of a bête noire of journalists, politicians and even its audience than it was under the leadership of his two postrevolution predecessors, Dragos Aurel Munteanu and Razvan Theodorescu. Both the precommunist *and* communist journalism tradition is still alive and well at Romanian Television, where there is a "monumental lack of professionalism" and "purposeful disinformation," "discrete manipulation," with an "anesthetic effect" (Antonesei, Jan. 21–27, 1993). In November 1993, Iuga (Nov. 2, 1993) even accused RTV of trampling on the constitutional guarantee of all Romanians to "correct and impartial" information, and of carrying out its duties contrary to the Audio-Visual Law (Article 1, line 2).

There is somewhat of a contradiction in the condemnation of TV as being unprofessional, manipulative and disinforming at the same time. Some argue that it is quite professional—indeed, that it has to be professional—in the way it manipulates and disinforms its audience. Professionalism did not significantly improve in the wake of Dumitru Popa's appointment to head RTV and the defection of 30 journalists, editors and producers to the new, commercial national network, Tele 7 ABC, in April 1994.

Local television is also generally recognized as harboring the same professional deficiencies, carried out with fewer technical capabilities and with staffs that are even shorter on experience. General Manager Andrei Dorobantu[26] of SOTI TV (the local Bucharest station that gave some competition to RTV and aspired to become a national station) described his news program in 1993 as "trying to do what theirs [Romanian Television] does not." He added a telling description of the station's independent news approach: "SOTI is 75 percent politically oriented in favor of the opposition."

Interestingly, and tellingly, the same critics of Romanian Television were slower in criticizing SOTI for its lack of journalistic professionalism.

In part, the absence of independent, professional television with a national reach has been the rationale vigorously advanced in the first three post-1989 years by many editors, journalists and media critics for a press that cannot be neutral and objective. The press, they argued, has to be in active opposition to the perceived still-communist mentalities and inclinations of the nation's president and the government and the television they control. (By fall 1993 the Romanian Parliament took on the oversight of RTV.) For instance, in 1991, Adamesteanu (April 26, 1991, 7) argued that no matter how amateurish the press may be, it has "corrected and completed as much as it could the information corrupted by television." That argument received only somewhat less assiduous and widespread support among journalists by 1993. The sentiments expressed by *Cotidianul's* Petru Ionescu (Aug. 6, 1993) regarding the necessity for a nonobjective, proactive, partisan press and the difficulty of making a transition to a more professional, information press, are more or less still shared by most journalists and their editors:

> However, in a world in "transition," in which nothing is stable and the revolution is in process, the press fights—alongside the other "powers" of the dreamt of nation of laws—so that a real relationship is reached, to the state of the real Western democracies based on individual rights and, in the first place, private property.

In fact, journalists point out that, at the very least in their first post-Ceausescu year when they admit a professional journalism was not practiced, they provided a service to society by producing a press that was the only counterbalance to the new political power (the National Salvation Front) until a political opposition was established and had an opportunity to evolve. Initially, by the end of January 1990, the corps of journalists became divided between those who supported the NSF and those who opposed it, a situation which was to persist until 1992–93 and the slow beginnings of a re-evaluation of journalism tenets and the traditional role of the journalist as a political fighter.

Cezar Tabarcea,[27] the head of the Association of Romanian Journalists' Higher School of Journalism from its inception in 1991 until 1992, asked the journalists assembled at the 1992 Costinesti colloquium whether they will "move forward or will hold to tradition that will not allow you to become effective and important" in the new society. By 1993, the public and private arguments over the nature of an effective, responsible news media and journalistic professionalism had taken on new urgency and visibility, as evidenced by the number of articles published and colloquia and seminars on media held throughout Romania. Chaos still reigned in Romanian journalism given the absence of journalistic criteria, admitted or not. As Rompres's Udroiu[28] correctly assessed the state of journalism in the second half of 1993, journalists still "can't find their compass."

Unfortunately, while in 1992 and 1993 the process of consciousness-raising regarding professionalization sped up, there was no sign that a major change in the circumstance of the media, in the mentalities of the majority of journalists and editors or in their products had occurred. Indeed, no *dramatic* changes could be recorded by the end of 1995. Changes were discernible, as already mentioned, such as better economic reporting, a move away from the most blatantly subjective and political biased reporting and a greater variety of items. There was the addition of more information (and less commentary) in news articles and the initiation of a search for universally acceptable journalistic standards.

In Romania, as in the rest of East-Central Europe, journalism was also part and parcel of its literary and intellectual tradition. This fact, too, now compounds the problem in making the leap from "traditional" journalism to a new professionalism capable of aiding the transition to a democracy and supporting its evolution. In this tradition, poets, writers and university professors were always engaged in an aesthetic exercise serving a sociopolitical or national-cultural purpose, and in the self-arrogated function of being the exclusive flag bearers of culture, morality, nationhood and intellectualism. This tradition experienced a rebirth in the post-1989 period and a reinjection in Romanian journalism. The "intellectualization," or reintellectualization, of the Romanian press was particularly and visibly acute in 1990 and 1991. It was exemplified in both the form and the substance of newspaper and magazine articles, and it provided yet another "traditional" model for the young journalists. Coman (1994) points out that the reinjection of intellectuals in the media system was helped along by the polarization of political life in the aftermath of the 1989 revolution:

> [B]eing deeply engaged in political fights, media communication turned into an opinion discourse, and this was an accessible genre for every intellectual. ... [T]he richness of events brought the illusion that newsgathering is very easy work which does not require any professional training or strong ethical conscience. ... This kind of journalist is devoted to ideological values, uses opinion discourse and mixes opinions with information, and is less sensitive to the criteria of objectivity. So, paradoxically old journalists and newcomers shared as a common, unifying value the same devotion to propaganda.

It is a classic European model of journalism married to literature. Romania has undergone one transitionary period after another since its establishment in 1859, experiencing a brief and solitary moment of quasi democracy in the 1920s before making the leap to regal despotism, then to neofascism and then to communism. Journalism never had an opportunity to evolve, to establish itself into a viable model capable of serving a democracy or democratic development now in the 1990s.

Janos Horvat (1991), a Hungarian television journalist, describes this European journalism tradition as being accentuated in the East-Central European milieu:

> [C]ommon in Europe is the concept of the active or participant journalist, the journalist who sees himself as someone who wants to influence politics and audiences according to his own political beliefs. This sense is even stronger in Eastern Europe, where journalists are closer to artists and writers, and many poets and writers contribute regularly to daily publications. Together with the journalists, they feel a sort of messianic vocation: They want to become a mouthpiece for the people.

The (natural) return to "traditional" journalism practices and concepts is also intimately related to the return to an only marginally developed civil society, whose characteristics are heavily tinged by the Marxist-Leninist experience (Jowitt 1992), itself affected by a specific Romanian interpretation and application. While post–December 1989 Romanian journalism contributed to the re-establishment of civil society by way of its diversity of opinions and the symbolism such fare offers, it is a civil society in an incipient stage once again. It shares some of the characteristics of its precommunist-era cousin: it is small and lacking any real power and constitutes a shaky and immature political culture. Almost four years after the anti-Ceausescu revolution, Tia Serbanescu[29] still had cause to state that "what has not been created is a just measure of and fidelity to democracy, the rights of man and civil society." The absence of a Romanian Magna Carta is sorely felt in Romania. And there can be no talk of democratizing Romanian society until and unless such a social contract is "made explicit and guarantees the freedom for civil society to evolve, juridically recognizes the existence and encourages an enlargement of the separation between civil society and state" (Gross 1991a).

The consequences of an absence of "a shared public identity as citizens, an identity that would have equalized rules and ruled, and allowed for truthful discussion and debate" (Jowitt 1992) are telling on the nature of journalism. From 1990 to 1992, on the whole, Romanian journalism was either completely loyal to the forces in power or completely opposed to them. By 1995, that loyalty had not disappeared but was somewhat diluted.

Yet, given the process of self-examination that Romanian journalism has embarked upon, the changes occurring in Romanian society and the progress made by individual journalists, the return to traditions or prepro-fessionalism may only be a springboard to the evolution of a journalism that is both democratic and capable of serving a democracy. Indeed, Professor Ion Dragan,[30] director of the Institute of Sociology of the Romanian Acad-emy, who has conducted some media studies in the early 1990s, opines that "we missed what has been positive since December 1989. There is a new press in Romania. And as far as returning to traditions is concerned, there is nothing wrong in starting from the past."

The Journalistic Discourse

The literary feature of Romanian journalistic discourse, married to its politicized nature, places overwhelming emphasis on the use of strong verbs, adverbs, adjectives and metaphors, creating a "parallel reality to the one which the facts alone create" (Coman 1993). Some, like Dorel Sandor,[31] take Coman's characterization one step further and talk about the journalistic discourse producing myth and countermyth and of presenting in-formation in a language of extremes. Together with the purposeful manipu-lation of the images being presented and the tone of the majority of print and television news items, these features, too, constitute a symbiosis of the pre-communist- and communist-era journalism.

Language

In the summer of 1990, *Romania Libera*'s editor, Petre Mihai Bacanu,[32] described Romanian reporting not only as being more polemical than jour-nalistic, but also its presentation being "in vague terms" and in "the old vo-cabulary learned during years of communist control." The use of the "wooden language" of the communist lexicon, to which was added a vitu-perative character, and precommunist symbols and modes of presentation seems to be counterproductive in presenting new ideas and messages. Henri Wald, writing in the weekly *22* (Sept. 28, 1990), argues that the fall of to-talitarianism has left behind, among other legacies, a crisis of individualism or individuality which, "for now, does not permit but a passage from the old wooden language to a new wooden language."

Actually, in Romania, unlike in other transitional or developing soci-eties where new ideas and messages "may be more readily accepted if they are related to old symbols and concepts" (Pye 1972, 127), the old symbols and concepts are rejected, yet at the same time are effective and still used. The communist symbols and concepts are rejected for being communist, and the precommunist ones because they are, at the very least, only vaguely known to the generations that were raised without them. The latter are also inappropriate to the transition period and to the claimed desire to move toward democracy because (1) they were never clearly defined and developed nor firmly established during the 1920s, the only period in which there was a beginning to a Romanian move to democracy, and (2) the situation of the 1990s is completely different from that of the 1920s, as are their respective preceding years and their effects on society, as well as the needs of the transition periods.

Yet, the return to tradition—to the noncommunist past, its concepts, symbols, and the adoption of a new "wooden language"—is interpreted even by those who are democratically minded and intellectually competent as a move to democracy and a journalism capable of serving that transition. Thus, Manolescu (1991, 155) mistakenly suggested in 1991 that "The *re-learning* of democracy's alphabet coincides with the re-learning of the press's alphabet (emphasis added)," when, in fact, democracy's alphabet was never absorbed in that society and the press's alphabet was never consonant with a democracy.

Elites are distinguished from the masses, and traditional elites are distinguished from "modern" ones, by language, a defining element in transitional societies (Passin 1972). Four types of Romanian languages are present and utilized.

1. The old "wooden language" (Associated Press, March 29, 1993), its unique Orwellian Newspeak, is still used by many journalists, politicians and other public figures, as well as by the public. As Rompres's Udroiu[33] pointed out in 1993, while journalists "are accused of not being able to use a language other than the old language, neither is the public."

2. On the other hand, a highly intellectualized language is used by the intelligentsia involved in journalism, particularly those who are democratically oriented, which tends to accentuate the division (a) between the educated professional and intellectual class and the still predominantly peasant population,[34] (b) between the educated professional class and the intellectual class, and (c) between the old communist-educated elite wishing to hang on to power and the educated elite who advocate a radical change to a democratic open society.

3. There is the third variant of the language increasingly used by journalists in the continually sensationalizing press. Dragos Seuleanu[35] from Romanian Radio explains this variant as the use of "language at the level of the street to escape the traditional [communist] language." That, too, aggravates

the division between the elites and the general population.

4. Finally, there is Wald's "new wooden" language (Sept. 28, 1990), a mixture of the old and the new, whose parentage rests with the psychological wounds left by communism and the uncertainty of the transition period.

The lack of a common media language makes it difficult to establish universal information media. Conversely, the general absence of an informational media or the failure to develop one in the first six post-Ceausescu years, therefore also excluded the formation and adoption of a commonly understood, accepted and used language. For instance, every journalist, when addressing the need for or using terms such as *democracy, freedom, human rights* or *free enterprise,* has a different definition and interpretation of these concepts. Therefore, the language used in informing and educating people in this transitionary period becomes precise only in its ambiguity. However, the language(s) used in journalism is (are) not the only contributor(s) to the problem faced by Romanian journalism.

Story and Discourse

"A popular myth was created by the press: they were not going to inform but were only to 'tell stories,'" lamented *Cotidianul*'s Doina Basca,[36] herself the editor of a daily newspaper engaged in telling stories, in summer 1993. Six years after the Ceausescus' overthrow, while still less a myth than it is a reality, the absence of sources, of information and its verification, and the presence of subjectivity, incompleteness, rumors, one-sidedness and inaccuracies of various degrees were slowly being turned around. However, the majority of press and television reports still have the feel of "Once upon a time"-type stories. Overt, politically motivated subjectivity also is still injected in the selection process as well as in the presentation of news.

In fact, as story and discourse (Genette 1983, 11), print and broadcast were overwhelmingly in the first two post-Ceausescu years far more the former than the latter, and only gradually and selectively less so by the end of 1993. To a lesser degree in 1992 and 1993 than in the previous two to three years, they still tended to be exercises in aesthetics, commentary and politics more often than not built around an inaccurate, unsubstantiated, incomplete, one-sided story. This situation prompted *Expres* editor Nistorescu[37] to complain in mid-1992, "There is never getting the other side of a story." One year later, Rompres's Udroiu[38] observed that "precision is missing and, therefore, there is manipulation and no one is satisfied with information" disseminated by the media.

The presumption that reporting or journalism is depersonalized or depoliticized is not applicable in Romania, partly because these first post-

Ceausescu years have been an exercise in the affirmation of the journalists' hard-won freedom, of empowerment and of catharsis on behalf of the individual, the various communities and the whole nation. As a result, a news story rarely gives "only information or its sources, and very quickly the story becomes commentary," observes Manolescu.[39] Out of step with the majority of Romanian media people, Lazescu,[40] publisher of *Monitorul de Iasi,* sees the majority of journalists commenting and criticizing rather than reporting, a situation which "is ridiculous, because no one can know that much and be so right all of the time."

There is sharp disagreement with these characterizations of the tone and content of the journalistic discourse on the part of a handful of young reporters working in the national and local or regional media. Lia Trandafir,[41] formerly of the weekly *Tinerama,* for example, contends that a comparison made of the contents of her news articles with those of a Western reporter covering the same stories will show that the same information, facts, data and sources will be present in both sets of articles, albeit the presentation will be differently packaged for cultural-linguistic reasons.

Yet, these young mavericks do admit that many of the media contain a profusion of rumors, opinions, polemics, personal attacks on individuals, propaganda, subjective reporting and writing, mobilization messages and pure fiction passed along as bona fide information and fact. This package is often enveloped in belletristic writing or attempts at such writing. More often than not, it is published only for the sake of such writing. George Carpat-Foche (Aug. 6, 1993) provides cohesion to the various criticisms of postrevolution problems in journalism, assigning it to the communist and pre–World War II period. He echoes the most negative views about media when he states,

> Rare are the newspapers that are capable of relating an event or diverse fact without seasoning it with asides and with more or less inspired interpretations. Stories with belletristic pretentions take the place of news reports, the isolated case is elevated (even in the economic pages) to the rank of a symptom with general significance; every newspaper perceives through its own prism the world's political reality.

This "minimal narrative" (Genette 1988, 18) in which the story is only marginal to the narration itself seeks to be interesting only by virtue of the writing and the authors' political stance, rather than the contents for their information or factual value. By 1994, the exceptions to this rule were increasing.

The belletristic aspects of Romanian journalism have to be understood in the larger context of a Romanian culture, which is in great measure a Latin one, and the already mentioned traditional marriage between journalism and literature. The presentation is appreciated as much as or more so than the content, and without the former, the latter might not get any attention. The lead of the story is one of the most noticeable examples of this belletristic writing with little or no journalistic value in the Romanian press. Rarely does it report anything, but it is often pleasant to read, intellectually challenging and pleasing, signaling an opinion or conclusion. In fact, some young journalists who in the 1990–93 period had occasion to journey to the West and partake in training courses can often be recognized by the Westernized feel and content of their leads. They tend not to bury the most important, the latest, the consequential facts somewhere in paragraph three or four and preface them with the flourishes of literary virtuosity.

Pseudonews

The notion that "all newspapers lie" is relatively well entrenched, according to *Romania Libera*'s Iordache.[42] Romanian journalism, at the very least, as Serbanescu[43] accurately contends, is in "a fight against 'false news.'" This struggle against "false news" is not meant to point the finger only at the fringe, extremist publication like *Romania Mare* or the scandal sheet *Evenimentul Zilei*. Mainstream publications such as *Adevarul* and *Romania Libera,* among others, have sometimes carried "news stories" that were intended to provoke, to make a political point and to manipulate. The entire Romanian media, concludes the University of Bucharest School of Journalism's Dean Coman (Coman 1994),

> raise the false-event, the theoretical discourse, the irrelevant daily facts, offer barren interviews and theoretical analysis. To all of this one can add the almost complete lack of utilitarian news—print and broadcast media seem to be produced by journalists for journalists but not for the people and the people's troubles.

Television, the most pervasive medium, throughout its first four post-Ceausescu years continued to offer pseudonews as its main fare. As Steriade (Dec. 7, 1990) among others describes it, the fare is characterized by news "such as the ritualized presentation of [diplomatic] credentials or official departures and arrivals from visits abroad." RTV is apt to spend 15 minutes on a story, complete with visuals, of an overturned horse cart in the middle of a Bucharest street, yet ignore an event in which the main participants are opponents of President Iliescu or the government. Worse yet, by 1993 it did not cease to most often disinform its audience and to "dress-up the truth, which presented only by half, derails into a falsehood" (Bucuroiu, Feb. 15, 1991). Serbanescu (June 3–9, 1993) speaks for those in and out of the media who see no redeeming value in Romanian television, who see it as "moral and professional misery," a partisan mouthpiece of the people now in power: "Perhaps the total lack of connection with reality is not surpassed at TV but by the stupidity with which contradictory announcements are strung together one after the other, and that, in its turn, is not surpassed but by the defiant character of the news."

RTV's Victor Ionescu disagreed in mid-1993 with most all criticism of television's news programs and claimed that RTV had become "more objective now than before in all respects, covering the news much better."[44] That may be true for individual journalists such as Ionescu, who in December 1993 was temporarily suspended from his post of foreign news editor because he gave "too much time" to the opposition during a December 1 program he hosted (Baesu, Dec. 13, 1993). There are few media people outside a small group of RTV leaders, journalists or politicians and other public figures who will agree with Ionescu. Radu Cosarca, a former RTV anchorman who was taken off the air for a number of days in spring 1992 and called on the carpet for broadcasting a news program on exiled King Michael's visit to Romania,[45] says that television tilts toward the entrenched political power, partly because RTV's leaders will not permit neutrality and partly, he claims (Palade, July 8–14, 1993), because Article 9 of the Audio-Visual Law (see chapter 3) was very quickly adopted at RTV as part of a "minimal resistance" editorial policy that gives priority of dissemination to anything that comes from elements of the ruling power.

Neutrality and Objectivity

Neutrality and objectivity also did not play a major role in local television in 1990–95. At SOTI in Bucharest, which Dorobanti[46] claims is mostly oriented ("75 percent") to the "opposition," "the choices of news stories [covered and broadcast] are made by personal notions of what is important." The same kind of "professionalism" dominates the work of television journalists and editors in Timisoara, Constanta, Oradea, Brasov and the other 11 cities in which local television was established between 1990 and 1993.

Editor Dumitru Tircob[47] of *Libertatea* reported in 1990 that journalists "come with all sorts of stories full of exaggerations, few facts, and unverified facts." The former head of Romania's Society of Professional Journalists, *Adevarul*'s Sergiu Andon,[48] argued in 1990 that it is "difficult to present news. They [the public] don't know how to understand news. People need commentaries." Three years later, in 1993, the journalists' levels of neutrality and objectivity, as exemplified by the absence of commentaries in news reports, fairness, balance, accuracy, completeness and attributions offered their audiences, has generally improved. The improvement has been only a slight one and among only a select few journalists and national and local or regional publications. More significantly, the need for objectivity and neutrality is still contested by a majority of editors and journalists.

There are three discernible reasons for this attitude. First and foremost, as *Expres*' editor Nistorescu[49] said in 1992, "the press answers the demands of society and the press perceives that its audience would be revolted at simply getting information." The lack of information in the media, of neutrality and objectivity in news gathering and newswriting are blamed by those who recognize these shortcomings on the entire Romanian society, on government and its officials. It is also blamed on the people and their perceived informational needs, on politicians and political parties and finally on the "Balkan culture."

Second, journalists' attitudes on neutrality and objectivity are tied to their notion that journalists must "find the truth" rather than reporting accurate, verifiable, attributed information and allowing the audience to decide what is true or false. Romanian Radio's adjunct director general, Paul Grigoriu,[50] for instance, argues that "objectivity is not truth. Absolute objectivity would mean absolute truth." He is among a majority of Romanian journalists whose definition of objectivity is tied to truth or falsity as judged by journalists, rather than to a process which insists on complete, evenhanded treatment of an issue, event or person and accuracy, attribution and the absence of editorializing. It illustrates a propensity for a black-or-white, truth-vs.-falsity interpretation of objectivity, rather than viewing it as a process with rules designed to minimize subjectivity, unfairness, imbalance and inaccuracies. Florin Iaru,[51] formerly with *Cotidianul* and now a free-lancer, speaks for many journalists when he says that if "objectivity is achieved it would mean only one newspaper would be necessary. Many opinions define society and democracy." There is no mention of information as the basis for an informed citizenry, defining a democracy.

Cristoiu, whose publication's journalism (*Evenimentul Zilei*) is the subject of scorn among most if not all press critics in Romania, makes no secret of his view that there is no such thing as objective news and applies this viewpoint in his daily paper by allowing the publication of "news" about a man raping a chicken, and a maid in the city of Iasi having been raped by seven men and declaring she had discovered the "joy of life." His newspaper offers readers the full names and addresses of rape victims and more often than not allows "news" items to be published without identifying any source(s) or verifying the information offered the public. For instance, among many other examples, on Sept. 28, 1993, the British Embassy in Bucharest was obliged to send out a news release (one was published in *Romania Libera,* Sept. 29, 1993, 8) stating that the contents of a September 27 *Evenimentul Zilei* article on British policy vis-à-vis Romania and Hungary were in effect false and the sources quoted were neither part of the British government nor spokesmen or spokeswomen for it.

Third and finally, contesting the need for neutrality and objectivity is also part and parcel of the prevalent attitude that journalism and journalists have to be active rather than neutral in sociopolitical terms, and participants rather than observers and recorders of history, militants in the service of a cause or a politico-ideology. Serbanescu[52] asks rhetorically, "Can the press be neutral? In relation to what? Truth or lies? All (political) parties?"

Cristian Popisteanu,[53] a journalist who wrote for *Adevarul* and *Curierul National,* answering on behalf of a majority of journalists, concludes that neutrality is "impossible" and "perhaps undesirable." Such a conclusion allows for selective accuracy or inaccuracy in reporting, incompleteness and rumors in the service of a goal, including outright fallacious reports, and frequent additions of journalists' judgments and views in what are billed as news stories.

It is important to reiterate that there are exceptions among journalists whose attitudes on the need and practice of objectivity are akin to those of their European and American colleagues. It is also important to note that journalists and editors who are quick to accurately identify the professional shortcomings of the majority of their colleagues are often guilty of practicing more or less the same type of journalism. And there are few newspapers that are moving in the general direction of increasing professionalism, such as *Monitorul de Iasi,* which has visibly "adopted an orientation on the opinion page, but not on the news pages, where there is equilibrium in reporting."[54]

Ethics

From 1990 through 1995, the confusion of values in general, partly inherited from the Ceausescu period and partly as a natural consequence of a major societal transition, made it difficult to develop a professional ethic or a universally accepted professional code, one that is consonant with the stated desire to move society toward democracy and provides that process with a necessary, professional journalism. Says Romanian Radio's Sylvia Ilies,[55] "At first we were all very aggressive. There was much freedom and, therefore, we had to begin setting some parameters and define our professional ethics."

They did begin the process, but they have not yet completed it, let alone refined it, or gained universal understanding and acceptance for the end product or adherence to it. During the revolution, graffiti appeared all over the major cities celebrating "Freedom of the Press" and "Freedom of Speech," which in the journalistic realm were translated into publishing anything and everything, violating individual privacy and the confidentiality of sources. The profession itself lacks certain, accepted definition: What is journalism? How is it to be practiced? What are the parameters of its practice? What role is it to play in society? Without defining the profession and its role, it is difficult if not impossible to outline an ethic for it *and* enforce it. To put it another way, while the search for a definition of journalism, for an ethos and a role, is still in progress, outlining a universally accepted ethic for it is put off.

Journalistic responsibility and impetus in the first five to six post-Ceausescu years have been defined rather narrowly: (1) the journalist is primarily responsible to the party whose paper he or she represents, (2) the journalist is responsible for a general cause (i.e., being in opposition—see other sections of this chapter as well as chapter 5), (3) the journalist is responsible to the entity that employs him or her and to the exigencies of his or her economic survival and progress, and (4) the journalist is responsible to his or her own egoism. This definition makes for a rather Machiavellian journalistic ethic.

Codes of ethics have been enacted by the major journalistic unions and societies, as well as by or for individual news organizations (e.g., the Ethical Code for Radio Journalists, *Tineretul Liber*'s Ethical Code which, for instance, specifies that its journalists cannot belong to a political party). These codes were partly in response to the "anything goes" attitude adopted by journalists and partly as a defensive measure against those in government, in the media and among their audiences who had been calling for the enactment of a press law since early 1990 (see chapter 3). In 1991, the major journalistic organizations and unions banded together and agreed on an ethical code. Published in *Romania Libera* ("Ziaristii isi apara si va apara onoarea," March 5, 1991), the Code of Ethics was introduced to the public (and to the Parliamentary Commission on Mass Media) by editors of the newspaper.

> Above any press law, which can become dangerous to freedom of opinion through its restrictive character, journalists have in this instrument that is the Code of Ethics the possibility of heightening their moral and professional standards, to radically better the climate in the print and audiovisual media in the not-too-distant future.

That "not-too-distant future" had not been reached by the end of 1995. The echoes of this Code of Ethics are only faintly heard in day-to-day journalism. Despite the called-for formation of professional commissions and honors juries in every journalistic union and association, enforcing the code is virtually impossible and by 1995 no attempt had been made to do so. The key to better journalistic ethics may be the individual journalist's self-discipline. That may come over time. The media themselves have failed to enforce the codes and punish offenders. There is a quasi-cynical notion that the codes are used in the same manner as Ceausescu's quotes that used to be posted on office walls: they were visible proof of good behavior that was disrespected whenever possible.

As a result, the journalistic discourse remains completely unprofessional, tentatively professional or only partially professional. If the necessity of an ethical discipline, personal and professional, would be unanimously recognized in the media, argues Carpat-Foche (Aug. 6, 1993), it would constitute great progress. The consequences would include

> an attenuation of egomania, in which the spirits that are still dizzy from the communist collectivist nightmare basked, the frenetic subjectivity would abate, [a subjectivity] which does nothing but display its insignificance and, ultimately, its inutility, [and] the provincialism of so many newspapers with excellent intentions would scatter.

Sources for and Access to Media

Finally, the journalistic discourse has two voices: that of the journalists and that of a limited, select few sources (Coman and Gross, spring 1994). Dependence on the same sources, mostly on those who are in leadership positions and those who fit the proper bias profile necessary to the subjectivity of the news report, is far more accentuated in Romania than in the West (Brown et.al. 1987, Giffard 1989, Shoemaker 1983, 1984). The legitimation and use of a larger pool of sources that encompasses more than just the officially recognized party leaders, government officials and representatives of various government and nongovernment institutions have not yet been accomplished. This failure is partly a legacy of the communist times and partly due to the largely unchanged personnel at all levels of government, industry and other (old) institutions. It adds to the bias of the journalistic discourse, and therefore the journalist once again, as Coman (1993) describes him/her, "succeeds to re-create, paradoxically, the habits of propaganda, a phenomenon with deep roots both in the social and *professional networks* of the communist times (emphasis added)."

In the aftermath of the 1989 revolution, government officials, including ministers, became highly accessible to journalists, as Tircob of *Libertatea* and Stanescu of *Adevarul,* among many others, testified in 1990.[56] By 1993, governmental institutions, from the police, army and even the Romanian Information Service to the various ministries, all opened press offices and appointed spokesmen and spokeswomen to deal with the media. Despite the changes, journalists say it is difficult if not impossible to access records which, in any case, are randomly kept. The hearings in parliamentary committees and permanent commissions are still closed to the public and to journalists.

Yet some progress was achieved by the end of 1993 when the president of the Chamber of Deputies, Adrian Nastase, decided to permit press access to the working of that legislative arm of Parliament, a step not yet taken by the Senate (Uncu, Nov. 26, 1993). The legal support for the journalists' access to information or for the right of journalists to protect their sources is missing (see chapter 3).

Access to information is used as a weapon or as a reward by government officials and institutions. For instance, in a letter addressed to Hans Goren Franck of the Council of Europe's delegation to Romania, 21 print, broadcast, and news agency journalists (including the BBC Romanian Service representative, Razvan Popescu) accredited to the Romanian Senate gave the following examples of control over access to information:

1. Following a protest by journalists accredited to the Chamber of Deputies in December 1992 regarding unacceptable working conditions at that institution, on Feb. 1, 1993, the number of minimum accreditations, already very low, was further reduced;

2. After signaling these problems to a delegation from the Council of Europe in March 1993, also as a reprisal, the institution's Protection Service (Serviciul de Paza) limited access to the institution to journalists, invoking an order by Aurel Zamfirescu, chief of the Press Bureau. Ultimately Zamfirescu was replaced and the working conditions for journalists were ameliorated—without, however, lessening the pressure against them.

3. On April 26, 1993, Stefan Ionita, the photographer for *Expres,* while taking a picture of Corneliu Vadim Tudor, the secretary of the Senate, was stopped by Senator Ion Circiumaru (Socialist Workers Party) who threatened to confiscate the film. When Ionita refused to cease his picture taking, he was threatened with the loss of his accreditation to the Senate.

Government and parliamentary information more often than not is passed to journalists by individuals for political and personal reasons. In 1992, Nistorescu[57] of the weekly *Expres* described a situation in which there were "leaks on the part of one institution to 'get' another institution or an individual. And there is selling of information on the part of sources." Instances in which the selective release and publication of incriminating documents from the files of the former Securitate to manipulate issues and people are well recorded in the 1990–95 post-Ceausescu period.

In general, the ordinary Romanian, the newly established businessman, lower-level bureaucrat or government official and others who have less than a high-level official function have little interest in cooperating with the press. Ion Itu of *Tinerama*[58] describes access to sources of information as one of the biggest problems for the Romanian media, a problem at once tied to still-existent fears learned in the past as well as to present perceptions of people regarding the power of the media.

> People are still afraid to talk. After three years [of post-Ceausescu life] many are still afraid to talk and present the media with the documents they have. It doesn't matter what we reveal in the press because nothing happens and no one wants to come forward to give us more information. If people would see that something comes of news stories, they will lose their fear and talk to us.

That fear on the part of sources and prospective sources is often given as a reason why sources are not identified in news stories. "Protecting sources in Romania means more than in the West, and there is a constant questioning of what sources we should give [identify] or not," argues Max Banus, publisher of the weekly *Tinerama*.[59]

The ordinary Romanian has little opportunity to have access to the media and only seldom to be part of the journalistic discourse. The introduction of talk radio in mid-1993 has somewhat changed that situation, and the "right of reply" included in the Penal Code does provide some media access to Romanians and an opportunity to be heard. Feedback is possible via letters to the editors of newspapers and phone calls to the television and radio stations. Yet the news reports, particularly in the print media, generally deal with the ordinary citizens mostly as parts of crowds (Coman and Gross, spring 1994). Surveys and polls were few and far between in 1990–93, adding to the absence of voices that allow ordinary citizens to hear from one another on the issues of the day.

In short, while civil society has been resurrected in Romania, Splichal's (1992a) observation of postsocialist civil society's access to mass communication outlets in East-Central Europe is in great measure apropos to Romania:

> The access of both oppositional parties and particularly autonomous groups from civil society to national broadcast media and mainstream print media is being limited. ... [P]arliamentary mechanisms of party pluralism and formal democracy are considered as the only legitimate way to articulate the interests and opinions of "society," while non-institutional arrangements of civil society are ignored.

The notion of media freedom, for so long a rallying cry of the anti-communists of every stripe, is not accompanied by any notion of media democratization, that is, widespread, direct, diverse access to media outlets and to the public discourse. The first postrevolution access to media by ordinary people, that experiment in community media and particularly broadcasting, is gone. Jakubowicz (1993a, b) pinpoints the commonality of these trends in all of East-Central Europe in this first stage of media evolution (1989–93). His summation (1993b) concerning the broadcast media in East-Central Europe could have been written solely to describe the situation in Romania:

> Thus, equality, access to public discourse and the politics of inclusion are not really a priority in remodeling broadcasting in Central and Eastern Europe—except in a very special sense. Elites of all ideological persuasions are clearly determined to make sure that political clout won thanks to popular support translate also into involvement in running and/or overseeing broadcasting and access to air time.

The effects of the journalism practiced in the six post-Ceausescu years, this preprofessionalism together with the first stage of the media's evolution, have had a telling consequence on mass media credibility as well as on their role in the transition. The journalistic discourse, while improved somewhat by 1995, feeds the most negative perceptions of the news media's professionalism and capabilities to contribute to a transition to a democracy.

CHAPTER 5

The Role, Effectiveness and Influence of News Media

Freedom of the press was the first—and some will argue, the only—immediately tangible result of the 1989 revolution in Romania. Ideally, it was to serve as one of the primary vehicles for democratizing and modernizing society. The evolution of the new, post-Ceausescu journalism and of the mass media by which it is practiced compressed into four years the rough equivalent of 200 years of U.S. journalism history. The press constituted the first private, commercial enterprise in postrevolution Romania and from a pamphletlike, polemical, strictly political press it moved very quickly to a stage at which by 1993 yellow journalism came to dominate, and the main impetus became economic survival.

In the aftermath of the Ceausescus' unceremonious exit from Bucharest, the news media instantly became populist in nature only to be converted within a short few weeks to a type of specialized media thanks to their politicization. By 1993, they again assumed a politico-populist character, heavily delineated by sensationalism, a cross between English and American tabloids, with only sporadic and selective elements of serious, professional, informational journalism.

Journalism's reputation and therefore the mass media's standing, its function and role in Romania's transitionary society, had between 1989 and 1995 undergone a drastic and important change. Specifically, journalism was first applauded, then damned. It was first considered an essential tool of surveying the melange of political views, contending realities and near-realities

125

and the recovering of Romania's long-suppressed history. Then it was viewed increasingly as entertainment with some dubious informational value, and highly sensationalist. In Coman's (1994) words, media were "being praised ... as the core for the revolution, as a weapon of our democratic metamorphosis and as an agent of our freedom. It ended up being often considered as a weapon against democracy and freedom, and misleading."

The public began viewing the media as entertainment, voyeuristic, sensational, and marginally informative, questionably or distantly relevant. Journalism generally evolved within the parameters of the television docudrama: literary and fictional license being taken with real events, personalities and issues. The exceptions were notable, but they were "powerless to counteract the moral poison of the bad," as Charles Dickens wrote of the "influence of the good" press in the midst of a generally scurrilous, polemical, partisan, unprofessional 19th-century American press.

At the same time, the powers-that-be, as elsewhere in East-Central Europe by 1993 (Splichal 1992a, b), again looked upon the media as something to be controlled through direct and indirect means. From directly and indirectly manipulating the press's distribution, newsprint availability, broadcast licenses and frequencies to attempts at enacting restrictive laws (see chapter 3), the powers-that-be in Romania made subtle and not-so-subtle attempts at bringing the media back under their control. Their efforts were directed mainly at the press and radio which quickly multiplied and became independent starting in December 1989.

This chapter examines the course that media credibility has taken in Romania, the media's functions and roles and their effectiveness as means of communication and information, of education and socialization and of democratization. A brief case study of the media's functions, roles and effectiveness in Romania's two major post-Ceausescu national elections is offered, as is a brief examination of their possible future evolution.

Consequences of Post-1989 Journalism

The findings of a weeklong examination of Romanian Television (RTV) news conducted in May 1993 by sociologist Pavel Campeanu (July 29–Aug. 4, 1993) led to the conclusion that, during the week studied, the station's performance had "more chances of having weakened rather than strengthened its credibility." This conclusion was yet another affirmation of the widely held view evolving since the first few months of 1990 that television was not credible. It was a sentiment also held in regard to the press whose evolution, in terms of both the kind of new publications being introduced and the content of the existing ones, increasingly decreased audience confidence in the media. For instance, the introduction in 1992 of the sensationalist tabloid *Evenimentul Zilei* created and answered a voyeuristic and entertainment demand. Concurrently, it also added to the view that the press is not credible and "contributed to a climate in which credibility was already lacking," as *Curierul National*'s Mioara Iordache, along with other journalists, recognized.[1]

Campeanu's conclusions and the opinions of journalists and politicians on the subject of media credibility are confirmed by all the surveys conducted in Romania in the years 1990 to 1993. They point to the audiences' net loss in confidence in the indigenous media. Romanian Radio (RR) is the only relative winner in this race for the respect and the sustained attention of the audience, perhaps because of its more professional approach to journalism. Cristinel Popa, RR's secretary general, rightly argues that "you gain respect when you send the message you are looking for information rather than something on which to comment."[2]

Nationwide polls conducted by the Bucharest-based Center for Urban and Regional Studies on behalf of the U.S. Information Agency show the Romanians' confidence in their own media to have drastically dropped from a relative high in the first four months after the revolution to mid-1993 (see table 5.1).

The largest drop in confidence was registered by the print media, which already lagged behind television and radio in early 1990. Only 59 percent of the adult population had "a great deal" or "a fair amount" of confidence in the press in April 1990, and that percentage shrank to 31 percent by May 1993. Romanian Television did not fare any better, albeit having been considered more credible than the press from the moment the media were freed from Communist Party control. In April 1990, a full 70 percent of Romanians had "a great deal" or "a fair amount" of confidence in RTV, but by May 1993 that figure lost 25 percentage points, with only 45 percent of the adult population expressing confidence in the medium. Romanian Radio lost only 7 percentage points between April 1990 (76 percent said they had "a great deal" or "a fair amount" of confidence in RR) and May 1993 (69 percent said they had confidence in RR).

The low level of audience confidence in Romania's television and press by 1993 was upheld by a Gallup poll published in *Romania Libera* ("Majoritatea populatiei Romaniei nu are incredere in Televiziune," March 3, 1993). It showed that a total of 43 percent of Romanians had "a great deal" or "a fair amount" of confidence in Romanian Television. For the press, the total of those expressing "a great deal" and "a fair amount" of confidence was only 28 percent. Radio, inclusive of Romanian Radio and the new in-

TABLE **5.1.**   **Confidence in Romanian Media** (in percentage)

	April 1990	Dec. 1990	Nov. 1991	April 1992	May 1993
Romanian Radio					
A great deal	23	11	13	8	15
A fair amount	53	57	50	51	54
Not very much	14	21	25	25	19
No confidence	2	5	4	5	3
Don't know/NA	8	6	9	12	9
Romanian TV					
A great deal	26	9	7	5	8
A fair amount	44	50	38	37	37
Not very much	19	26	33	34	36
No confidence	5	11	15	13	12
Don't know/NA	6	4	8	11	5
Romanian Press					
A great deal	9	3	2	3	4
A fair amount	50	34	21	26	27
Not very much	24	39	45	37	38
No confidence	4	15	17	15	15
Don't know/NA	13	9	16	19	16

Source: U.S.Information Agency, 1993.
NA = not applicable.

dependent stations, received a respectable but not a brilliant report card. The Gallup Poll showed that for all radio stations in Romania, a total of 53 percent of the audience had "a great deal" or "a fair amount" of confidence— better than the figures for TV and the press, but still showing that, conversely, nearly half the population did *not* have much confidence in the medium.

The results of the polls measuring confidence in indigenous news media are further supported by a study conducted by Professor Ioan Dragan of the Romanian Academy's Institute of Sociology. He reported in the summer of 1992[3] that among those who in 1990 had confidence in the television, 27 percent had lost confidence in the medium two years later. Similarly, 25 percent of those who showed confidence in the press in 1990 no longer held the same sentiments by 1992. Confidence in the mass media had not changed much by 1995.

The exhilaration of being liberated and finally able to overtly think, say, write, read, listen and view whatever media program they desired allowed journalists and their audiences to enjoy a special relationship in the first few weeks after the revolution. During this honeymoon period, news media credibility was not questioned and confidence in them was relatively high. News media were sought after out of curiosity and sheer hunger for a free, indigenous media, one that had been missing from Romanian society since the early 1930s. The political polarization, which quickly began to take hold by the end of January 1990 and achieved warp speed by the time the May elections rolled around, together with the media's practical need to begin covering something other than the revolution, the Ceausescus and the past, signaled a lack of professionalism. It triggered a steady decline in audience confidence in the news media.

Mihailescu (July 27, 1990) argues that the new, old leadership or power and the general state of corruption contributed to the crisis of media credibility. This crisis of credibility was tied to a crisis of identity with which journalism and journalists were struggling in the first postrevolution year. It may be argued that it was also tied to the audience's identity crisis. Furthermore, the old mentalities of fear, nepotism and careerism led to a crisis of initiative on the part of journalists and journalism. This crisis of initiative was severely aggravated by the crisis of gerontocracy and (Mihailescu, July 27, 1990) "the suffocation of the new hires [journalists], the embargo on debates, protectionism, and the stubborn perpetuation of the 'mandarin' mentality, the obsession to belong to a [political] group, the gorging on columns and grandious subjects."

The passage of time and the drastic change in the makeup of the corps of Romanian journalists did not resolve this crisis of confidence and credibility. They worsened it, as statistics demonstrate. Journalists and public officials point to a number of specific and general factors contributing to the media's standing in this post-Ceausescu society. Some, like Sergiu Andon of *Adevarul*,[4] argue that the "loss of credibility is natural at this time [in a transition] in which there are no certainties and the value system is in the process of being rebuilt." Along the same line, others contend that no Romanian institution has much credibility. And, they maintain, the nature of Romanian journalism and mass media, derived from its reflecting a transitionary society and its not-too-credible institutions and power players, contributes to the media's loss of credibility.

Additionally, it was argued that the paradox of having a free press in a still-communist country, in Alina Mungiu's (June 8, 1990) rather extreme characterization of postrevolution Romania, contributed to the distrust of the media. Some observers inside and outside the media speculate that the overall high expectations the events of December 1989 engendered, including the anticipation of a professional, effective news media, brought about an equally extreme disappointment and a general malaise given the lack of quick and definitive progress. For the news media, it meant they had to deal with a public which became increasingly distrustful of the messengers as well as of the messages they brought. According to Manolescu (1991),

> The credibility crisis is evident. People have become accustomed with the lies told by journalists and no longer pay attention to them. ... People have forgotten how *Scinteia* [the Romanian Communist Party newspaper]

lied, as did the other newspapers until December [1989]. Today's press
seems incomparably more dishonest, probably because of its diversity.

The prestige of the journalists had plummeted in tandem with audience
loss of confidence in the media, or vice versa. At first, as Coman (1994) argues, the journalist was seen as a hero, martyr, revolutionary and person of
justice, only to be viewed by 1991 as quite ordinary, a liar, a clown, and im-
moral to boot. The journalists' personal battles carried out in the pages of the
press and on the airwaves made them "less credible from the moral and social point of view" (Coman 1994). Other factors may have cumulatively
contributed to the negative image of the journalist. For instance, the revelations that at least two of the best known among them were Securitate informers during the Ceausescu years did not foster any great trust in the journalists' corps, particularly because these individuals continued their
journalistic work after their public confessions.[5] Reports of journalists taking bribes to write specific stories and to publicize certain products, busi-
nesses and organizations,[6] as well as rumors of the chronic drunkenness of
some reporters and editors, further eroded the public image of the profession
and its members.

This loss of faith in journalists brought a concomitant reduction in the
willingness to act in concert with the journalists, to seek their help, rely on
them and expect them to bring about changes or contribute to them. It also
heightened the interest in entertainment and the voyeurism satisfied by a
sensationalist news media. And, one point on which most journalists can
agree, the absence of an echo to what is reported, particularly from the government and its ministers, contributes to the lack of credibility on the part of
most people. It also contributes to the perception of the media institution and
its journalists as wholly ineffective (as will be detailed in the next section of
this chapter).

Supported by media researchers and critics, journalists also argue that
a contributing factor to the loss of media credibility was an overall failure of
the young information system in the country. The image of disorganization,
inconsistency and amateurishness became a specter haunting the nation's reorganized news agency, Rompres, the new private news agencies, the new
press offices opened by the various governmental and nongovernmental institutions and the nature and professionalism of news conferences.

Cornel Nistorescu of *Expres,*[7] who recognizes the shortcomings of the
news media and their journalists, makes the point that the press's sagging
credibility is also a reflection of the low credibility of Romania's politicians
and government officials who serve as sources for and focal points of news
stories, analysis, commentary and editorials. At the very least, as former
Prime Minister Petre Roman[8] sees it, government officials were not able to

"explain basic concepts of democracy and open markets." Few journalists will implicitly point to the low level of professionalism in their journalism as the driving force behind their loss of credibility, or to their disrespect of readers and viewers, as evidenced by their need to tell them how to think instead of what to think about. *Monitorul de Iasi*'s Andy Lazescu[9] is among only a handful of journalists who views the lack of "equilibrium in reporting" and the "injection of subjectivity and commentary" in what is meant to be reporting as the principal cause of the loss in credibility (see chapter 4). On the other hand, the higher credibility assigned to Romanian Radio is credited by its director, Eugen Preda, to saying "*no* to commentary, *yes* to information."[10]

Public officials, too, the principal subject of many news reports, seem to feel that the media in general and the press in particular have a credibility problem. Former Prime Minister Theodore Stolojan[11] assigns this problem to the concepts and mentalities of Romanians in the transition period, ones that the press reflects in the way it carries out its journalism. Politicians like Petre Roman and Nicolae Manolescu speak for those who view the absence of a clear distinction between information and commentary as the main wellspring for the loss of confidence in the media.[12]

Iolanda Staniloiu,[13] Prime Minister Stolojan's spokesperson, who was viewed by most of the Romanian press as credible and open, assigns the media's lack of credibility to six perceived failings or characteristics:

1. A lack of effectiveness.
2. The tone of the media.
3. Continuous scandal surrounding the media themselves and that which was portrayed by the media.
4. A lack of professionalism, which exhibited itself at the most basic level of grammar and the level of the language used.
5. The perception that the media are elements of discord.
6. The plethora of media, which simply became overwhelming and fatiguing.

The perceptions of Romania's journalists regarding the population's confidence in the media for which they work is also instructive in that it implies an astuteness regarding the audience that was not generally translated into a widespread self-examination—the latter, presumably, leading to a corrective change in the way journalism is practiced. Professor Dragan[14] reports that 60 percent of journalists felt the RTV lost credibility, and 63 to 72 percent said the press had lost credibility since those early postrevolution days.

Yet, despite these dismal statistics regarding confidence in and the credibility of Romania's news media, television still serves as the major source of information for 60 percent of Romanians (Center for Urban and Regional Sociology, December 1995). This is partly because it reaches a larger audience than the print media that continue to battle with distribution problems. Furthermore, as a visual medium, it simply attracts a larger audience. This audience, whose mentalities have hardly undergone a major change since December 1989, because of or despite knowing that RTV directly or indirectly speaks for "The Power," seems to find a certain amount of paternal comfort in it.

Of course, there is yet another argument that could be made: Lack of credibility may, perversely, also be desirable in the sense that society needs a questioning, unaccepting public. Therefore, the steady loss of credibility in the mass media may indicate a change in the audience's mentalities, an evolution that bodes well for the resocialization process.

Radio, in general, was considered more credible than RTV or the press throughout the 1990–95 period. Like its visual cousin, radio is also able to penetrate the country's every nook and cranny, yet radio serves as a source (national) of information for only 20 percent of the population, as reported by the Center for Urban and Regional Sociology (December 1995). According to that same source, the press takes a close third place, with 19 percent of the population using it as its major source of news.

While newspapers are constantly disappearing and new ones are being launched, by 1995 circulation figures were dismally low (see chapter 3, The Press section). In part, the ever-increasing cost of these newspapers severely challenged the abilities of people living with a high inflation rate to afford them. In part, the high newsprint costs cut down on printing runs. However, data consistently showing low confidence in media at the very least suggest the possibility that the credibility of the press may also be a contributing factor to decreasing circulation. It may also explain the continuous introduction of and welcoming by audiences of new publications. Readers appear to be searching and hoping for a credible newspaper to come along and establish new standards of journalism.

The broadcast media, while not being that much more credible than the press, are also in a state of flux. Audiences were eagerly looking forward in 1993–95 to the new radio and television stations expected to begin their operations after being granted licenses and frequencies beginning in spring 1993. The question journalists, public officials and audience members were asking is whether these new broadcasting outlets would offer carbon copies of existing news programs or would improve professional standards and thus contribute to changing the news media and their role, effectiveness and influence in society. By the end of 1995, the answer was clear: change had occurred, but it was minimal.

News Media and the 1990 and 1992 Presidential and Parliamentary Elections

On May 20, 1990, Romanians had the opportunity to select from among some 80 political parties and hundreds of candidates for parliamentary seats. It was the first free election since the early 1930s. Two years later, on September 27, 1992, the second postcommunist election was held in Romania with voters being courted by 151 sometime overlapping, mostly irrelevant, registered political parties (Rompres, 1992). The news media's role and effectiveness in these elections provide a microcosm of their everyday role and effectiveness in the first six years of postcommunist existence.

The May 1990 Election

While free, the Romanian press prior to the May 1990 election still had to contend with government control of (a) printing facilities, (b) newsprint production and distribution, and (c) the national distribution system for all publications. The effects were telling.

The interim National Salvation Front (NSF) government, via its appointed minister of culture, decided to decrease newsprint allocations to and press time for opposition party publications and independent publications opposed to the NSF and its candidates. In April 1990, the NSF actually decreed that with the exception of its own daily newspaper, *Azi*, newspapers should cut their circulations in half (Ruston, September 1990, 4). Consequently, national newspapers that were decidedly anti-NSF, such as *Romania Libera*, had their circulation cut by as much as 30 percent prior to the May 1990 elections (Gross 1991b). Worse yet, independent and opposition newspapers reported their dailies delivered late, burned, discarded or stored in warehouses yet reported distributed (Gross 1991b; Ruston, September 1990; U.S. Commission on Security and Cooperation in Europe, May 30, 1990).

Contextually, daily and weekly newspapers gave their readers few brief or in-depth sketches of the candidates or interviews with them. Their news coverage was polemical, subjective and partisan. It concentrated predominantly on political matters, social conflicts, (politicized) economic issues, trade union and other nonpolitical organizations (yet politically active and important), the rehashing of the revolution and its victims and alleged villains, and communist history and personalities (their trials, denunciations, and so forth). The extreme politicization and polarization in the wake of the Jan. 23, 1990, the NSF announcement that it would renege on its Dec. 29, 1989 promise not to constitute itself as a party and be a contestant in the up-coming elections, were a predominant feature of the press. It zeroed in on is-sues that served as a daily focus for newspapers, in a pro or con fashion:

1. NSF's membership, the hordes of former Communist Party officials.

2. NSF members' still ambiguous role in the December 1989 revolu-tion.

3. NSF's manipulation of the newly constituted electorate and the con-trol and use of RTV by the NSF in this context.

4. The violence the NSF government and the president's office al-legedly, directly or indirectly, engendered against the opposition party (in-clusive of the miners' first rampage through Bucharest in support of the NSF on Feb. 19, 1990).

5. NSF leader Ion Iliescu's communist pedigree.

In broadcasting, the control exerted over Romanian Television (RTV) by the interim government before the elections was also telling: it allowed the more than 80 political parties[15] to equally share 50 percent of airtime on RTV while the NSF used the other 50 percent for its own campaign. The In-ternational Center on Censorship, "Article 19," reports (1991, 304) that "the government manipulated events throughout the election campaign, using ex-clusive television coverage, with extremely limited airtime allowed to other parties, and then at times of minimum viewing." RTV news reports on mat-ters concerning the campaign or the parties and candidates lacked balance and the absence of bias, favoring the NSF and Ion Iliescu. While most view-ers still assigned more credibility to RTV, only 25 percent thought it could contribute to the establishment of democracy in Romania (Campeanu et al. 1991, 85).

On May 17, a debate between the three presidential candidates (the NSF's Ion Iliescu, the Liberal Party's Radu Campeanu and the Peasant Party's Ion Ratiu) was televised by RTV. Ninety-six percent of RTV's pos-sible audience viewed the event (Campeanu et al. 1991, 69). It was a unique event for Romanians. The "panel" that ran this debate was composed of Emanuel Valeriu, Victor Ionescu and Razvan Theodorescu, all three RTV executives. Ionescu was the only working journalist among them, serving as head of the Foreign News Department. All three went well beyond putting questions to the candidates, embarking on their own speeches and analyses. Ultimately, according to Campeanu et al. (1991, 72),

Television was not satisfied with its role as host, arrogating for itself

also [the role of] the sole representative of [Romanian] mass media. ... Assuming in exclusivity this role, Television exposed itself to all manner of
suspicion: the improbable hypothesis that it favors one of the three candidates, that it offered him in advance a scenario of questions. ... One more
proof of how difficult it is for Television to take upon itself the crisis of
credibility, which it deepens by ignoring it. In the case to which I refer, it
[RTV] reserves for itself an area of manipulation even if it has no intention
to manipulate.

The effectiveness and influence of the news media in presenting candidates and political parties and their platforms to the voters is unclear. Given
that in April and May 1990 (the Romanian election campaign spanned eight
weeks) the Romanian press established itself as a party press, with even its
"independent" element being firmly and overtly entrenched as a supporter of
a particular candidate or party, it acted more as a combination public relations representative and advertiser for its chosen champions. During this period, circulation was still relatively high. Romanians were still at a stage
where they could afford and had an interest in purchasing more than one
newspaper. Therefore, they were exposed to a diversity of views and presentations of various happenings.

In this way they were able to discover, not without some effort, the
many newly established political parties and their often changing, ambiguous platforms. However, the news media appear to have played more of a reinforcing role, catering to the real or imaginary fears of voters, thus adding
to the feeling of postrevolution chaos and social unrest that the majority
(85.9 percent) felt served as the background for the election campaign
(Campeanu et al. 1991, 55). This majority was unable to discover the candidates, their platforms or the major, pressing issues via the news media, beyond the presentations that were politically one-sided or banal (e.g., Radu
Campeanu's viability as a candidate given that he spent the last years of the
Ceausescu regime in exile in Paris; Ion Ratiu's bow tie, which in Romania
is more a symbol of a waiter than a respectable politician; the imminent return of totalitarianism, and so on).

An IRSOP poll on opinion change (Gheorghiu 1991, 80) shows few al-
terations in voter choices from March 26–28 to May 4–6, just before the
election. It speaks at least partially to the limited effectiveness and influence
of the news media or, from a positive perspective, their effectiveness and influence in retaining followers for the candidates and party they championed.
Only two significant changes occurred: (1) a drastic loss of interest in the
National Liberal Party and its candidate Radu Campeanu (from 24 percent
to 14 percent) and (2) a somewhat increased interest in parties other than the
six most-supported ones[16] (from 1 percent to 7 percent). The Liberal Party's
loss of support may be assigned to the public actions and statements of its

candidate, Campeanu. These were positively publicized by the party's own publication and those supporting it and used as a political punching bag by those in the other camps. The increased interest in other than the major political parties is due primarily to the dissemination of these groups' own publications rather than the coverage afforded them by what was shaping up to be the major national press.

The NSF, loaded with former Communist Party members and other apparatchiks, won the majority of seats in Parliament.[17] Ion Iliescu, a former Ceausescu regime official, was elected president of the country with 85.07 percent of the votes. The explanations for their win ranges far and wide, from the economic to the political, from the cultural to the sociopsychological. From a mass communication or news media perspective, they won because they controlled the dissemination of the press outside the large cities and RTV with its ability to reach the majority of Romanians. Additionally, the (politicized) news media served as the communication apparatus of the parties and candidates. As the public relations representatives of the parties and candidates, the independent news media were no match for the few among their ranks who supported the regime and the president and were staffed by experienced propagandists inherited from the communist period. In short, both the reach of the NSF-Iliescu mass communication machine and the effectiveness of its message conceptualization and delivery outperformed that of the opposition. *Romania Libera*'s Eugen Serbanescu's summary[18] is representative of that of many in and out of journalism: "The communist elites, now the new noncommunist elites, are more skillful at manipulation; therefore the 1990 and 1992 election results."

Once again the news media, by their very diversity, as official or unofficial representatives of one or another political party and candidate, served as recruiters to an incipient civil society. However, the news media failed as purposeful and symbolic educators of a new democratic life and order. They failed because they showed intolerance, partisanship, lack of balance and a disrespect for the audience by assuming that it needed to be directed in its deliberations rather than informed. They did not present readers or viewers with news but rather with views on the events and issues of the day, and thus were only indirectly and incompletely informative. Their adversarial role was carried out vis-à-vis each other and the candidates and parties they opposed—that is, it was a battle between them on behalf of their champions, couched in terms of service to their audience and society.

The September 1992 Election

There was general agreement among Romanian and foreign observers that the Sept. 27, 1992 parliamentary and presidential election and the subsequent October 11 runoff for president, as a whole, were fair and better organized than in 1990. The media, "while offering qualitatively and quantitatively better coverage in 1992, continued to serve an ambiguous role in the democratization process and intrinsically in the political election" (Coman and Gross, spring 1994). More to the point, the international observer delegation, organized by the National Democratic Institute for International Affairs and the International Republican Institute, in a generally positive statement (*Preliminary Statement by the International Observer Delegation*) released on September 29 said, "Although access to television by political parties and candidates has greatly improved, the news broadcasts on national television reflected overt and subtle political biases."

As in 1990, television was the pervasive medium accessed by Romanians, followed by radio and the press, a fact averred by Romanian and foreign polls. Campeanu's survey (Oct. 1, 1992) shows 71.6 percent of those polled getting their election information from RTV, 34.1 percent from Romanian Radio and 30.1 percent from the press. RTV's own audience research[19] carried out August 17–23, 1992, showed that 40 percent of its viewers used television as their main source of election news, 8.2 percent used the press and only 5 percent radio. This pattern of general news media usage is also supported by a late 1991 survey conducted by Bucharest's Center for Urban and Regional Sociology on behalf of the U.S. Information Agency (February 1992). It shows 58 percent of Romanians relying on television as their main source of information, 24 percent on radio and 14 percent on the press. Therefore, the main focus of attention on the part of domestic and foreign observers was RTV.

Compared to 1990, television and radio coverage were far more equitable in 1992, partly thanks to new legislation. Access to the news media and how the media campaign was to be carried out were spelled out in two 1992 laws passed by Parliament: Chapter 7 of Law No. 68 (On the Election to the Chamber of Deputies and the Senate) and Section 4 of Law No. 69 (On the Election of the President of Romania). The Audio-Visual Law enacted on May 21, 1992 (Law No. 48) called for the newly established National Audiovisual Council to work out a timetable for electoral campaign programs (Article 32, Section 2). A special Parliamentary Commission,[20] composed of 11 members from the Chamber of Deputies, 4 Senators, one representative from RTV and one from RR, established a timetable for the electoral campaign and airtime assignments for those parties in and outside of Parliament, as well as for the presidential candidates.

The seven parties holding seats in the Romanian Parliament[21] each received 4.4 percent of all the RR and RTV airtime allocated to the electoral campaign. The two Liberal parties (National Liberal Party-Democratic Convention and the New Liberal Party), split up shortly before the elections, were assigned an aggregate 6.5 percent of airtime reserved for the campaign. All other parties active in the electoral campaign, some 50 of them, were allotted a total of 67.2 percent of airtime. Each of the six presidential candidates (I. Iliescu, E. Constantinescu, G. Funar, I. Manzatu, C. T. Dragomir, M. Druc) was allotted 16.6 percent of television and radio airtime. During the runoff campaign after September 27, each of the two candidates (Iliescu and Constantinescu) received 50 percent of the electoral campaign airtime. Prior to the runoff presidential election on October 11, four debates between the two candidates were televised by RTV (October 5, 6, 7 and 8). These occasions turned out to be lively, uninhibited give-and-takes with less interference from the moderators than in the one 1990 (May 17) debate. Significantly, 12 percent of viewers said they decided how to vote in the presidential contest after watching the debate (Media Monitoring Unit 1992, 40).

There were noticeable disparities between allocated airtime and that which was actually used. Some of these disparities were blamed on the failure of the parties or candidates to provide RR or RTV with audio- or videotape of their messages (Media Monitoring Unit 1992). The Media Monitoring Unit study shows there were also disparities in the coverage afforded the parties and the presidential candidates in RTV and RR news and current affairs broadcasts. Among the presidential candidates, not surprisingly, the incumbent (Iliescu) received a larger share of coverage by virtue of his "news making" as president of Romania.

In its conclusion, the European Institute of the Media's Media Monitoring Unit (1992) found that RTV in particular was biased in favor of Iliescu and against the main opposition party (Democratic Convention) on a number of occasions. This bias was expressed in terms of omissions of important news items regarding the main opposition parties and candidates, camera angles when filming candidates and more coverage allotted to the incumbent presidential candidate. However, the Media Monitoring Unit (1992, 43) also concluded that it could not prove "consistent interference" and that "the frequency and tendency of the imperfections revealed" were not "likely to have significantly affected the outcome of the election." Romanian Radio was praised for its professional competence, balance and autonomy, while RTV was diplomatically judged to have "failed to achieve its potential."

The press, while moving away from being a party press per se, continued to exhibit the kind of party-press parallelism that stopped it from being a neutral purveyor of news instead of a disseminator of partisan interpretations and advocacy messages. The findings of a U.S. Information Agency survey conducted by a Bucharest-based group, SOCIOBIT (November 13, 1992), were therefore not surprising. For instance, the survey showed that 55 percent of the supporters of the nationalist parties read the xenophobic, nationalist *Romania Mare* and 23 percent the somewhat more neutral yet still Democratic National Salvation Front (DNSF)[22] sympathizer *Adevarul*; 30 percent of Democratic Convention supporters read the decidedly anti-government, anti-president *Romania Libera,* 19 percent the aforementioned *Adevarul* and 9 percent the opposition weekly *Expres*; 29 percent and 11 percent of the DNSF supporters read *Adevarul* and *Romania Mare,* respectively.

While offering more coverage of the campaign, issues, candidates and parties, the Romanian daily and weekly press demonstrated four general characteristics (Coman and Gross, spring 1994):

1. Its journalists and editors were unable to divorce themselves from the "magic" of opinion writing, mixing opinion, commentary and other evaluative judgments in their news and feature writing.

2. It reflected the political polarization in the country by being itself polarized politically and encouraging this polarization. Thus, given its biased presentation of limited, incomplete facts, it proved incapable of carrying out its mission of informing the public.

3. There was a selective indifference in newspaper items to external voices such as news releases, interviews and press conference materials, as well as to the readers and voters.

4. There was a general tendency to evade dealing with larger, more substantive political issues or political education. Instead, the press concentrated on the relatively minor but more spectacular ones: internal party dissension, outrageous statements by politicians, accidents involving politicians, the conduct of the election campaign—all of it tied to candidates and parties the newspapers opposed.

As a consequence of the press's approach to and manner in which it covered the election, it (Coman and Gross, spring 1994) "again contributed to an atmosphere of confusion, rumormongering, partisanship, and emotionalism. Its efficacy as a tool of re-education, resocialization, and information is at best highly questionable and most likely non-existent."

According to Lia Trandafir,[23] a *Tinerama* reporter in 1992, while Romanian journalists "desperately tried to introduce neutrality," they failed. That neutrality was essentially translated in more or less equally beating on the opposition and on the opposition to the opposition. Journalists and their news media made four mistakes:

1. They compromised themselves as independent, neutral professionals. They did so by becoming "house journalists" or "lapdogs" rather than

"watchdogs" and not publishing the negative aspects of events, issues and candidates of the parties they (or their newspaper) supported.

2. They embarked on partisan campaigns against certain fringe or extreme parties and candidates,[24] often losing track of reporting election news, and elevating them in the public's consciousness.

3. They "suffocated with love" the Democratic Convention, according to Trandafir and other journalists. By running the media campaign for them, by avoiding publishing negatives about their candidates or platforms, journalists "did not allow the DC to develop its own modern, efficient communication."

4. They concentrated almost exclusively on the presidential race, disregarding the much more consequential parliamentary races. This is perhaps an indication of the greater symbolism each presidential candidate, in comparison to the political parties, was assigned in regard to ideology and political leanings and for or against which the news media battled.

Still, many Romanian journalists claim that election results show that they and the news media made a significant difference between 1990 and 1992 (see table 5.2, Election Results, at the end of this chapter). Specifically, they point to Ion Iliescu's loss of 23.67 percentage points since 1990 (from 85.07 to 61.4 percent of votes). Yet, on the most basic level, to assign such a loss in votes to the press would have meant that

a. more people read newspapers at a time *when circulations actually decreased* (see chapter 3),

b. the various newspapers' readership became more diverse or stayed at least as diverse as in 1990 (i.e., readers buying the various newspapers even if they did not agree with their obvious political biases), which *cannot be substantiated because the decrease in circulation suggests a cutback in the number of newspapers bought each day by any one reader,* and

c. both print and broadcast news media's journalism provided significantly more information whose credibility increased since 1990, *when in fact polls show credibility decreased* (see first section of this chapter).

In conclusion, the press and radio's level of contribution to political information or its impact was not changed by the election campaign itself, remaining limited. This fact, together with the increased impact of visual propaganda versus information, strengthened the primacy of television (Campeanu, Oct. 1, 1992). But it did not strengthen its credibility. Therefore, its effectiveness and influence on election results are questionable, particularly in view of its biases. That is, President Iliescu was re-elected, this time in a runoff, and by a smaller margin than in 1990, and the DNSF (partly because of the NSF-DNSF split) received fewer parliamentary seats.

News Media Roles
After December 1989

Senator Gheorghe Dumitrascu,[25] a mustachioed, portly, comedic figure from the Black Sea port city of Constanta, opined in 1992 that the press "doesn't inform, neither does it disinform, the press deforms." In great measure and to varying degrees in the course of the first six post-Ceausescu years, that statement applied to the entire Romanian news media.

The majority of journalists disagree to one degree or another. They point out that since December 1989 the mass media and their journalism have served significant educational and informational roles in politics, culture, the economy and social development by

a. pioneering in the discovery of the market economy;

b. serving as a litmus test for the relationship between the new powers and the population and destroying the myths surrounding them, that is, that they are not immune from scrutiny;

c. facilitating a change in mentalities, the elimination of fear and the promotion of questioning as a way of life, changing voters into constituents, transforming the group and class reflex into individual and national reflexes;

d. providing audiences with the European and world context of Romania's existence;

e. educating audiences on history (and its consequences to their contemporary lives), geography, legislation, the rights of individuals, the rights of minorities, extremism and nationalism;

f. presenting audiences with the new civil society and the new middle class, and

g. mediating the political dialogue.

Virginia Gheorghiu (1991, 2) is more specific. She defines four roles for Romania's media:

1. They are actors in other institutions, in political and industrial life.

2. They are communicators explaining institutions to the people involved in them by both vertical and horizontal communication.

3. They are information brokers, conveying messages in and through social processes.

4. They are legitimizers of values and institutions in the public arena, conferring status and validity and setting the agenda for political debate.

These views of the roles played by the Romanian media in the 1990–95 period are far too broad and generous, perhaps more a matter of hubris than of reality. As a whole, the media only partially fulfilled some of these roles, mostly as an unintended consequence of preprofessional journalism, of solid journalism that was an exception to the rule and of the very existence of a diverse, freewheeling press.

The symbols of a diverse, changing press, of a national television that generated nothing but controversy and local television that offered a poor alternative with some local news and views, and of an expanding and experimenting radio industry, played significant roles in a society accustomed to a media graveyard. Minimally, this media diversity allowed for autodidacticism on the part of the audience and was as successful in marginally and haphazardly fulfilling the roles listed earlier as were the contents of the media. The diversity and largely negative nature of the media's contents and approach to journalism had the (additional) unintended role of indirectly educating the audience to be more selective and better media consumers. Their falling confidence in existing media and continued receptivity to and search for new media partly support this argument.

In the immediate aftermath of the December 1989 revolution and the national and individual catharsis the mass media facilitated, they were divided into two distinctive camps, according to Mungiu (Jan. 18, 1991). Part of the press took anti-Securitate and anti-nomenclatura positions. Other publications, she writes, promptly forgot the sins of the past regime and zeroed in on the "phantom enemies of communism: land owners, the masters/bosses, Legionairs, dissidents of the Ceausescu regime, the (Romanian) Diaspora, etc." In the more simplistic political jargon of the post-Ceausescu period, and as an expression of the level of maturation of Romanian democracy, the news media took either the pro or the con view of the NSF, later the DNSF, and President Iliescu. In both cases, instead of supplying their audiences with complete, verifiable, sourced information, the new Romanian journalism had at its core the expression of the journalists' opinions (see chapter 4). It was an "extreme diversity of opinions" that illustrated "the grave socio-political crisis" of the transition period (Szabo, July 27, 1990). By offering up this diversity of opinions in the nation, they incompletely mirrored the changes occurring. And these media and the society in which they functioned were only fractionally mutually influencing. Therefore, they only partially fit into two possible media–social structure relationship types posited by Rosengren (1981): they are mirrors of change, and at the same time media and society are mutually influencing.

From 1990 to the end of 1992, Romanian journalism created an advocacy and not simply an adversarial media. It was a media of mobilization for specific politico-ideological groups and ideas and not for a transition to a well-defined, generally agreed upon democratic ideal. While the media and their journalism represented newly found freedoms, as well as the socio-political, cultural and economic crisis in which the nation found itself, they did not reflect or legitimize a newly institutionalized democracy and its consonant values.

First, these subjective, partisan, often caustic news media failed to be symbols of a more democratic life and values: tolerance, civility, balance. Second, they substantively failed to inform public opinion, to educate and socialize the public in the tenets of a democracy and to give Romanians the wherewithal, the information, the facts, the choices they needed to participate in an informed national conversation regarding their future.

For instance, democracy, its ideal meaning, its processes and required mentalities and behaviors were ill-communicated to the point of creating confusion about the political terms and concepts being used as well as their practical applications and exigencies (Campeanu, June 28, 1991). The persistence of media whose loyalties were defined in terms belonging either to "The Power" or to "The Opposition," instead of to the audience and the ideal of a Fourth Estate, made for a strictly partisan journalism and media. Or, as Tia Serbanescu (Aug. 6, 1993) sees the "independent" press, it was either in opposition to "The Power" or in opposition to the opposition.

A boycott of the government as a news beat, called in the summer of 1993 by the Association of Romanian Journalists and widely observed by the press, best illustrates the self-assigned partisan, political role of reporters and the news media and their lack of professionalism. The boycott was in response to the government failure to "provide answers or explications" to the press's multiple and continuous discoveries of alleged corruption in the government and to its continuing "protection of the accused." ("Guvernul—supus sanctiunilor presei," July 14, 1993). It was also a political statement, yet another shot by the "opposition" press against "The Power."

However, while highly politicized and partisan, this does not mean that the media and their journalism were either supporters or opponents of a status quo (Peterson et al. 1966). After all, a status quo did not exist in the first four post-Ceausescu years. For instance, the media that supported the party in power and the president were not necessarily supporting the postrevolution political system per se. In general, media were the standard-bearers for the sociopolitical views and political players fighting to establish a status quo—that is, a sociopolitical system with dominant, definable and accepted institutions, culture, politics and ideology. However, as mobilizers for and advocates of the newly established parties and newly formed elements of civil society, the media did play a significant role in the first phase of laying the groundwork for a possible democracy.

In the first three post-Ceausescu years, the press in particular exemplified the public's political fragmentation and polarization and encouraged and nurtured it. Far from mediating the political dialogue, the media's intent was reinforcing and indoctrinating in nature, tending to temporarily mobilize and whip up sentiments against a party, a program, an idea or an individual. In the 1993–95 years, signs of a move toward a semblance of balance, of neutrality, of further diversification in some news media's contents softened their politicized nature. However, even in 1993 Adamesteanu (April 8–14, 1993) still argued that the press was divided into two general camps: publications that manipulate inaccurate news with a precise goal in mind and those that allow this news to be further deformed because they are indifferent or wish to capture readers with scandalmongering. Indeed, the operative definition of *adversarial* seems to have been equated with being scandalous and in opposition to "The Power." Still, a third camp slowly made its appearance: publications that sought to bring a variety of information to their audience and began the process of presenting it in a less stridently subjective way.

In the first three post-Ceausescu years, the opposition to "The Power" was an opposition to who or what politics or ideology may be attempting to dominate society. In 1993 and 1994, general opposition to the structure of power was added to the former targets. Consequently, the agenda-setting power of the media was severely weakened because, in part, they first couched everything in an anti-communism and anti-communists context. Subsequently, they couched everything in a general anti–power structure context, when the general public was concerned with the more practical issues of day-to-day survival and struggling to formulate a vision of its future.

If the media served as a litmus test for the relationship between the new powers and the population, the message was not entirely a positive one. The news media's mostly futile fight against corruption (as described in the next section) showed that though the new powers are not immune to scrutiny, they are largely immune from any meaningful consequences to this scrutiny. Thus, the news media reinforced rather than destroyed the myths surrounding those with political power. In fact, they managed to append another chapter by adding the economically powerful to the ranks of the perceived quasi untouchables with their description of the nouveaux riches and their newly acquired clout. The mentality of fear was inadvertently reinforced; "questioning as a way of life" may have been encouraged by the symbolism of a diverse media but discouraged by the nature and content of their reports. The group and class reflexes remained generally unchanged thanks to the overt introduction of the new economic *and* political divisions, those with power versus those without.

Equally damning, Coman (1993) sees the news media being entertaining rather than informative and the journalists as "sort of magicians who have been able to bewitch them—for one or more moments" in order to get "applause, glory and ... who knows?" Television was even worse, contends Cornea (Aug. 12–18, 1993): "As far as the capacity of television to distort facts, to serve as a means of propaganda for the Power, it [this capacity] has not remained static, quite the contrary, it has recently been considerably accentuated."

Dan Vardie,[26] editor of *Tineretul Liber,* concluded in 1993 that the Romanian press "had not fulfilled the role of a press in a national transition." It failed to play the educational and informational role required in the transition period, according to Vardie and a handful of other journalists and editors. Yet, none of the journalists is able to clearly define what the media's role should be in the kind of transition Romania is undergoing. What seemed to have been missing was only identified ex post facto. For instance, says former Prime Minister Petre Roman,[27] "the educational programs to change mentalities were missing. Not only did they not do anything, but they were counterproductive."

The atomization of the totalitarian mentality, the main intent (again as in the precommunist era and, even more so, communist era) on political mobilization, reinforcement and proselytizing, manipulation, dissimulation and rumormongering in the service of its political biases, made for a journalism that had the one-sidedness of public relations releases with an added touch of holy writ and a dash of Machiavellianism (Gross 1993b). Growing commercial interests since 1990 reinforced this type of journalism. Cornel Nistorescu, editor of *Expres,* pointed out in 1990 (July 27) a trend among journalists which only very slowly began changing two to three years later when he said that journalists "instead of being teamsters carrying information from reality to readers, transformed themselves into political gunslingers." Echoing these sentiments in 1992, Grigore Marian[28] of the Romanian Society of Journalists, decried the fact that "everything is still turned into politics."

The continuous campaign by the National Salvation Front government, the presidency and the press supporting them to discredit the "opposition" press (Uncu, July 11, 1991), accusing it of being a destabilizing factor, of being supported by foreign powers, and wanting to "sell the nation," added to the press's polarization and politicization. Both the opposition and the pro-government, pro-president media ignored or deformed events and information or embarked on the sort of disinformation campaigns familiar during the communist era (Bacanu, April 6, 1993). For instance, information regarding the Democratic Convention's first presidential candidate (Manolescu) in 1992 was simply not presented to the public by the "opposition" media so as not to damage his candidacy.[29] On the other hand, the media that supported the National Salvation Front that controlled the government ignored or deformed the machinations of the president and the government that involved the miners' rampages through Bucharest, the slowness of reforms, the corruption, the obstruction of justice and other issues and events (Berindei et al. 1991). The introduction of sensationalism in the service of politico-ideological inclination, as Coman (1994) says, led to the publication of gossip about politicians and their private lives, "secret and unexpected political papers (the sources of information is [*sic*] still a mystery for everybody) ... the most vehement social responses, ... the most worrying data about the new prices ... wages."

By the end of 1992, after the second postrevolution parliamentary and presidential elections, the so-called "press of the barricades" began giving way to a less obviously partisan one. That is to say, with the exception of the government-issued *Vocea Romaniei*, the majority of the press set itself more or less in "opposition." But, it was a general opposition to the power structure and not necessarily against the party and individuals in power or their philosophies and politics. At least the necessity for some degree of neutrality was being recognized. The marriage of information with opinion was acknowledged as a journalistic combination that had to be dissolved to some degree. Rompres's head, Neagu Udroiu,[30] agreed in 1993 that Romanian journalism began (in December 1989) "with commentaries, and information marginalized." Yet, he added that with sufficient justification, commentaries have become less important in the four years since the revolution, and "we will reverse this traditional approach as soon as information takes center stage in society."

The general absence of information as a centerpiece of the evolving Romanian society is also a telling reason for the nonexistence of the concept of the Fourth Estate. It never existed in Romanian journalism or mass media and does not exist now in the postrevolution period, despite continuous discussions on the subject among journalists and editors and its treatment in the press itself. Dan Pavel (July 11, 1991) points out that if the power of the Fourth Estate is not exercised, it is neither a power nor free. Yet, he argues, in Romania the media cannot become the "Fourth Power/Estate" under conditions in which "the other three powers make up a deformed amalgam, a teratological unity, a Leviathan with ambiguous organic functions."

Furthermore, without acceptance of the concept of a Fourth Estate in Romania, together with the present notion of professionalism, there is no ideological construct capable of enhancing the political or occupational status of journalism, as Schiller (1981), for instance, posits the role of the Fourth Estate in his study of commercial journalism in the United States. The traditional notion of the media as an institution that is not part of the national checks and balances, but only a weapon of political warfare, contributes to the absence of the Fourth Estate concept. This notion is encouraged even by the most enlightened and intelligent observers of the Romanian media and political scene, such as Gabriel Andreescu (Dec. 10–16, 1992). He acknowledges that mass media do not represent a Fourth

Estate, but are "in any case, the first power of the opposition."

An additional contributor to this situation is the idea of journalists whose status is secured by their success and stature as political fighters or creators of literary prose in and outside the fictional genre, and not on that of reporters. The "traditional" and very European idea of the journalist being an activist, an advocate, is not surprising given that the best-known and most "successful" journalists of the precommunist era, as was the case elsewhere in Europe, were also Romania's literary or intellectual giants and political activists (e.g,. N. Iorga, I. H. Radulescu, M. Eminescu, M. Eliade, C. A. Rosetti, I. L. Caragiale, M. Kogalnicianu, P. Istrati, B. P. Hasdeu). Intimately related to this outlook on media professionalism (the literary, activist, advocate, polemical journalism) is the deeply ingrained belief that journalists are born and not made, and therefore, that "talent is everything," as *Evenimentul Zilei*'s Cristoiu has repeatedly said.[31]

The often repeated words of Caragiale, one of Romania's foremost playwrights, a novelist and a journalist, that the only requirement to being a journalist is "bun simt si gramatica"—common sense and grammar—was taken literally by a sizable segment of the post-Ceausescu journalistic community, despite the fact that both common sense and good grammar are often missing in the new journalistic product. It is an outlook that makes it difficult to accept the idea of journalism training or universally accepted professional standards.

The news media's role in the modernization and development process has to be decidedly different from that of their counterparts in the Third World. In Romania's type of traditional society, new ideas and new information need to be disseminated to "stimulate people to want to behave in new ways" (Lerner 1972, 348). But there is a twist to it, in the sense that the Romanians *want* to behave in new ways. The stimulation to do so has existed for years. But (a) they are afraid to do so, (b) they don't know how, and (c) they need to be convinced that there is a real opportunity to do so in the political, social and economic realms. There is no need to stimulate "the peasant to want to be a freeholding farmer, the farmer's son to want to learn reading, ... the farmer's wife to want to stop bearing children, the farmer's daughter to want to wear a dress and do her hair" (348). Those attitudes, desires and outlooks already exist. Lerner's "new public communication" leading "directly to new articulation of private, interests" is not a goal in Romania where private interest has been expressed all too well in various negative ways before and after the 1989 revolution. Rather, there was a need, not met by the new mass media, for a type of new public communication that redefined private interests, the way to meet these interests and how private interests can be successfully married to public interests. Given their contents, mode of presentation and general approach to journalism and the messages embodied in the form and symbol of their existence, the media have been limited agents of resocialization in Romania.

Finally, the social, political and economic turmoil in the nation made it an urgent need for the media and their journalism to perform a normative and integrating sociopolitical and cultural role (Alexander 1981). Yet they failed to perform such a role, and, in fact, they were forces of dispersion, individuation and isolation. This situation is partly because the sociopolitical culture had and still has ill-defined tenets from which few principles can be derived by the system that, in turn, defines and regulates media roles (Gurevitch and Blumler 1983, 282). Lacking a clear definition of news media and journalism and the function they ought to carry out, their roles constantly change (within narrow parameters) as the sociopolitical system and its incipient culture experimentally, tentatively and restrictively mold and remold themselves.

In positive terms, the news media and their journalism's normative role in 1990–95 can be defined as one of recruiters for elements of the reforming civil society and the sociopolitical and economic landscape and as symbols of a departure from a monolithic or near-monolithic media system.

By their diversity and their politicization they proved to their audiences that it was possible to speak freely—an important lesson to those emerging from a communist system as Stalinist as the Romanian one was under the Ceausescus. As recruiters, the media were mobilizers and manipulators involved in education and information of a very narrow range, that of the party or political philosophy they supported. Only their diversity in terms of their originating points (e.g., a party, a philosophy or ideology, a particular intent) increased that range and made their role a positive one in regard to their contribution to civil society and the political culture's establishment and growth. Beginning in 1993, when the news media, with the exception of RTV, became somewhat more neutral and informative and more diverse in their content, media also saw their role as agents of change probably increasing.

News Media Effectiveness and Influence

Opposition and anti-communist themes, the recruiting, mobilization, reinforcement and proselytizing intent pervading the very nature of news reporting and writing did not make for an effective media in a transitionary society. Romania was and still is a transitionary society whose unarticulated expectations of the news media are that they be different from the communist ones and be from diverse origins.

The ineffectiveness and counterproductivity of the news media were exemplified in the loss of confidence as sources of complete and truthful information, as well as in their inability to form a public opinion consonant with the stated aspiration for a transition to democracy. Since December 1989, media consumers have increasingly found the press to be more entertaining[32] than utilitarian from an informational point of view (Ionescu, Feb. 15, 1991).

A great part of the problem was that post-Ceausescu journalism and news media remained creators or reinforcers of public opinion and did not transform themselves into informers of public opinion. This situation did create some notable successes for the mass media, such as the resignation of Prime Minister Petre Roman in 1990 after an extensive media campaign against him.

Yet, on the whole, media and their journalism and the audiences reinforced one another. They created an almost static situation in the first three post-Ceausescu years, one which only began to slightly change in the fourth and fifth years, were it not for other factors influencing both. Pye (1972, 125) argues that such a media and audience "limits educational potentialities of mass media ... casts in doubt the possibility that ... the process of consensus building can be rapidly realized by the employment of the media."

Generally, on the macro level, their influence can best be defined as quasi-passive in regard to a significant transition to a democratic society. If they are stimulating, they are so only because they catered to the perceived beliefs, attitudes and psychology of their audience, thus reinforcing them and becoming allies, companions or soul mates instead of educators, informers or stimulators. But there was a positive side, as Gheorghiu (1991, 71) points out: a more active influence on the micro level. According to Gheorghiu, the media's diversity, or each media outlet's own biases,

> enables the individuals to nourish their own points of view by finding support for them ... ; it makes it possible for those with similar attitudes to learn about each other and to get in touch with each other, and it thus facilitates the growth of public opinion, the formation of new political groupings, and the modification of the programs of existing groups.

However, as creators and reinforcers of public opinion, instead of informers, their moral and professional authority was missing. Their authority has not been established with a public whose combination communist-era and transition-instigated paranoia and split personality disorder have it believe, on the one hand, that everything disseminated by the media is credible and, on the other hand, that all information is but propaganda and not to be believed (Horasangian, Feb. 8, 1991). The public's psychological ailments are, in fact, also telling in regard to what the public really wants from the news media. Addressing the nature, effectiveness and influence of the press, which is easily applicable to television as well, Tudor Octavian (May 16, 1990) expresses what many news media observers, in and out of the media, have said:

> The press lies because, exactly as all of us do, it does not disseminate ideas and information, but invectives and sentiments. It is not the press' fault. It gives, in fact, what is asked of it. People want to feel intensely through words and images. People do not need the truth, because now truth hurts.

This state of mind has had a telling effect on the formation and expression of public opinion. Ominously, Campeanu (May 3, 1991) warns that Romanian public opinion has gone "from candor to circumspection," which is not negative unless this circumspection is transformed into "a general suspicion, one that is paralyzing." He concludes, "Having reached this state, public opinion no longer allows itself to be seduced—it has to be convinced. This presupposes a substantial change in how public dialogue is registered ... which depends in greatest measure on the press, on television and on radio."

There are no indications that the Romanian public is paralyzed because of the news media and its journalism. Yet, circumspection and general suspicion did re-emerge after only a short hiatus between Dec. 22, 1989, and the end of January 1990. What also took root since the revolution was an increased political polarization and the rise in demagogy and public apathy. The former two result from agendas being set by politicized, biased news media gatekeepers and power-hungry special interest groups and politicians, rather than by national consensus arrived at in public debates and facilitated by bona fide journalism that informs. Most of them use a large segment, if not all, of the media for demagogic purposes, as Shils (1972) posits will occur in new states.

Apathy in Romania has its roots in lingering traditional attitudes, those described by Radulescu-Motru (1936, 1976) and others (Shafir 1985), as well as in the "deep resentment and frustration over how the modern world has been communicated" (Pye 1972, 150). In turn, the media's inability to effectively convey public opinion rests in the already discussed lack of professionalism, confidence in it on the part of audiences, and unwillingness or reluctance of government to share power with the governed. Also hampering media effectiveness in conveying public opinion is the legitimate suspicion that the new and old political elites seek to monopolize information and its means of dissemination, or at the very least attempt to retain significant control.[33]

The news media's power to affect public opinion for a unified sociopolitical, economic and cultural development policy was nullified by

1. The presidency and the government ignoring media reports of corruption, thus creating a perception of media powerlessness. In fact, as Tia Serbanescu (Nov. 17–23, 1993) correctly assessed the damage, "the Power ... aggravates the press's illnesses as well as those of this society." It does so because, as *Romania Libera*'s editor in chief, Petre Mihai Bacanu,[34] says, "The press can publish articles on corruption, with proof, and there is no effect."

2. The lack of a political culture that makes elected officials responsible to the electorate. The news media were not able to significantly contribute to a change in mentalities or to a political culture allowing individuals to view themselves as citizens with power.

3. The public's general lack of response to news media's presentations of corruption cases and lack of awareness of its own power also contributed to a perception of media weakness. Eugen Serbanescu[35] of *Romania Libera* says, "Before you could not talk; now you can but no one listens."

4. The news media's own lack of professionalism and its attendant lack of credibility.

Consequently, the news media not only reflected the absence of a national consensus on an issue or of a mainstream of views on important issues, they encouraged it and contributed to it. That includes an absence of a national consensus as to the role the new news media should play and their worth in a society that has not yet defined itself. Therefore, whatever power the news media and journalism garnered in 1990–95 is not institutionalized. It exists but is difficult to define and never approaches a modicum of constancy on the national level or significantly cuts across lines of sociopolitical, economic and cultural segmentation. The news media's would-be power—or, more accurately, its harassing, potentially spoiling nature—is recognized only in political terms. Witness, for example, the miners' destruction of opposition newspaper headquarters in 1990, the demands for independent television and the indirect control and politicization of Romanian Television.

The news media's general lack of effectiveness has drastically minimized the ability of reformers (of whatever persuasion, whether political or economic) to gain support from a public that is not informed. As a result, economic reform was difficult if not impossible even if and when the government attempted it, because people were not being educated to the process, meaning, benefits and drawbacks of such reform (Cornea, Sept. 28,

1990). For instance, a survey published in *22* (Campeanu, April 1991) reveals that 63 percent of respondents felt that information about the liberalization of prices was insufficient. Only 25 percent indicated they were sufficiently well-informed to be able to form an opinion. Eugen Dijmarescu,[36] a finance minister in 1992 and later an ambassador, claims that "reform was presented as unemployment, high prices and corruption." This presentation had the effect of further demoralizing the people, turning them against any meaningful reforms and perpetuating the "class warfare" mentality of the communists.

One other reason the media were less effective and influencing was their sheer number. If, as Pye (1972, 126) suggests, scarcity of media in transitional societies means audiences do not develop attitudes of selectivity and the media play a more potent role, in Romania the opposite was and is true. The number of news media, particularly print and by 1995 radio and television, allows for high selectivity among already fragmented audiences, contributes to the dilution of media's power and is an additional limitation of possible effectiveness in the transition phase.

Furthermore, the Romanian mass media, with their catering to specific audiences, entered the specialized stage, bypassing the elitist and popular stages in media development (Merrill and Lowenstein 1971, 33). This development was not a reflection on the high evolutionary stage achieved by Romanian society. Rather, it was a specialized stage based more on the sociopolitical than the commercial aspects of Romanian society and its media system in 1990–93. In the context of a transition period, being in the specialized stage, the media and their journalism's opportunity to be universal educators, socializers and influencers on and for a national consensus on basic sociopolitical tenets was again largely lost or, at the very least, minimized. By 1993, the media generally stepped back into a popular stage, yet their educational role, their influence in the transition period changed, but it is not yet clear to what extent.

It is also notable that while many subjects related to democracy and democratization were discussed in the media, these analytical and philosophical discussions were carried out largely by a journalistic or intellectual elite. Furthermore, these discussions were targeted at their brethren more than the public at large, whose interests and capabilities to follow the intellectualized discussions were relatively minimal.

While the negatives were covered here, some positives warrant mentioning. The news media had a modicum of success resolving some problems via their presentation, as long as there was no political component involved. The unearthings of corruption were clear cases of journalistic success for which the media can justifiably take credit, even if consequences were noneffective in most cases involving those who were politically sensi-

tive or politically connected individuals. Much of the reporting was professional even if the manner of its presentation itself was again intended to gain
political advantage for the "opposition" or lessen the impact against "The
Power" in the case of RTV and other media supportive of the government
and the president. The influence of media in this case was marginal: the government did not respond to the revelations, and public opinion was affected
but with no overt resulting action. Lia Trandafir,[37] speaking on behalf of a
considerable number of journalists, says, "They ["The Power"] say the Romanian press is free but weak; we [the journalists] say it is not free but powerful." In this case, The Power's assessment of the state of the news media,
as expressed by Trandafir, is accurate—which has as much to do with the
news media as with the public and the Romanian political culture.

A second area in which the media's journalism was successful and effective was in the presentation of Romania's precommunist history,[38] stifled
or distorted by the communists, and the ensuing public debates. Their presentation of General Ion Antonescu's regime, the persecution and killing of
Jews and the Romanian fascist movement engendered a robust debate based
on far more verifiable information than ever reached the public.

The overt rebirth of nationalism, with its xenophobic, anti-Semitic,
anti-Hungarian characteristics, gave rise to publications representing it. To
their credit, elements of what might be called the mainstream press took up
the fight against this type of nationalism and contributed to the debate on the
subject and the search for a definition of the character of the country. They
fought on two anti-nationalism fronts, one anti-communist and the other
anti-fascist.

Moreover, the media successfully and effectively presented the nation's
42-year-long communist legacy. In this respect, Romanian news media were
representative of the region's mass media which were "filled with detailed
accounts of massive mistreatment, interrogation, and of the discovery after
discovery of new mass graves of tens of thousands of secretly buried victims." (Brzezinski 1993, 15). Importantly, the media regained for their audience a history, a legacy and a truth with which they had to come to grips. By
doing so, they served as the only moral conscience of the nation vis-à-vis the
communist era in the absence of any significant accounting for the latter's
crimes (much less a Nuremberg-like trial of the crime and criminals that
would have constituted a closure of and for the communist era).

Gheorghiu (1991, 77) argues that the press campaigns against former
communist officials constitute "the most visible effects of the press activity
... affecting individual politicians." At best, this contention is only partially
supportable. While Dumitru Mazilu[39] was forced to resign from the new
leadership group in January 1990 after revelations by the press of his activities during the communist period, President Ion Iliescu and others who held

high posts in Ceausescu's communist regime and against whom a continuous press campaign has been waged since 1990 are still in power.

The admittedly sensationalistic presentation of poverty and crime in cities and towns and the destruction of the environment, with all their attendant affects, brought Romanians face to face with a social reality long ignored and denied under Ceausescu's communist regime. The news media were successful in bringing this aspect of society to their audiences, but their effectiveness in eliciting reasonable public debate or marshaling public opinion was questionable at best. The news media also introduced the various new and old national and international aid agencies to the public, establishing them as meaningful elements of civil society, of civilization.

Another area of success in 1990–95 was the presentation of foreign news and of other nations in general. It was a qualified success because the overwhelming majority of these news items were received from international news agencies and not from the various media's own correspondents. The economic situation of Romanian media outlets did not and does not allow them to support a permanent corps of foreign correspondents. Only on certain occasions (e.g., trips made by the president of the country, major political or economic meetings or conferences, the World Cup soccer championships and the Olympics) will significant numbers of journalists be sent abroad to provide Romanian reports on international happenings.

By 1995, as already mentioned, the topics covered in a handful of major newspapers, led by *Romania Libera,* increased in number and variety. Local news became a much more important component in a news media culture that has most journalists wanting to deal with national and international issues rather than local or regional ones. Altogether, these developments constitute a step forward for the mass media and their journalism. The local media were far more informative on local issues than the national media were on national issues. However, they too mirrored the partisanship and the other negative aspects of their cousins at the national level. Also by 1995, the news media, unwittingly by virtue of their preprofessional journalism, educated the public at least to what they did not want from them. Therefore, they contributed to a more critical audience and, in that sense, to the beginnings of change in the mentalities inculcated by the communist era. Moreover, the diverse partisanship of the news media aided each Romanian's ability to identify with a particular group, social or political, professional or cultural. Thus, they served as mobilizers for an incipient civil society and democracy.

Finally, the battle over control of the news media in the 1990–95 period, as evidenced by the Audio-Visual Law, the attempted changes in the Penal Code, attempts at enacting a press law, and the machinations of RTV vis-à-vis the independent local television stations, was a battle over their imagined and potential, rather than real, powers in the first five post-Ceausescu years. Their effectiveness and influence were only in an incipient stage, and their importance in this regard were judged still more from a communist perspective than a democratic one.

TABLE 5.2. **Election Results**

	1990		1992	
	Chamber	Senate	Chamber	Senate
Political Parties				
National Salvation Front*	263	91	43	14
Democratic National				
Salvation Front	0	0	117	49
Democratic Convention**	0	0	82	34
Hungarian Democratic Union	29	12	28	12
National Liberal Party	29	10	0	0
National Peasant Party	12	1	0	0
Ecological Movement	12	1	0	0
Romanian Unity Alliance	9	2	0	0
Agrarian Democratic Party	9	0	0	5
Romanian Ecological Party	8	1	0	0
Socialist Democratic Party	5	0	0	0
Romanian National Unity Party	0	0	30	14
Greater Romania Party	0	0	16	6
Socialist Workers Party	0	0	13	5
Presidential Candidates	1990		1992	
Ion Iliescu	85.07%		61.4%	
Emil Constantinescu***			38.6%	

* The National Salvation Front split in 1992 into the Petre Roman–led National Salvation Front and the larger Democratic National Salvation Front.

** The Democratic Convention encompassed the National Peasant Party, the Liberal Party, the Liberal Party–Democratic Convention, the Romanian Ecological Party, the Social Democratic Party, the Civic Alliance Party, and the Hungarian Democratic Union (the latter only for purposes of the presidential election).

*** Constantinescu did not run in 1990.

CHAPTER 6

The Laboratory and Its Lessons

It is never easy to prognosticate the future. In East-Central Europe that task is complicated by the unpredictability of present developments and the ever-present volatile legacy of the past. More than six years have passed since the overthrow of communism, and economic and sociopolitical development have been slow or stagnant and certainly uneven throughout the region. Mass media growth has been spectacular, yet quantity has not been matched by quality. As in economics and politics, Western models of mass media and journalism and their societal roles, and solutions to news media problems, were not uniformly applicable and only marginally successful.

The evolution of Romania's media and journalism from 1989 to 1995 provides one example of a transition from the communist era. How mass media and journalism will evolve and with what consequences to various aspects of Romanian society, or vice versa, is minimally suggested by the summation of the lessons learned in the first six years of freedom.

Lessons Learned

Romania is a nation in transition. It is a traditional society, an underdeveloped one in need of political, economic and social evolution. Yet studies of development or modernization, of transition from traditional to modern, and of mass media in this context, provide little help in understanding or explaining the process. They certainly do not provide a model for it.

Most studies have been carried out in the realm of the traditional, underdeveloped Third World, in Asia, Africa and Latin America. Romania is not in the Third World. Or, if it is to be considered as such, it is a special type of Third Worldliness, created by communism and shared by other East-Central European countries. On the most elementary level, for instance, Lerner's (1958) required elements for a transition from a traditional society, for modernization (e.g., urbanization, literacy, mass media development, political participation) already exist in Romania. So do the appreciation and respect for education, for cultural refinement and for "the modern." Universities and newspaper and book publishing are old features in the Romanian landscape.

A level of modernity, or modern thinking, at certain strata and in certain aspects of society is already interwoven with remnants of the traditional, both that which survived communism and that which was established by it. During the communist period, Romania's mass media were developed and assigned significant roles, albeit none consonant with the requisites of an open, democratic society. In the post-1989 era, media are far more numerous and consumption is higher, yet the roles and the process by which they are to be carried out remain ill defined, or undefined, and preprofessional.

There are perhaps three salient aspects of immediate postcommunist Romanian news media and their journalism and journalists:

1. The elimination of a communist regime simply opened the cage, allowing its former inhabitants to run amok in a veritable jungle.

2. There was an almost instant proliferation of media outlets and of journalists without any training (formal or informal) in reporting and newswriting or understanding of their role in a free society.

3. The new kings of the jungle, many among them princes in the former cage, almost immediately began probing for ways of controlling or, at the very least, manipulating the news media and their journalism.

Romania's media in the still-revolutionary period from Dec. 22, 1989, through January 1990 provided a lesson in community media and journalism. It was amateur hour on a national scale. There were no professional news media offering professional journalistic products. Radio in some ways constituted the only limited exception.

Mass media, in general, provided a lesson in manipulation. The news media and journalists were manipulated and in turn manipulated their audiences. In this December 1989–January 1990 period, this manipulation was less by design than by virtue of the media's amorphous nature, their anything-goes, rumor mill quality, their dominance by an opinion or commentary type of journalism and the absence of professional leadership, defined roles and rules. Their unwitting manipulation (e.g., being fed a variety of opinions and information from myriad sources with the assurance they would be unquestioningly disseminated) had the salutary effect of signaling the reawakening of civil society and of a generally sociopolitically and culturally diverse nation. In turn, news media manipulation of audiences (e.g., the dissemination of unverified, outrageously high numbers of victims and rumors of rogue Securitate elements, among others) served to inflame the population, encourage it, convince it a meaningful change was in progress and was worthy and safe to actively support.

As the debris of the revolutionary explosion settled, there was the expectation that the newly freed media would contribute to "building democracy." It was a radically misplaced expectation, despite their almost instant, extensive proliferation and widening audience consumption rates. Much of what occurred in Romanian news media and journalism since December 1989 was driven directly by

1. The needs of the incipient civil society to (a) blow off steam, recoup a sense of individual and national identity, and simply provide background noise once the possibility to do so arose, and (b) transmit new messages (i.e., views and not necessarily news or information).

2. The establishment of diverse political parties, jockeying for power, attempting to establish power bases and influence.

3. The still unresolved issues surrounding the revolution (e.g., what really happened? who was involved?) and the predominance of former communists in the nation's institutions of leadership.

4. The individual and group focus on acquiring and securing economic power.

5. Editors, publishers, and journalists' ambitions, egos, sociopolitical zeal and the very possibility of entering a hitherto restricted and restrictive field.

6. The overall crisis of values engendered by communism, sudden postcommunism and the transition to a future that still begs for definition.

Thus, news media moved from a catharsis role to clear-cut political partisanship, to a simply politicized press. Then, still politicized, they refocused on the lowest common denominator. They attempted neutrality and in large measure failed. In the process, they became blander or more entertainment oriented and sensationalistic. This latter stage was partly driven by the need to increase audience size and survive economically. Additionally, it was a consequence of the end of the amateur stage and of the intellectuals' predominance in and dominance of the media. It was also the result of the settling in of the preprofessional stage and, subsequently, of a slow, limited beginning of professionalization. Thus, tentatively, the serious search for a role and appropriate attendant professional processes began.

LESSON 1. Undemocratic democracy is served by partisan journalism, a pluralism of opinions and little information.

The agendas of the news media's new owners, publishers, editors and journalists were not tied to a Western understanding of democracy or a transition to it. They were tied to a particular view of democracy, induced by communism and sudden postcommunism. This view was of a democracy of separate, selfish, singular political interests, a "my turn to dictate" democracy. It was a view of democracy which defined it as opportunities for political or economic power by their denial to others; a democracy of the individual and not of society. It was a far cry from Dahrendorf's (spring 1990) open society. The deep and widespread effects of communism were underestimated.

As a result of this interpretation of democracy's meaning, partisanship in journalism was a natural attribute of journalists. And the democratization of media, its absence decried in other East-Central European countries (Jakubowicz 1993a, b; Splichal 1992b), was also missing in Romania. The communist proposition, "you are either with us or you are against us," simply remained operative in the postrevolution battles for political and economic power. It was atomized and expressed in day-to-day journalism. In itself, that made for a news media of mobilization serving varied sociopolitical interests but not directly serving cohesive societal, transitionary, development interests. It was a news media and a journalism that stressed opinion and subjective interpretation over information. Ironically, it was an approach faithful to the ideas expressed by the very founders and most avid supporters of democratic philosophy, enlightenment and experience. Milton, Voltaire, de Tocqueville and the like stressed the notion of freedom of opinion and of expression—without, however, stressing the press's task of accurately informing its readers or of the need for information.

In short, the Romanian laboratory showed that rapid growth of news and mass media in a transitionary period is testimony to newly won freedoms and the possibility of establishing a pluralist media. And this pluralistic media presented a pluralism of opinion. However, they failed to offer accurate information which, by its very definition, cannot be pluralist in nature. Can democracy be established or flourish only on the basis of pluralist opinions but without accurate information? Lippmann's (1965, 202) answer to the question is equally valid for Romanian society as it was and is for American society: "Truth is not easily recognized simply from a competition of opinion." This pluralist news media, this journalism of opinion, subjectivity and rumors, symbolized the promise of and possibilities in democracy and is part of the process, but did not directly aid the transition to democratic society.

LESSON **2.   Mass media are a not-so-important significant institution.**

The insistence that mass media play a direct and uniform role as educators, information disseminators and mobilizers on a national scale for transition and development purposes was misplaced. Mass media in transitionary Romania are not and cannot be the single isolated variable that affects the speed and nature of the transition. Other institutions have as much or greater significance in the transition, in addition to affecting the media's own transformation. There is no single isolated variable that affects the speed and nature of the mass media and journalism's change—unless an extreme situation arises, such as a new totalitarianism or authoritarianism of the Left or Right. The crisis of values needs to be resolved, as does the larger crisis that encompasses the social contract. Much of how the news media's role will be defined and how the professional parameters of journalism will be outlined and complied with are a function of resolving these crises.

John Keane (1991), an articulate presenter of the philosophical or conceptual origins of media freedom and one of its staunch supporters, recognizes media as being one of the most important institutions. He points out (1991, 193), however, that "the courage and independence they display are always a register of the state of morale, and vigor of other bodies, from schools, trade unions and churches to legislatures, governments and courts of justice."

LESSON **3.   News media have been transformed from lapdogs to lapdogs/attack dogs.**

A related lesson was the mistaken emphasis placed on defining the role of news media as a watchdog and as a Fourth Estate. The existing sociopolitical and (pre)professional culture misinterpreted such emphasis and definition to mean a news media that can best serve a transition by being partisan, an attack dog, and a "counterpower." It became a double negative when the frustration of being unsuccessful as a counterpower resulted in the news media generally degenerating into sensationalism, entertainment, superficiality, even banality. The need to simply inform, thus serving the notion of watchdog or Fourth Estate, was lost in the exuberance of freedom, in egos and in the zeal, anger and goals of emerging sociopolitical battles.

This situation fuels an ongoing debate in Romania, as in the rest of East-Central Europe and, indeed, the rest of the world. The debate relates to freedom versus responsibility, opinion versus information, subjectivity versus objectivity. The debate's birth in Romania is a salutary development in the process of professionalization.

LESSON **4.   Attempts at defining journalistic responsibility and media roles by laws carry a sense of déjà vu.**

Much of the proposed and enacted laws addressing mass media and journalists are, at least superficially, explained as attempts to ensure responsible reporting and responsible mass media. Attempts at enacting press laws and at altering of the Penal Code were intended to regulate "responsibility" and professionalism and to muzzle reporting of certain issues and public figures. In short, the justifiable argument for a more responsible, professional journalism was being used for unjustifiable, attempted and realized acts of censoring and forcing self-censorship on the newly freed news media.

In 1990, Vaclav Havel, one of the most enlightened and credible East-Central European leaders, became a sharp critic of the media, suggesting the need for a definition of journalistic responsibility which had detrimental implications for journalistic and media freedom (Horvat and Roskin, fall 1990). Goban-Klas (1994, 259), in his excellent, detailed work on the Polish media and their transition from communism, responded that "Freedom comes first, then responsibility, not the other way round." Fair enough. Freedom of media should not be curtailed; it is at the very marrow of democracy, as Keane (1991) so eloquently demonstrates. And, responsibility or professionalism cannot be defined by governments or states. But it still leaves unanswered questions. If the news media are not responsible in exercising their freedoms, what substantive and symbolic contributions can they make to the resocialization of their audiences toward an open, democratic society, to development? And, will responsibility necessarily be an outgrowth of freedom? Is it even important?

The Romanian example has also demonstrated that the debate over deregulation, regulation, and reregulation in broadcasting is a controversial issue, rife with possibilities for manipulating radio and television. Splichal (1992b) and Jakubowicz (1993c) demonstrate that these issues are not uniquely Romanian but, to differing degrees, shared by other postcommunist societies.

LESSON **5.   Local media are more useful than national media.**

The predominant attention paid the national news media was not helpful to the development of a mass communication system and a journalism capable of aiding in the transition. National news media in the first few post-Ceausescu years concerned themselves with large philosophical and political issues revolving around the journalists' own political inclinations and loyalties, outright partisanship, egos and ambitions. The national press also experienced severe distribution problems, and an alternative to state-controlled national broadcasting was not established.

On the other hand, the slowly developing local media, at first also paralleling national media in content and approach, incrementally pioneered a focus on more substantive, practical, day-to-day issues of personal concern to audiences. They began focusing on the transition at the micro level. With few exceptions, they were no more professional or less politicized than their national cousins. Yet, given their focus, they provided more useful information, better lessons for resocialization purposes and in the mechanisms of incipient democratic process and their requirements, than did national media. It took the national media until 1993 to catch up to the local media in this respect—at least at the philosophical or conceptual level.

The "Think globally, act locally" slogan in American politics, slightly altered to "Think nationally, act locally," should be applied to the restructuring and retooling of mass media systems and journalism in transitions similar to Romania's. Local rather than national mass or news media are far more useful and effective in aiding the transitional process. Use of local media also provides for decentralization, an important aspect of the diversification of mass media so crucial to their distancing from the centralized communist system.

LESSON 6. The wrong premise guided the introduction of Western journalism.

Western aid to Romanian news media, well meant and generously offered, seems to have started from Fukuyama's (1992) premise that democracy is inevitable. Initially, Romanians and their Western helpers expected positive change in mass media and journalism, and in their role in the transition, to come quickly. There was the assumption that there was a common interpretation of concepts such as "democracy," "freedom," "journalism" and so on, and the only requirement of the new situation was retraining in the technicalities of journalistic processes, or a Western approach to them.

It turned out that the establishment of a Western-type media and journalism was impossible in Romania because the social, political, cultural and economic conditions to host them did not exist and because the nature of the journalists', editors', politicians', civil servants', and audiences' psychology, mentalities, interests, training or habits did not lend themselves to the establishment and acceptance of a news media and a journalism of information. There was simply no leadership; there were no examples provided from within the journalistic community and none from outside to establish a journalism of information rather than one of opinion.

LESSON **7.   More is not better.**

Consequently, one of the lessons learned was that the sudden acquisition of journalistic freedom and heightened news media consumption does not mean a better informed population. In fact, it may mean a more confused and cynical population. Partly, the confusion is a result of the avalanche of communication, the sheer size of it making it difficult to sift through and digest. But here, also, is where the issues of freedom versus responsibility, opinion versus information, subjectivity versus objectivity are revisited. Contributing to the creation of confusion, the Romanian mass media also increased their audiences' fears, predilections toward negativity, passivity and even antipathy to "democracy" and resistance to change, provoking a barrage of questions: Where are we going? How are we getting there? When are we getting there? What is the price or sacrifice? Why should I pay the price and make the sacrifice?

LESSON **8.   Retooling is a family affair.**

The retooling of journalism had to proceed along autodidactic lines, by trial and error. It was a process affected by political or financial exigencies on the personal and institutional levels, egotism and the sheer need to produce something to fill space and time. Foreign assistance in this process was secondary in importance to the indigenous impetus for a step-by-step evolution or, more accurately stated, step-by-step changes. Western—and, specifically, American—journalism and its professional standards and ethics are not exportable to Romania, as Muravchik (1991) and others have claimed they can be to all postcommunist nations.

The "new" journalism was first introduced by old, communist-trained journalists, by vague memories of precommunist journalism, by personal notions and ambitions. Examples from and exposure to Western journalism and journalists helped and were in a limited way adapted here and there. Postcommunist journalism was also introduced in and by a culture that stressed the values of intellectualism or intellectual approaches to journalism, while at the same time resented it and felt alienated from it. Furthermore, it was introduced by and in a culture that has been schooled in the value of the absolute, the black and white without any shades of gray, the winner and loser, the importance of the (elegantly stated) opinion versus the verifiable fact.

LESSON **9.** **Training is necessary for leaders as well as for the rank and file.**

Western contributions to retraining journalists failed to take into account, as already intimated, their education, civic sense and understanding of media roles, meaning, importance and uses in a democracy. They did not address the retooling of the newly established news media's leadership (e.g., publishers, editors, producers) and that of audiences. Training sessions were geared to make Romanian journalists and journalism servants of democracy. Covering elections and government, "objective" journalism, "freedom of the press" were some of the primary foci of news reporting and writing training sessions, seminars and colloquia sponsored by various foreign groups.

The overwhelming majority of these contributions were introduced as processes to be adopted in cultural, sociopolitical and professional contexts that were inhospitable to them, even if conceptually attractive in a far-off, fairyland manner. Or, they were inapplicable and incomprehensible to Romanians except in the academic, intellectual sense. Many of them were simply rejected, because they went counter to the intent of some journalists, editors and publishers and the role they envisioned for a new mass media in a new Romania.

Very few Western forms of aid to journalists and journalism were predicated on an understanding of Romanian culture and history or of the dynamics of an (admittedly) hitherto unknown type of transition. More helpful was the Romanian journalists' exposure to Western society and news media provided by trips to the West. Such trips afforded an opportunity for them to absorb for themselves some lessons, digest them in their own way and attempt to slowly adapt some. While initially helpful in exposing Romanian journalists to Western journalism, these colloquia, seminars and training sessions describing Western journalism and its practices got to be old hat. The relevancy was missing for the Romanian journalists' own attempts to understand what they were doing, why, with what results and for whom.

LESSON **10.** **The education of media consumers is also necessary.**

One aspect of the postcommunist transition that was not factored into Romanian or Western visions of resocialization or retraining was, specifically, the Romanians as news media consumers, as an audience. What should this audience demand from their news media? Why and how should and could it make certain demands? What relationship do the news media have to the audience as citizens, voters, consumers? Romanians received no help from their own news media or the educational systems, ones that were also in the process of beginning a transition. Since 1989, Romanians learned what they did not want, but they could not define what they did want and why. Consequently, the number of media stayed high, as did turnover. Ultimately, the audience settled for entertainment and distractions which were provided in various forms, including scandals, controversies, crime and sports. Yet, judging by the continuous introduction of new newspapers, magazines and radio and television stations, the search for meaningful, credible new media never abated.

LESSON 11. Instability in employment and the absence of an elite press to serve as a standard make professionalization difficult.

Yet another lesson offered by the Romanian laboratory is that in a situation of constant growth and change, economic instability and preprofessionalism, there is a regular game of musical chairs played by journalists. This constant movement by journalists from one media outlet to another, from one medium to another, looking for a place to roost and make more money, also curtailed professional development.

Coupled with the absence of an elite press that has achieved a high standard commensurate with the elite press of the world or of Europe, the journalists are lacking a goal to be achieved as they evolve. An elite press would set those high standards to which all journalists would aspire and provide a measuring stick for their professionalization.

LESSON 12.   Technology does not improve journalism.

Western aid, which also included the introduction of Western media technologies, had limited consequences. In fact, the introduction of new media technologies, while eagerly sought and badly needed from a technical standpoint, only provided a distraction for the news media from their principal need: better journalism. Better equipment simply allowed Romanian media to better technically produce preprofessional products.

LESSON 13.   The transitionary concept of media is a mixture of other concepts and then some.

There was an unmistakable need for media to have an active role in the transition and development of the country. Yet, the development concept of the mass media (Hachten 1981, 72–75) was not applicable in Romania. There, coming from a controlled and controlling media system, there was little possibility of successfully arguing for a system that is centrally harnessed for centrally defined transition or development goals. Since December 1989, the postcommunist Romanian mass media system and its functioning have been based on an odd mixture of the revolutionary and libertarian concepts (Siebert, Peterson and Schramm 1956), with a not-always-small dash of actual or attempted authoritarianism. This transitionary concept of the mass media and journalism in Romanian was characterized by (1) constant motion, experimentation and manipulation, (2) the recent and distant past's heavy influence, (3) the overall culture, societal and individual psychology and mentality, and (4) dependency on the nature of and the changes in other institutions and general societal progress germane to but outside the realm of mass media and journalism.

A search for a more permanent, definable, cohesive philosophy, role, form and process is yet to be a unified goal for mass media and their journalists. One thing is certain, the process has to be carried out indigenously, it will be slow, and the outcome is uncertain.

LESSON 14.   Economic and management dimensions of mass media have been relegated to the back burner.

The five-year plan having disappeared along with state management, how does one manage a media enterprise? The absence of media managers, or the special skills and knowledge required of them, was self-evident. The operative approach to media management was the trial-and-error, fly-by-the-seat-of-your-pants mode. Nepotism, friendship, loose accounting, helter-skelter organization, lack of organizational discipline and an overall amateurish way of running an organization were some of the hallmarks of Romanian media in their first few years of postcommunism. Few in Romania deviated from this path, and few Western aid programs zeroed in on this important aspect of successful mass media development.

LESSON 15.   The transition is proceeding along well-known lines.

When all is said and done, the changes in Romanian journalism have been rapid and followed a pattern discernible in other Western and East-Central European societies. There was a quick passage from a journalism of comment and opinion to a form of yellow journalism and muckraking, one heavy on subjectivity. That is a transition from forms of editorial and commentary writing to forms of reporting and transmitting information. The process and presentation was, more often than not, incomplete, subjective, shallow, inaccurate or banal. Yet, it did contribute to the fermenting process that represents transitions.

The Future

Unquestionably, economics and politics play a significant role in the development of mass media and their journalism. As the market economy expands, support for mass media will also expand and be far more reliable. This is, perhaps, a singularly important development. It will allow for the kind of relative stability that, in turn, permits journalism to progress from a purely commercial or political endeavor to one that is societal in scope. How far this expansion will proceed and how reliable subsequent support for media will be are impossible to gauge. They are important issues, particularly pertinent to the survival and evolution of the small, local media.

The streamlining of editorial and technical staffs that the Romanian media began implementing in the spring and summer of 1994 will create some unemployment among journalists. The market is finally impacting on each newspaper, radio station and television station's organization, staff size, and productivity. It is part of the process of professionalization, both journalistic and managerial. It will limit the revolving-door situation and create some stability because journalists will find it more difficult to move from one editorial room to another. It will also heighten the power of editors and publishers over journalists, with all the possible negative connotations suggested, in part for other East-Central European media, by Splichal (1992b) and Jakubowicz (1993a, b), among others.

As civil society continues to grow, the diversity of the mass media should receive considerable sustenance. And as political life continues to be lively and extreme, the number of diverse media outlets will remain relatively high. Journalism is going to evolve incrementally as new priorities arise, as journalists gain more confidence, knowledge and understanding, to demand a more professional definition of standards and adherence to them. The establishment and evolution of the many new journalism education and training programs may be one small addition to the eventual professionalization of journalism in Romania. So is continued contact with foreign journalists and news media. They will influence the Romanian journalists as much as Romanian audiences and indigenous economic, social, political, and cultural development.

We have already witnessed a change from a purely political pamphlet–like press and journalism to a sensationalistic, muckraking news media format within three to four short years. The beginnings of professionalization will slowly bring a news media system in which the sensationalistic news media will coexist side by side with a more serious, yet small, informational and analytical media. The rapid growth of television (inclusive of cable) and radio will first and foremost mean more entertainment choices and only secondarily more news. If nothing else, it will mean increased attention to local issues. The professionalization of information gathering and presentation—indeed, the separation of opinion from information—will be incremental and much affected by the sociopolitical culture. This culture will reform itself over time. It will do so by virtue of the sociopolitical leadership, unforeseen political, economic or foreign crises and the nature of life each citizen envisions for himself or herself and their willingness to act.

Despite the negatives already described, some progress has been achieved. More will be achieved, even if two steps forward are followed by a step backward. Romanian society and its mass media and journalism have a dynamism of their own which provides for adjustments, movement and, therefore, progress. However, there can be no expectation that the news media and their journalism can be harnessed or can play a concerted role in the transition and in development. They are simply one factor in this process, albeit more visible, noisy and potentially negative.

The news media became instantly popular in nature, even communitarian, highly accessible, then just as quickly changed to a specialized press, a party press, accessible to self-select readers. The current move to a more popular press and broadcasting bodes well for a less overtly subjective journalism, a certainly less partisan one, because of its focus on the lowest common denominator.

An elite news media, represented to date by publications such as 22, may also evolve as professionalization continues in print and broadcast journalism and as society fails to close the gap between various strata of society, particularly between the intellectuals and the rest of the population. A truly professional elite press would be a useful and welcomed addition to Romania. It would set standards to be emulated and to which the rest of the press would aspire.

It is quite possible that Romanian society will have elite, popular and specialized press systems existing side by side. The popular press will be predominant. It will focus primarily on entertainment, British and American tabloid-type journalism that mixes several approaches to journalism and caters to the lowest common denominator.

Radio will remain a source of news and entertainment, but it may play second fiddle to television. Romanians are as attracted by television as Westerners are, and the introduction of interactive technologies heightens the interest in the visual medium. The success or failure of the many new local television stations will be a deciding factor in how much of a role radio will play in Romanian society. The search for national television that will offer a bona fide alternative and competition to RTV will continue.

The rapid expansion of communication technologies increasingly provides a way of supplementing the existing news media, of accessing information: cable and satellite broadcasting, VCRs, E-Mail, fax and so on. These sources of information and entertainment, together with access to foreign radio, television, and press, constitute one variable that will continue to influence journalism and its professionalization. They will also influence audiences and what they will seek to receive from their mass media. If entertainment culture is becoming increasingly internationalized, or at the very least regionalized, so can professional journalistic culture.

This culture is a living one, constantly changing, adapting, struggling. Romanian journalism and journalists have now joined it.

NOTES

Chapter 1

1. Romanian newspapers from the 1920s and early 1930s are available to researchers at the Hoover Institution, Stanford University, Palo Alto, CA.

2. For a description of the Communist Party's takeover in the aftermath of World War II, see Stephen Fischer-Galati, *20th Century Rumania* (New York: Columbia University Press, 1970) and Vladimir Tismaneanu, *Reinventing Politics* (New York: Free Press, 1992).

3. Information gathered on Agerpres in 1979 by the author during a (dissertation) research trip to Bucharest, sponsored by the Kaltenborn Foundation.

4. As told to the author by editors of *Adevarul,* the former Communist Party newspaper *Scinteia* which in the afternoon of December 22 came out with a second edition under a new flag, *Scinteia Poporului,* only to change its name again three days later.

5. One example is Cornel Nistorescu, the editor in chief and publisher of the national weekly, *Expres.* He told the author in 1990 that during the Ceausescu regime he chose to be a sports reporter because it was the only way to escape stringent scrutiny by the censor, carry out a less than political function and have the occasional opportunity to travel abroad to cover athletic events.

6. The general consensus among Romanian journalists is that Romanian Radio was more professional because Ceausescu paid little attention to it. Editors and journalists told the author in 1990 and 1991 that many competent journalists gravitated to radio because there was a slight improvement in the atmosphere, tone and circumstance in which they could practice journalism. This view was confirmed in a conversation with the director of Romanian Radio, Eugen Preda, in 1991.

7. From a conversation with Eugen Preda, director of Romanian Radio, in July 1993.

8. From interviews with Victor Ionescu in May and August 1990. He was then head of the News Department at Romanian Television.

9. From interviews with editors and journalists of newspapers in Timisoara, Iasi, Brasov and Bucharest in January, May and August 1990.

10. Ibid.

11. The list of Romanian dissidents, at least those who took a public stand, is small but significant. It includes writers Paul Goma and Aurel Dragos Munteanu, historian Vlad Georgescu, poets Mircea Dinescu, Dorin Tudoran, Dan Desliu and Ana Blandiana, Father Gheorghe Calciu Dumitreasa, teacher Doina Cornea and other intellectuals such as Dan Petrescu, Gabriel Andreescu and Mihai Botez. This small group was joined in the last two years of the Ceausescu regime by former party-state officials Silviu Brucan, Dumitru Mazilu and a handful of others. For a description of dissident activities, see Nestor Ratesh, *Romania: The Entangled Revolution,* 1991, and H. Gordon Skilling, *Samizdat and an Independent Society in Central and Eastern Europe,* 1989. The story of Romanian dissidence, as small as it may be, and of a more widespread passive resistance to the regime is yet to be written.

12. From an interview with Viorel Salagean, one of the editors of *Adevarul,* in January 1990.

13. Radu Filipescu, a young Bucharest-based engineer, distributed anti-Ceausescu leaflets.

14. From an interview with Petre Mihai Bacanu, editor in chief of *Romania Libera,* and recollections by Stefan Niculescu-Maier, one of the vice presidents of the "R" Company that publishes *Romania Libera,* in January 1990.

15. In 1990, Petre Mihai Bacanu (*Romania Libera*), Constantin Stanescu and Viorel Salagean (*Adevarul*) and Dumitru Tircob (*Libertatea*), among many other Romanian editors, complained that journalists used the old language and structures associated with the communist era.

16. Bacanu interview, January 1990.

17. From remarks made at the 1992 government-sponsored colloquium on "Press and Transition and the Transition of the Press" held in Costinesti.

18. From an interview with Viorel Salagean, one of the editors of *Adevarul*, in January 1990. The same descriptions, in the same language, were given to the author by other editors and journalists in interviews carried out in January, May, August and November 1990.

Chapter 2

1. Those who began and continued the shooting against civilians and army personnel have still not been identified, and no one has yet stood trial for the killing of innocent people during those turbulent December 1989 days.

2. There are some indications that a movement within the Romanian Communist Party against the Ceausescus preceded the revolution (see, for example, "Fronda anti-Ceausescu nel partito. Un documento proclama: 'Liberiamo il Paese dal Tiranno,'" in *La Stampa,* Sept. 20, 1989, p. 5). The notion that the revolution was hijacked also has some support and was given voice by a number of writers including Andrei Codrescu (Sept. 2, 1990), at least in part because of the ultimate leadership and makeup of the National Salvation Front: former high-ranking members of the Communist Party. (See also Calinescu and Spulber, Dec. 30, 1989; Hoagland, April 26, 1990.)

3. People in Timisoara told the author in January, May, August and November 1991 that Hungarian radio and television played a major informational role. See also Socor (Feb. 2, 1990).

4. The author spoke to hundreds of Romanians in 1990 in meetings in their homes, on the streets, on trains, in taxis—wherever they were willing to talk.

5. It has still not been ascertained whether General Milea committed suicide or was shot after refusing to follow orders from the Ceausescus to have his army troops open fire on demonstrators. In any case, the news of his death actively placed the army on the side of the demonstrators.

6. Related by Gabriel Stanescu, a journalist with *Ziua,* July 17, 1994. Similar stories were told to the author by other journalists.

7. Several television journalists made the claim during discussion with the author in January and May 1990 that individuals within the RTV deliberately wanted to show the nation that Ceausescu had lost control. The immediate and manipulative use of the RTV (and its staff) by the leadership of the National Salvation Front beginning on Dec. 22, 1989, reinforces the claim to some degree.

8. This theory is in part supported by the open letter addressed to Ceausescu by six former top Romanian Communist Party members in spring 1989 and by a trip made in June 1989 to the Soviet Union by one of the signatories, Silviu Brucan, who again went to Moscow in November 1989 in a suggested attempt to shore up support for a coup d'etat engineered from within the party (see Falin, spring 1990). It is also supported by statements made by Brucan, a former Romanian foreign minister, and by former Minister of Defense Nicolae Militaru, published in *Adevarul* (August 1990). They claimed that members of the National Salvation Front had met in spring 1989 to set the stage for a coup.

9. Most of the bona fide dissidents resigned from the National Salvation Front and joined the opposition in early 1990. Iliescu was elected president of Romania in May 1990 and re-elected in September 1992.

10. From discussions with Victor Ionescu in January, May and August 1990.

11. From discussions with Romanian Television personnel in 1990, including Emanuel Valeriu, the then director general.

12. From discussions with Romanian Television personnel in 1990.

13. From interviews with Imre Gnandt, the station's "creator," Jan. 12–17, 1989 (Gross 1990a).

14. Ibid.

15. General Vlad claimed to have had undergone an instant conversion to the revolution on December 22. Under the guise of working with the National Salvation Front and the army, he purportedly directed the forces of the Securitate against the army and the revolutionaries on the street. He was ultimately arrested. As of 1993 he was still under house arrest, but no indictments had been brought against him and no trial examined his involvement in the fighting in December 1989 or his leadership of the Securitate before then.

16. These claims were made by the heads of the former regional stations of Romanian Radio after resuming their broadcasts Dec. 22, 1989, or shortly after. For example, these figures were given to the author by the leadership of Romanian Radio—in Iasi, Grigore Ilisei and Valentin Ciuca, and in Timisoara, Bogdan Herzog—during interviews in May, August and November 1990.

17. As related to the author in January 1990 by C. Stanescu and V. Salagean, two of *Adevarul*'s editors.

18. Ibid.

19. Ibid.

20. As told to the author in January 1990 by Dumitru Tircob, at that time editor in chief of *Libertatea.*

21. Bacanu interview, January 1990.

22. Ibid.

23. From an interview with George Serban in May 1990.

24. Tircob interview, January 1990.

25. Serban interview, May 1990.

26. Stanescu and Salagean interview, January 1990.

27. Bacanu interview, January 1990.

28. Ibid.

29. Ibid.

30. From the testimony of people from all walks of life in Timisoara, offered to the author in January and May 1990.

31. People in Timisoara, Bucharest, Cluj, Iasi, and Oradea told the author that if General Milea or children were not safe, then no one was. They reasoned that if they were all under a "constant" death sentence, they might as well join the fight and attempt to topple the leadership.

32. These are estimates offered by Romanians in the media industry.

Chapter 3

1. There was no definitive accounting of how many publications there were in Romania. The numbers are based on informal surveys of each region in the country by editors of the major publications who generally agreed on an approximate figure. Most other figures concerning

the size of the press, circulation and so on in this chapter, unless otherwise indicated, were obtained from editors or publishers.

2. In April 1990 the National Salvation Front "decreed that independent publications should halve their circulation and that weekly papers should issue fortnightly," according to London's Index on Censorship (Ruston, September 1990).

3. Editors of major newspapers in Bucharest, Timisoara, Brasov, Oradea and other cities argued that the two major paper-manufacturing operations in Romania purposely decreased production and sold paper to foreign buyers, thus decreasing available supplies to the Romanian press.

4. Meeting Nov. 25, 1991, with Ionel David and Adrian Firica of the Department of Socio-Political Structures attached to the Prime Minister's Office.

5. Bacanu interview, January 1990.

6. Data collected by author in an unpublished survey of newspaper costs in 1990–91. The major newspapers in each city were surveyed.

7. As related by Gabriel Stanescu, an editor of the new *Ziua,* on July 19, 1994. Before joining *Ziua,* Stanescu was a journalist with *Romania Libera.*

8. Alin Teodorescu spoke at an international colloquium on "Media in Transition and Transition of Media," held at Costinesti, Romania, May 28–31, 1992.

9. From discussion with *Ziua*'s Gabriel Stanescu and with Mihai Coman, dean of the School of Journalism and Mass Communication Studies at the University of Bucharest, in summer 1994.

10. Interview with Neagu Udroiu, head of Rompres, July 20, 1993.

11. From interviews with Romanian Radio (RR) personnel in 1990, 1991, 1992 and discussions with Eugen Preda, RR director, on Aug. 11, 1993.

12. From interview with Bogdan Herzog on May 18, 1990.

13. Ibid.

14. Interview with Grigore Ilisei on May 23, 1990.

15. The author toured Romanian Radio studios in 1990, 1991, 1992 and summer 1993.

16. The author was told about and shown foreign equipment donated in 1990 and 1991 in Iasi, Timisoara, Bucharest and Brasov.

17. Interview with Ministry of Communication officials on Jan. 22, 1991.

18. Interview with Bogdan Herzog on Dec. 25, 1991.

19. Interview with Adrian Ureche on Jan. 27, 1991.

20. From survey of radio and television stations carried out by author on behalf of Internews.

21. Interview with Dan Klinger, head of Uniplus Radio, on July 29, 1993.

22. From discussions with Max Banus, owner of the weekly *Tinerama* and Radio Tinerama, on July 22, 1993.

23. From discussions with Romanian Television personnel, journalists and political activists in January 1991.

24. From interview with Dumitru Iuga on July 26, 1993.

25. Dumitru Iuga provided the author with a copy written in French on July 26, 1993.

26. Iuga interview, July 26, 1993.

27. The leadership of SOTI in November 1990 provided the author with a copy of *Proposal. Establishment of an Independent National Television Company "Continental T.V." in Romania.*

28. The group included 88 persons who were representatives of already operational local television stations and of the cream of Romanian intellectuals, dissidents and journalists—Alexandru Paleologu, Octavian Paler, Mihai Sora, Stelian Tanase, Vartan Arachelian, Petre Mihai Bacanu, Pavel Cimpeanu, Gabriel Liceanu and Doina Cornea, to name but a few.

29. Mircea Stoian, one of the founding leaders of SOTI, told the author in November 1990

at a meeting held at the Group for Social Dialogue that millions of lei were deposited by Romanians from all over the country in SOTI's bank account.

30. President I. Iliescu stated that independent television is a "technical impossibility," according to Ruston's (September 1990, 9) report in London's *Index on Censorship.*

31. Letter from president of Parliamentary Commission on Culture, Art and Mass Media, I.V. Sandulescu to RTV President Razvan Theodorescu, April 11, 1991.

32. Letter from Senate President A. Birladeanu to RTV President R. Theodorescu, April 11, 1991.

33. Letter from RTV President Razvan Theodorescu to SOTI President Mircea Stoian, Aug. 30, 1991.

34. A letter from L. Tripcovici, member of SOTI's leadership council, to the author on Jan. 22, 1992, related some of the machinations, politics and troubles faced by SOTI and its leadership. See also Liana Ionescu (March 21–22, 1992) "Despartirea de SOTI," in *Romania Libera,* pp. 1, 3.

35. The author was involved in SOTI matters and gained a firsthand view of its troubles while acting as a consultant for the International Media Fund in 1991–92.

36. As a consultant to the International Media Fund and while carrying out training sessions for Romanian journalists in Romania and in the United States, the author was directly involved in media matters in Romania and with broadcasters in Timisoara, Oradea, Brasov, Constanta and Bucharest.

37. The author witnessed one such transmission in 1992.

38. From discussion with television personnel at local stations in 1992–93.

39. Discussions with Mircea Stoian, president of SOTI, in 1991, 1992 and 1993.

40. From discussions with local television personnel and newspaper journalists in Timisoara, Oradea and Constanta and with V. Ionescu, head of the News Section of Romanian Television on Aug. 5, 1993.

41. From August 1994 discussions with Cristian David, employed in the office of the Public Affairs Officer, U.S. Embassy, Bucharest, who was charged with gathering facts related to media development in Romania.

42. From Aug. 7, 1994 note to author from Iolanda Staniloiu, member of the NAVC until summer 1993.

43. Ibid.

44. From discussions with Iolanda Staniloiu on June 11, 1994, with Horia Murgu on July 25, 1993, and with Radu Cosarca on July 24, 1993.

45. Staniloiu discussion, June 11, 1994.

46. From an interview conducted by *Expres* reporter Harald Zimmerman with Petre Roman and conveyed to the author by fax on Dec. 13, 1994.

47. Udroiu interview, July 20, 1993.

Chapter 4

1. Eliade (1987), among other critics of the precommunist press, characterized it as an opinion-laden, know-nothing vehicle of publishers, editors and journalists to participate in politics, push their own ideas and carry out personal battles.

2. Iuga interview, July 26, 1993.

3. There was no exact count of how many people were engaged in what was called "journalism" during the communist era. Aside from regular staffs, Romanian mass media employed "contributors." Usually, they were factory workers or other state employees who contributed stories to the media. Some were simply hacks who graduated from the Stefan Gheorghiu Academy in Bucharest, the Communist Party's "university."

4. The Atheneum University is one of dozens such institutions. Their educational quality is suspect. Its journalism program consists of 80 percent literature courses and 20 percent journalism courses.

5. The U.S. Information Agency through its Voice of America International Training Program has hosted more than 50 Romanian journalists since 1990 in its three-week, monthlong or yearlong programs. It has sponsored other media-related training programs in Romania, as have the German Marshall Fund, the Soros Foundation, Internews, the International Media Fund and the National Endowment for Democracy, among a handful of other organizations.

6. From Doina Basca's comments at the July 24–25, 1993 "Mass Media and Society" international colloquium in Bucharest.

7. From discussions with print and broadcast journalists in 1990–93.

8. From Tia Serbanescu's comments at the Bucharest colloquium, July 24–25, 1993.

9. Iuga interview, July 26, 1993.

10. From presentation made by Dorel Sandor at the Black Sea University, Costinesti, Aug. 13, 1993.

11. This more honest self-examination was undertaken by a minority of journalists, and only after the 1992 presidential and parliamentary elections did they begin to overtly recognize some of their shortcomings.

12. Comments made by Nicolae Manolescu at the Costinesti colloquium, May 28–31, 1992.

13. From Silviu Brucan's presentation at the Costinesti colloquium, May 28–31, 1992.

14. From Nicolae Ulieru's comments at the Bucharest colloquium, July 24–25, 1993, and his elaboration of his view in conversation with the author.

15. From Petre Roman's comments at the Bucharest colloquium, July 24–25, 1993. As with most politicians worldwide, Roman did not think much of the news media. He told the author in a conversation on Aug. 16, 1993, that the shortcomings of the media were accentuated by the inability of people in government to explain the transition.

16. Comments by Roxana Iordache at the Bucharest colloquium, July 24–25, 1993.

17. Interview with Dan Vardie on July 23, 1993.

18. From discussion with Andy Lazescu on July 14, 1993.

19. The Costinesti colloquium, May 28–31, 1992, was organized by the government of Prime Minister Stolojan, ostensibly to improve relations with the mass media.

20. Ion Luca Caragiale was a Romanian journalist, novelist and playwright who, according to Magris (1989, 373) distorted reality "to scoff at it explicitly in order to reveal its falsity and vacuity."

21. From discussions with Harald Zimmerman, a journalist from Timisoara who spent a year at California State University–Chico on a U.S. Information Agency grant.

22. From comments made by Doru Ionescu at the Bucharest colloquium, July 24–25, 1993.

23. Udroiu interview, July 20, 1993.

24. Iuga interview, July 26, 1993.

25. Somehow these out-of-town miners also managed to obtain the home addresses of certain journalists and went looking for them. There is a great deal of justified suspicion, but no verifiable proof, that the attack on newspapers and journalists was orchestrated by the government or the president and that many of the "miners" were police or members of the new Romanian Information Service.

26. Discussion with Andrei Dorobantu on Aug. 12, 1993.

27. From Cezar Tabarcea's remarks at the Costinesti colloquium, May 28–31, 1992.

28. Udroiu interview, July 20, 1993.

29. Serbanescu comments, July 24–25, 1993.

30. From presentation by Professor Ion Dragan at the Costinesti colloquium, May 28–31, 1992.

31. Discussion with Dorel Sandor on July 30, 1993.

32. Interview with Petre Mihai Bacanu in January and May 1990.

33. Udroiu interview, July 20, 1993.

34. Nearly 50 percent of the population either lives in rural areas or are first-generation city dwellers.

35. From discussion with Dragos Seuleanu on July 24, 1993.

36. From discussion with Doina Basca on July 20, 1993.

37. From discussion with Cornel Nistorescu on May 28, 1993.

38. Udroiu interview, July 20, 1993.

39. Manolescu comments, May 28–31, 1992.

40. Lazescu discussion, July 14, 1993.

41. From discussions with Lia Trandafir in fall 1993 and spring 1994. Trandafir spent an academic year at California State University–Chico on a U.S. Information Agency grant.

42. Iordache comments, July 24–25, 1993.

43. Serbanescu comments, July 24–25, 1993.

44. Interview with Victor Ionescu on Aug. 5, 1993.

45. Romanian authorities have on several occasions refused an entry visa to King Michael of Romania, who had been forced to give up this throne on Dec. 30, 1947, after the Communist Party took over the government. In spring 1992, the king paid one of his rare visits and received wide news coverage. Cosarca's story was a straightforward report of the king's visit.

46. Dorobantu discussion, Aug. 12, 1993.

47. From interview with Dumitru Tircob on Jan. 18, 1990.

48. From interview with Andon on Jan. 17, 1990.

49. Remarks by Cornel Nistorescu at the Costinesti colloquium, May 28–31, 1992.

50. From remarks by Grigoriu at the Bucharest colloquium, July 24–25, 1993.

51. From remarks by Florin Iaru at the Bucharest colloquium, July 24–25, 1993, and private discussions with the author in February 1992 at California State University–Chico, where Iaru was participating in a three-week U.S. Information Agency-sponsored program.

52. Remarks made at the Bucharest colloquium, July 24–25, 1993.

53. From remarks by Cristian Popisteanu at the Bucharest colloquium, July 24–25, 1993.

54. Lazescu discussion, July 14, 1993.

55. From discussion with Sylvia Ilies on July 25, 1993.

56. From interviews with Tircob and Stanescu in January 1990.

57. Nistorescu remarks, May 28–31, 1992.

58. From remarks by Ion Itu at the Bucharest colloquium, July 24–25, 1993.

59. From discussion with Max Banus on July 24, 1993.

Chapter 5

1. Statement made by Mioara Iordache at the Bucharest colloquium, July 24, 1993.

2. From a discussion with Cristinel Popa, Aug. 11, 1993.

3. From Professor Dragan's presentation at the Costinesti colloquium, May 28–31, 1992.

4. Statement made by Sergiu Andon at the Costinesti colloquium, May 28–31, 1992.

5. Sorin Rosca-Stanescu and Florin Gabriel Marculescu admitted in May 1991 that they were informers for the Securitate.

6. Some of these accusations were allegedly made for political reasons. For example, the case of RTV's Vasile Tolcsvai and Mihai Predescu, who were accused of taking $15,000 in March 1994 to publicize certain products on television.

7. From Cornel Nistorescu on May 29, 1992.

8. From discussions with former Prime Minister Petre Roman on Aug. 16, 1993.

9. Lazescu discussion, July 14, 1993.

10. From discussions with Eugen Preda on July 15, 1993.

11. As stated by then Prime Minister Theodore Stolojan at the Costinesti colloquium on May 31, 1992.

12. Both expressed such views at the Costinesti colloquium in 1992 and subsequently in a number of their writings and interviews given Romanian newspapers. Roman reiterated such views in a discussion with the author on Aug. 16, 1993, and at a presentation the same day to a class at the Black Sea University.

13. From a discussion with Iolanda Staniloiu in Arlington, Va., on June 11, 1994.

14. As reported by Dragan, May 28, 1992.

15. The most important of these political parties were the traditional ones (e.g., the Peasant Party, the Liberal Party) and the newly constituted ones (e.g., the National Salvation Front, the Hungarian Democratic Union).

16. The National Salvation Front, National Liberal Party, Romanian Ecological Movement, National Peasant Party, Social Democratic Party and Republican Party.

17. The NSF won a total of 354 seats, 263 in the chamber and 91 in the senate.

18. From interview with Eugen Serbanescu on June 11, 1994.

19. As presented to the author by Victor Ionescu on Sept. 26, 1992.

20. As called for in Chapter 7, Article 46, Part 4 of Law No. 68, 1992.

21. Democratic National Salvation Front, Democratic Convention, National Salvation Front, Party of Romanian National Unity, Hungarian Democratic Union, MER, and National Liberal Party.

22. The Democratic National Salvation Front was so renamed after the Petre Roman wing split from the National Salvation Front, retaining the name.

23. From discussion with Lia Trandafir on May 12, 1994.

24. For instance, Gheorghe Funar and his Romanian Party of National Unity. Funar reportedly thanked the independent media for campaigning for him by virtue of all the negative articles they published about him.

25. Statement made by Senator Dumitrascu at the Costinesti colloquium on May 28, 1992.

26. Vardie interview, July 23, 1993.

27. Roman discussion, August 16, 1993.

28. Statement made by Grigore Marian at the Costinesti colloquium on May 28, 1992.

29. Several reporters for newspapers considered "in opposition" related how they had information about opposition candidates that, if published, could have damaged their candidacy. They chose not to publish this information because they were sympathetic to these candidates.

30. Udroiu interview, July 20, 1993.

31. As repeated by Ion Cristoiu at the Costinesti colloquium, May 28–31, 1992.

32. In more than 100 interviews with newspaper readers on trains, on buses, in taxis, and so on, they expressed the view that the press's stories "amuse" them, offer a voyeuristic view of events and people.

33. See chapter 3 and the discussion regarding the Audio-Visual Law, attempts to enact a press law, and the changes made to the Penal Code.

34. From a discussion with Petre Mihai Bacanu on Aug. 4, 1993.

35. Eugen Serbanescu interview, June 11, 1994.

36. As stated at the Costinesti colloquium on May 28, 1992.

37. Trandafir discussion, May 12, 1994.

38. It was particularly effective in presenting the younger generation with a history of their country. Therefore, the media presentations were eye-opening and provided a larger context for their lives and the understanding of their country.

39. Dumitru Mazilu was named vice president in the interim National Salvation Front government on Dec. 26, 1989.

BIBLIOGRAPHY

Adamesteanu, Gabriela. April 8-14, 1993. Unul dintre marile 'succese' ale presei: dezinformarea. *22*, p. 1.

Adamesteanu, Gabriela. April 26, 1991. Cind (si cum) s-a schimbat televiziunea noastra cea buna? *22*, p. 7.

Adamesteanu, Gabriela. March 29, 1991. Despre diletantism, disperare si agresivitate—II. *22*, p. 4.

Adamesteanu, Gabriela. March 22, 1991. Despre diletantism, disperare si agresivitate—I. *22*, pp. 4–5.

Alexander, J. C. 1981. The news media in systemic, historical and comparative perspective. In *Mass media and social change*, edited by E. Katz and T. Szescko. Beverly Hills, Calif.: Sage Publishing, pp. 17-52.

Alexandru, Alin. Aug. 13-19, 1990. Am fost amenintat si m-am hotarit sa vorbesc. *Expres*, p. 7.

Alter, Johnathan. Jan. 8, 1990. Prime-time revolution: How technology fueled a year of change. *Newsweek*, p. 25.

Amelunxen, Hubertus von, and Adrei Ujica. 1990. *Television/Revolution: Das Ultimatum des Bildes*. Marburg, Germany: Jonas Verlag.

A.M. Press. May 14, 1994. Doi ziaristi romani solicita protectia Amnesty International. *Romania Libera*, p. 3.

Andreescu, Gabriel. Dec. 10-16, 1992. Saptamana Politica: Spectacol, Discretie. *22*, p. 3.

Anghene, Mircea. 1974. Rolul si insemnatatea organelor cu dubla natura, de partid si de stat, in sistemul democratiei socialiste. *Revista Romana de Drept* 4:9-18.

Antica, Andrei. May 16, 1994. In sfarsit, Music Television. *Romania Libera*, p. 16.

Antip, C. 1979. *Istoria presei romane*. Bucharest: Academia Stefan Gheorghiu, Facultatea de Ziaristica.

Antip, C. 1964. *Contributii la istoria presei romane*. Bucharest: Union of Journalists of the Popular Republic of Romania.

Antonesei, Liviu. Jan. 21-27, 1993. Televiziunea intre ridicol, penibil si servilism. *22*, p. 4.

Armeanu, Oana. Feb. 25-March 3, 1993. Alin Teodorescu: Pe Piata Este Inca Loc Pentru Publicatii Profitabile. *22*, p. 11.

Article 19. International Centre on Censorship. 1991. *Information Freedom and Censorship*. Chicago: American Library Association.

Associated Press. March 29, 1993. In Romania, doubletalk rolls off the "wooden tongue." *Chico Enterprise-Record*, p. 7A.

Associated Press. Dec. 25, 1989. Two Americans and two European journalists shot and wounded. *New York Times*, p. 14.

AZR. Oct. 25, 1994. Legi abuzive. *Romania Libera*, p. 1.

Bacanu, Petre Mihai. April 6, 1993. Manipularea mass-media in strategia consensului. *Romania Libera*, p. 16.

Bacanu, Petre Mihai. March 3, 1993. Majoritatea populatiei Romaniei nu are incredere in Televiziune. *Romania Libera,* p. 3.

Baciu, Mircea. March 1993. Piata Audiovizualului in Romania. Realizari si Perspective. *Buletin. Consiliul National al Audiovizualului* 2 (3): 6-8.

Baesu, Dorina. Dec. 13, 1993. Victor Ionescu a fost suspendat din functie. *Romania
Libera,* p. 3.

Banta, K. W. Sept. 5, 1988. Where glasnost is still a dirty word. *Time,* pp. 31-32.

Berindei, Mihnea, et al. 1991. *Romania, Cartea Alba.* Bucharest: Humanitas.

Birladeanu, A. April 11, 1991. Letter to Razvan Theodorescu, President of RTV. Duplicated.

Bohlen, Celestine. Dec. 28, 1989. Romanians moving to abolish worst of repressive
era. *New York Times,* pp. A1, A12.

Bohlen, Celestine. Dec. 23, 1989. Hatred of security forces growing as Romanian
atrocities increase. *New York Times,* pp. 1, 14.

Bohlen, Celestine. Dec. 21, 1989. Ceausescu blames fascists for uproar in Romanian
city. *New York Times,* pp. A14.

Bohlen, Celestine. Dec. 20, 1989. Visitors horrified at protest scene. *New York Times,*
p. A17.

Bohlen, Celestine, and Clyde Haberman. Jan. 7, 1990. Revolt in Rumania: Days of
death and hope/A special report: How the Ceausescus fell: Harnessing popular
rage. *New York Times,* p. 1.

Boila, Romulus. 1956. Press and radio. In *Captive Romania,* edited by Alexander
Cretzianu. New York: Praeger, pp. 257—84.

Botez, Mihai. 1992. *Romanii despre ei insisi.* Bucharest: Editura Litera.

Boyle, Theresa. Dec. 26, 1989. Former PQ minister ponders role of video in uprising. *Toronto Globe and Mail,* p. 7.

Brown, J. D., et al. 1987. Invisible power: Newspaper news sources and the limits of
diversity. *Journalism Quarterly* 64:45-54.

Brown, J. F. 1994. *Hopes and Shadows: Eastern Europe After Communism.* Durham,
N.C.: Duke University Press.

Brucan, Silviu. 1992. *Generatia Irosita. Memorii.* Bucharest, Romania: Editurile
Universul & Calistrat Hogas.

Brzezinski, Zbigniew. 1993. *Out of Control: Global Turmoil on the Eve of the 21st
Century.* New York: Collier Books.

Brzezinski, Zbigniew. 1989. *The Grand Failure: The Birth and Death of Communism in the Twentieth Century.* New York: Macmillan Publishing Company.

Bucurescu, Adrian. Oct. 1, 1992. Pisicile aristocrate si Kmerii Rosii. *Romania Libera,* p. 2.

Bucuroiu, Razvan. Feb. 15, 1991. Postul mare si televiziunea. *22,* p. 5.

Burileanu, Bogdan. Nov. 15, 1994. Libertatea presei este in pericol. *Romania Libera,*
p. 3.

Burileanu, Bogdan. Aug. 3, 1993. Dupa demisia Jeanei Gheorghiu. Ziaristii si-au
demonstrat solidaritatea de breasla. *Romania Libera,* p. 9.

Busuioc, Ion. 1974. Organele de dubla natura—de partid si de stat. *Viitorul Socialist*
3: 5-11.

Buzek, Anthony. 1964. *How the Communist Press Works.* New York: Praeger, 1964.

Caliga, G. 1926. *Almanahul dictionar al presei din Romania si a celei romanesti din pretutindeni.* Bucharest: n.p., 1-24.

Calinescu, Matei, and Nicolas Spulber. Dec. 30, 1989. In Rumania, an old Stalinist charade? *New York Times,* p. 25.

Caluschi, Cezar. Sept. 26, 1994. Letter to Peter Gross.

Campeanu, P. Oct. 1, 1992. On the eve. *22,* pp. 5, 11.

Campeanu, P. July 29-Aug. 4, 1993. Credibilitatea Televiziunii Romane. *22,* p. 10.

Campeanu, P. June 28, 1991. Ecuatie cu doua necunoscute. *22,* p. 16.

Campeanu, P. May 3, 1991. Nelinistile opiniei publice. *22,* p. 16.

Campeanu, P. April 12 , 1991. Opinia Publica si Liberalizarea Preturilor. *22,* p. 5.

Campeanu, P., et al. 1991. *Romania inaite si dupe 20 mai.* Bucharest: Humanitas.

Capelle, Marc. Jan. 7-13, 1993. Jurnalismul: Este Permisa Orice Fel De Lovitura? *22,* p. 4.

Carpat-Foche, George. Aug. 6, 1993. Mentori si stentori. Reflectii despre publicistica noastra. *Alternativa,* p. 8.

Ceausescu, Nicolae. Sept. 10, 1977. Cuvintarea la consfatuirea de lucru cu activistii si cadrele din domeniul educatiei politice, al propagandei si ideologiei. *Scinteia,* p. 1.

Ceausescu, Nicolae. June 30, 1977. Speech to the Central Committee of the RCP and the Supreme Council for Socialist and Economic Development. *Scinteia,* p. 1.

Ceausescu, Nicolae. 1972. Raportul cu privire la dezvoltarea economica-social a Romaniei in urmatorii ani si in perspectiva la perfectionarea conducerii planificate a societatii si dezvoltarea democratiei socialiste, la cresterea rolului conducator al partidului in edificarea socialismului si comunismului, la activitatea internationala a partidului si statului. In *Conferinta Nationala a Partidului Comunist Roman.* Bucharest: Editura Politica.

Ceausescu, Nicolae. July 9, 1971. Expunerea la consfatuirea de lucru a activului de partid din domeniul ideologiei si al activitatii politice si culturale-educative. In *Romania pe drumul construirii societatii socialiste multilateral dezvoltate* 6.

Center for Urban and Regional Sociology. December 1995. *Public Opinion Barometer.*

Ceterchi, Ion. April 4, 1974. Legea presei: Un document important politic si juridic. *Romania Libera,* p. 12.

Chan, J. M., and C. C. Lee. 1991. *Mass Media and Political Transition: The Hong Kong Press in China's Orbit.* New York: Guilford Press.

Chendi, I. 1900. *Inceputurile ziaristicei noastre (1789-1895).* Orastie, Romania: Minerva.

Chirita, Elena. Feb. 11, 1994. Televiziunea prin cablu/Posturi partiu clare in Bucuresti. *Romania Libera* 5.

[No byline] June 6, 1994. Cine conduce TV Soti? O declaratie a unui membru al Consiliului de administratie. *Romania Libera,* p. 9.

Cioaca, Stefan. October 1992. La rascruce de drumuri: Alegerile parlamentare. *Curierul Romanesc,* p. 2.

Cismarescu, Michael. 1981. *Einfuhrung in das Rumanische Recht.* Darmstadt, Germany: Wissenschaftliche Buchgesellschaft.

Codrescu, Andrei. Sept. 2, 1990. Romania's Bogus Revolution. *Sacramento Bee*, Forum section, p. 1.

Coman, Mihai. 1994. Romanian journalism in a transition period, 1990-1992. In *Osten Europa Medienlandschaft im Umbruch*, edited by Gerd Hallemberger and Michael Krzeminski. Berlin, Germany: Vistas, pp. 81-98.

Coman, Mihai. 1993. Puterea si Carnavalul. *Romanian Journal of Sociology* 2:145—53.

Coman, Mihai, and Peter Gross. Spring 1994. The 1992 presidential/parliamentary elections in Romania's largest circulation dailies and weeklies. *Gazette*, pp. 223-40.

Comanescu, Serban. Aug. 13-19, 1993. Mass-media: Unde sint publicatiile sexy de altadata? *Tinerama*, p. 12.

Constitutia Romaniei. Nov. 21, 1991. In *Monitorul Oficial al Romaniei*, no. 233.

Cornea, A. Oct. 4-10, 1995. Deriva antidemocratica. *22*, p. 3.

Cornea, A. Aug. 12-18, 1993. A fost of vreme... *22*, p. 1.

Cornea, A. Sept. 28, 1990. Necesara demarcare. *22*, p. 4.

Cosarca, Radu. 1993. Televiziunea privata in Romania. Duplicated.

Cosma, Doru. March 8, 1991. Marginalii la proiectul legii audiovisualului: Dreptul la Antena. *22*, p. 14.

Cosma, Doru. March 1, 1991. Marginalii la proiectul legii audiovisualului: Consiliul National al Audiovisualului. *22*, p. 11.

Cosma, Doru. Feb. 22, 1991. Marginalii la proiectul legii audiovisualului: Ce se spune si ce se vrea. *22*, p. 7.

Cosma, Doru. Jan. 25, 1991. Proiectul Legii Audiovizualului: Transformarea monopolului de stat intr-un monopol de drept. *22*, p. 6.

Cosma, Doru. July 27, 1990. Dreptul la replica in proiectul noii legi a presei. *22*, p. 5.

Costandache, Iulian. Dec. 4, 1993. O lesa pentru cainele de paza al societatii. *Romania Libera*, p. 3.

Cretia, Petru. Aug. 3, 1990. Ce nu este vremelnic in ziaristica lui Eminescu. *22*, p. 4.

Cristea, Radu Calin. Oct. 25-Nov. 1, 1991. Poezie si contabilitate. *22*, p. 6.

Curry, Jane Leftwich. 1984. *The Polish Black Book*. New York: Vintage Press.

Dahlgren, P. 1981. TV News and the suppression of reflexivity. In *Mass media and social change*, edited by E. Katz and T. Szecsko. London, England: Sage Publications, pp. 101-14.

Dahrendorf, Ralf. 1991. *Reflections on the Revolutions in Europe*. New York: Random House, Inc.

Dahrendorf, Ralf. Spring 1990. Has the East joined the West? *New Perspectives Quarterly* 7 (2): 41-43.

David, Petru. Nov. 16, 1994. Sub pretextul defaimarii. *Timisoara*, p. 1.

[No byline] April 3-4, 1993. Declaratia in Favoarea Transparentei Procesului Legislative. *Alianta Civica*, p. 6.

Deutsch, Karl. 1966. *The Nerves of Government*. New York: Free Press.

Dinescu, Mircea. Nov. 16, 1990. Cel de-al doilea intuneric al culturii romane. *22*, p. 2.

Dumitrescu, Rodica. Nov. 12-18, 1993. Ziaristii balcanici despre adevar si toleranta. *Tinerama,* p. 5.

Echikson, William. Jan. 31, 1989a. Personality cult thrives in Romania, but economy withers under weight of grandiose projects and rush to repay debt. *Christian Science Monitor,* p. 5.

Echikson, William. Jan. 31, 1989b. Journalists find high barriers to serious reporting in Romania. *Christian Science Monitor,* p. 6.

Eliade, Mircea. 1987. *Despre Eminescu si Hasdeu.* Iasi, Romania: Junimea.

Epstein, L. K. 1973. *News From Nowhere.* New York: Random House.

[No named editor] Spring 1994. *Essays of the Hubert H. Humphrey Fellows.* Syracuse University. S. I. Newhouse School of Public Communication.

Falin, Valentin. Spring 1990. The Collapse of Eastern Europe: Moscow's View. *New Perspectives Quarterly,* pp. 22-26.

[No byline] May 5-11, 1992. Fara legea accesului la informatie, presa va fi obligata sa fure. *Expres,* p. 6.

Fein, Leonard, and Victoria E. Bonnell. 1965. Press and radio in Romania: Some recent developments. *Journalism Quarterly* 42:443.

Fischer-Galati, Stephen. 1970. *20th Century Romania.* New York: Columbia University Press.

Florea, Mirela. July 15, 1994. Victor Ionescu, din nou in proces. *Romania Libera,* p. 9.

Frankland, Mark. 1993. *The Patriots' Revolution.* Chicago: Ivan R. Dees.

Freedom Forum. 1994. *Looking to the Future: A Survey of Journalism Education in Central and Eastern Europe and the Former Soviet Union.* Arlington, Va.: Freedom Forum.

[No byline] Sept. 20, 1989. Fronda anti-Ceausescu nel partito. Un documento proclama: "Liberiamo il Paese dal Tiranno." *La Stampa,* p. 5.

Fukuyama, Francis. 1992. *The End of History and the Last Man.* New York: Free Press.

Gabanyi, A. U. 1990. *Die unvollendete Revolution: Rumanien zwischen Dictatur und Demokratie.* Munich: R. Piper.

Gabanyi, A. U. 1978. Das Zensursystem in Rumanien. *Wissenschaftlischer Dienst Sudosteuropa* 5:270-73.

Gans, H. J. 1979. *Deciding What's News.* New York: Free Press.

Garnham, Nicholas. 1990. *Capitalism and Communication.* London: Sage.

Gaspard, Armand. 1965. Das neue Gesicht der rumanischen Presse. Zurich, Switzerland. *IPI Review* 4-5.

Gaunt, P. 1990. *Choosing the News.* Westport, Conn.: Greenwood Press.

Genette, G. 1988. *Narrative Discourse Revisited.* Ithaca, N.Y.: Cornell University Press.

Genette, G. 1983. *Nouveau discours du recit.* Paris: Editions du Seuil.

Georgesco, J. 1936. *La Presse Periodique en Roumanie.* Oradea, Romania: Editura Sfanta Unire.

Gheorghiu, Virginia. 1991. *The Functions of Media During the Transition from Totalitarianism to Democracy.* Cluj, Romania. Photocopy.

Ghibutiu, Horia. Feb. 22, 1993. Deocamdata, bile albe... *Tineretul Liber,* p. 2.

Giffard, A. 1989. *Unesco and the Media.* New York: Longman.

Glasser, Theodore. 1988. Objectivity precludes responsibility. In *Impact of mass media: Current issues,* edited by R. E. Hiebert and C. Reuss. White Plains, N.Y.: Longman, pp. 44-51.

Goban-Klas, Tomasz. 1994. *The Orchestration of the Media: The Politics of Mass Communication in Communist Poland and the Aftermath.* Boulder, Colo.: Westview Press.

Golding, P., and P. Elliott. 1979. *Making the News.* London: Longman.

Gross, Peter. 1995. Romania. In *Glasnost and after: Media and change in Central and Eastern Europe,* edited by David Paletz, Karl Jakubowicz, and Pavao Novosel. Cresskill, N.J.: Hampton Press, pp. 195-214.

Gross, Peter. 1993a. Public opinion, media, and the transition process in Romania. In *Media in transition from totalitarianism to democracy,* edited by Oleg Manaev and Yuri Pryluk. Kiev, Ukraine: ABRIS, pp. 86-102.

Gross, Peter. 1993b. Mass media and public opinion in Romania: Forward to the past. *ARA Journal* 4:126-30.

Gross, Peter. May 8, 1992. Libertatea Presei Inseamna Putere Si Protectie Pentru Presa. *Romania Libera,* pp. 1, 3.

Gross, Peter. 1991a. Romania's poor orphans: Civil and information societies. *Media, Culture & Society* 13 (3): 407-14.

Gross, Peter. 1991b. Restricting the free press in Romania. *Orbis* 35 (3): 365-76.

Gross, Peter. 1990a. Small signs of great changes ... at a Romanian TV station. *Columbia Journalism Review* (May/June), pp. 37-39.

Gross, Peter. 1990b. Exercises in cynicism and propaganda: Law, legality, and foreign correspondence in Romania. *Political Communication and Persuasion* 6 (3): 179-90.

Gross, Peter. 1990c. The Soviet communist press theory—Romanian style. In *Democratization and media,* edited by S. Splichal et al. Ljubljana, Yugoslavia: Communication and Culture Colloquia, pp. 94-108.

Gross, Peter. 1990d. The USA as seen through the eyes of Romania's Scinteia. *East European Quarterly* 24 (3): 373-92.

Gross, Peter. 1988. Trials, tribulations and contributions: A brief history of the Romanian press. *East European Quarterly* 22 (1): 1-22.

Gross, Peter, and Stephen King. 1993. Romania's new journalism education programs: Beginning or beginning of the end? *Journalism Educator* (fall), pp. 24-32.

Gurevitch, M., and J. G. Blumler. 1983. Linkages between the mass media and politics: A model for the analysis of political communication systems. In *Mass Communication and Society,* edited by J. Curran et al. London: Edward Arnold, 270-90.

[No byline] July 14, 1993. Guvernul—supus sanctiunilor presei: Motiune de cenzura. *Romania Libera,* p. 1.

Hachten, W. A. 1981. *The World News Prism: Changing Media, Clashing Ideologies.* Ames: Iowa State University Press.

Hanes, Petre V. 1927. *Istoria literaturii.* Bucharest: Editura Ancora, S. Benvenisti and Co.

Harden, Blaine. Dec. 29, 1989. Shortwave radio shaped the revolution. *Washington Post,* pp. A1, A24.

Harsanyi, D., and N. Harsanyi. 1992. Story/discourse in the Romanian daily press. *European Studies Journal* 9 (2): 27-39.

Havel, Vaclav. 1989. *Living in Truth.* London: Faber and Faber.

Helsinki Watch/Association for the Protection of Human Rights in Romania. Nov. 29, 1994. Comentariile APADOR-CH privind limitarile aduse de parlamentul Romaniei libertatii de exprimare. Photocopy.

Hetherington, A. 1984. *News, Newspapers and Television.* London: Macmillan.

Hoagland, Jim. April 26, 1990. Off to a rough start. *Washington Post,* p. A23.

Horasangian, Bedros. Feb. 8, 1991. Autoritate, autoritarism, autoritati. *22,* p. 4.

Horlamus, Sepp, ed. 1976. *Mass Media in C.M.E.A. Countries.* Prague: International Organization of Journalists.

Horvat, Janos. 1991. The East European journalist. *Journal of International Affairs* 45:191-200.

Horvat, Janos, and Jay Roskin. 1990. Singlethink: Thoughts on the Havel episode. *Gannet Center Journals* (fall), pp. 31-52.

Hoyer, Svennik, Epp Lauk, and Peeter Vihalemm. 1993. *Towards a Civic Society. The Baltic Media's Long Road to Freedom.* Tartu, Estonia: Nota Baltica Ltd.

Ierunca, Virgil. 1994. Mitologiile stingii romanesti. In *Dimpotriva,* edited by V. Ierunca. Bucharest: Humanitas, pp. 36-52.

Illyes, Elemer. 1982. *National Minorities in Romania: Change in Transylvania.* East European Monographs. New York: Columbia University Press.

[No byline] Dec. 17, 1992. In Camera Deputatilor: Pe usa din dos intra ... legea presei. *Romania Libera,* p. 1.

Ion, Andrei Remus. Jan. 7-13, 1993. Al treilea an pentru a patra putere in stat. *22,* p. 7.

Ion, M. June 12, 1993. Televiziunea prin cablu: Patru firme private au contribuit la extinderea receptarii prin satelit. *Romania Libera,* p. 9.

Ionescu, A. A. 1913. *Publicatiunile periodice romanesti.* Bucharest: SOCEC.

Ionescu, Costel. Aug. 6, 1993. Functia mediatoare spiritual a presei in democratie. *Alternativa,* p. 7.

Ionescu, D. Oct. 2, 1992. Romania. *Radio Free Europe/ Radio Liberty Research Report* 1 (39): 55-57.

Ionescu, Liana. March 21-22, 1992. Despartirea de SOTI. *Romania Libera,* pp. 1, 3.

Ionescu, Petru. Aug. 6, 1993. Presa 'de schimbare.' *Alternativa,* p. 3.

Ionescu, Petru. Feb. 15, 1991. Utilitatea presei. *22,* p. 11.

Ionescu-Dolj, I. 1914. *Presa si regimul ei in Romania, 1859-1914.* Bucharest: n.p.

Iorga, Nicolae. 1922. *Istoria presei romanesti.* Bucharest: Union of Journalists.

IRSOP. December 1994. *Public Opinion Barometer.* Bucharest: Romanian Institute for Public Opinion Research.

Iuga, Dumitru. Nov. 2, 1993. Incalcare grosolana a Constitutiei prin dezinformare. *Romania Libera,* p. 3.

Ivascu, G. 1964. *Reflector peste timp: Din istoria reportajului romanesc.* Bucharest: Editura pentru literatura, vol. 1 (1829-1866).

Jakubowicz, Karol. 1993a. Access to the media and democratic communication:

Theory and practice in Central and Eastern European broadcasting. Paper presented at "The Development of Rights of Access to the Media" conference, June 19-21, at the Institute for Constitutional and Legislative Policy, Central European University, Budapest.

Jakubowicz, Karol. 1993b. Equality for the downtrodden, freedom for the free: Changing perspectives on social communication in Central and Eastern Europe. Lecture at the Institute of Journalism, University of Warsaw. Photocopy.

Jakubowicz, Karol. 1993c. The case for decisive regulation of broadcasting in post-communist countries: A Polish case study. Photocopy.

Jakubowicz, Karol. 1992. From party propaganda to corporate speech? Polish journalism in search of a new identity. *Journal of Communication* 42 (3): 64-107.

Jakubowicz, Karol, 1990. Media and culture in the information society. *Gazette* 42 (2): 71-88.

Jakubowicz, Karol. 1989. Between communism and post-communism: How many varieties of glasnost. Paper presented at the third International Colloquium on Communication and Culture, Sept. 22-26, in Piran, Yugoslavia.

Jowitt, G., and V. O'Donnell. 1986. *Propaganda and Persuasion*. Beverly Hills, Calif.: Sage Publications.

Jowitt, Ken. 1992. The Leninist legacy. In *Eastern Europe in revolution*, edited by Ivo Banac. Ithaca, N.Y.: Cornell University Press, pp. 207-24.

Kaplan, Robert D. 1993. *Balkan Ghosts. A Journey Through History*. New York: St. Martin's Press.

Keane, John. 1991. *The Media and Democracy.* Cambridge, England: Polity Press.

Kecskemeti, Paul. 1950. Totalitarian Communication as a Means of Control. *Public Opinion Quarterly* 14:224-34.

Kepplinger, H. M., and R. Kocher. 1990. Professionalism in the media world? *European Journal of Communication* 5 (2-3): 285-311.

Kifner, John. Dec. 28, 1989. Rumanian revolt, live and uncensored. *New York Times,* p. A1.

Kifner, John. Dec. 25, 1989. Romanian army gains in capital but battle goes on. *New York Times,* p. A1.

Klapper, J. T. 1949. *The Effects of Mass Media*. New York: Bureau of Applied Social Research, Columbia University.

Klapper, J. T. 1948. Mass media and the engineering of consent. *American Scholar* 4:419-29.

Klebnikov, Peter. Feb. 8, 1989. For newsmen in Romania, glasnost is in short supply. *New York City Tribune,* pp. 1, 3.

Kolakowski, L. 1989. On total control and its contradictions: The power of information. *Encounter* 2:65-71.

Kolakowski, L. 1983. Totalitarianism and the virtue of the lie. In *1984 revisited*, edited by I. Howe. New York: Harper and Row, pp. 122-35.

Kolakowski, L. 1978. *Main Currents of Marxism.* New York: Oxford, vol. 3.

Konrad, Gyorgy. 1984. L'ecrivain etatisse. *Lettre Internationale* 2:40-44. As quoted in Jacques Rupnik (1988), "Totalitarianism Revisited," in *Civil Society and the State*, edited by John Keane, London, England: Verso, pp. 263-90.

Kruglak, T. E. Summer 1958. Agerpres: The Romanian national news agency. *Jour-*

nalism Quarterly 35:343-47.

Kubik, Jan. 1994. *The Power of Symbols Against the Symbols of Power.* University Park: Penn State University Press.

Lazar, Virgil. May 4, 1993. Clujenii prefera televiziunea prin cablu. *Romania Libera,* p. 16.

Lazarsfeld, P., and E. Katz. 1955. *Personal Influence.* Glencoe, Ill.: Free Press.

Leahu, Valentin. April 29, 1994. Televiziunea romana, data in judecata de CBN. *Romania Libera,* p. 9.

Leca, Cristina. June 1995. The Newsprint Crisis Continues. *Times—Romanian Monitor,* p. 1.

[No author] June 18, 1994. Legea privind organizarea si functionarea Societatii Romane de Radiodifuziune si Societatii Romane de Televiziune. *Monitorul Oficial al Romaniei* no. 153.

[No author] May 25, 1992. Legea Audiovisualului. *Monitorul Oficial al Romaniei* no. 104.

[No byline] Feb. 3, 1993. Legea Audiovizualului nu poate defini activitatea TVR. *Cotidianul,* p. 2.

Lendvai, Paul. 1981. *The Bureaucracy of Truth: How Communist Governments Manage the News.* London: Burnett Books Ltd.

Leonhardt, Peter. 1974. Das rumanische Presserecht nach dem Gesetz vom 28.3.1974. *Jahrbuch fur Ostrecht* 15:199-229.

Lerner, D. 1972. Toward a communication theory of modernization. In *Communications and Political Development,* edited by Lucien W. Pye. Princeton, N.J.: Princeton University Press, pp. 327-50.

Lerner, D. 1958. *The Passing of Traditional Society. Modernizing the Middle East.* Glencoe, Ill.: Free Press.

Lippmann, Walter. 1965. *Public Opinion.* New York: Free Press.

Longworth, R. C. Jan. 7, 1990. In Eastern Europe, TV was the tool of revolution. *Chicago Tribune,* p. 1.

Lucan, Cristina, June 1995. SRI: Information source or political police. *Times—Romanian Monitor* 9.

Lunin, Luis F. June/July 1990. Information from Radio Free Europe helps free Romania. *Bulletin of the American Society for Information Society* 16 (5): 23.

Magris, Claudio. 1989. *Danube.* New York: Farrar, Straus, Giroux.

Mainland, E. 1986. The Voice present and future: VOA, the USSR and communist Europe. In *Western Broadcasting Over the Iron Curtain,* edited by K. R. M. Short. New York: St. Martin's Press, pp. 113-33.

Maioreanu, Bogdan. March 30, April 5, 1993. Cine apara demnitatea cetateanului calomniat? *Expres,* p. 12.

March 3, 1993. Majoritatea populatiei Romaniei nu are incredere in Televiziune. *Romania Libera,* p. 3.

Man, Liviu. Summer 1993. The independent press in Romania: Against the grain. *Uncaptive Minds,* pp. 89-96.

Manaev, Oleg, and Yuri Pryluk, eds. 1993. *Media in Transition from Totalitarianism to Democracy.* Kiev, Ukraine: ABRIS.

Manea, Ion. 1986. Does the Romanian press exist in today's Romania? Why are Romanian foreign correspondents nowhere to be found? *ARA Journal* 8-9:149-55.

Manea, Ion. 1985. Does the Romanian press exist in today's Romania? *ARA Journal* 6-7:142-47.

Manea, Norman. 1992. *On Clowns: The Dictator and the Artist*. New York: Grove Weidenfeld.

Manolescu, Nicolae. 1991. *Dreptul la normalitate: Discursul politic si realitatea*. Bucharest: Litera.

Maratu, Bianca. 1993. *Publicitatea in Televiziune*. University of Bucharest. Duplicated.

Marinescu, Valentina. 1993. *Private versus State Television in Romania: Regulations and Achievements*. Duplicated.

McIntosh, M. 1986. Public opinion assessment and Radio Free Europe's effectiveness in Eastern Europe. In *Western Broadcasting Over the Iron Curtain*, edited by K. R. M. Short. New York: St. Martin's Press, pp. 245-63.

McQuail, Denis. 1992. *Media Performance: Mass Communication and the Public Interest*. Newbury Park, Calif.: Sage Publications.

McQuail, Denis. 1987. *Mass Communication Theory: An Introduction*. Beverly Hills, Calif.: Sage Publishing.

Mediafax. Aug. 5, 1994. Hartia de ziar se va scumpi din nou. *Adevarul*, p. 1.

Media Monitoring Unit. November 1992. *The 1992 National Elections in Romania: Coverage by Radio and Television*. Manchester, England, and Düsseldorf: European Institute for the Media.

Menard, Robert. Sept. 27-Oct. 3, 1995. Protest. *22*, p. 7.

Merrill, J. C. 1983. *Global Journalism: A Survey of the World's Mass Media*. New York: Longman.

Merrill, J. C. 1974. *The Imperatives of Freedom*. New York: Hastings House.

Merrill, J. C., and R. L. Lowenstein. 1971. *Media, Messages and Men: New Perspectives on Communication*. New York: David McKay.

Middleton, Kent R. 1993. Applying Europe's "First Amendment" to Romanian libel and access law. In *Creating a free press in Eastern Europe*, edited by Al Hester and Kristina White. Athens: James M. Cox, Jr., Center for International Mass Communication Training and Research, University of Georgia, pp. 405-30.

Mihailescu, Dan C. July 27, 1990. Dam din cap, sau nu? *22*, p. 4.

Milin, Miodrag. 1990. *Timisoara. 15-21 decembrie '89*. Timisoara, Romania: n.p.

Mills, Rilla Dean. 1983. Mass media as vehicles of education, persuasion, and opinion making ... in the communist world. In *Comparative mass media systems*, edited by L. John Martin and A. G. Chaudhary. New York: Longman.

Milosz, Czeslaw. 1981. *The Captive Mind*. New York: Vintage Books.

Ministerul Postelor si Telecomunicatiilor—Directia Generala a Postelor si Difuzare a Presei. 1990. *Lista Publicatiilor Interna (difuzate prin unitatile de posta si telecomincatii). Nr. 43 A—Pentru uz intern*. Duplicated.

[No byline] August 1994. Mixed report from Romania. *CFJ Clearinghouse On The Central & East European Press* 15:215.

Monitorul Oficial. June 18, 1994. *The Law Concerning the Organization and Functioning of the Romanian Radio Society and of the Romanian Television Society*.

Moyers, Bill. 1992. Old news is good news. *New Perspectives Quarterly* 9 (4): 35-37.

Mungiu, Alina. June 1-7, 1993. Daca TVR n-ar exista, *Expres,* pp. 1, 3.

Mungiu, Alina. March 8, 1991. Diletantism jurnalistic de interes national. *22,* p. 2.

Mungiu, Alina. Jan. 18, 1991. Sintem gazetari sau psihoterapeuti. *22,* p. 6.

Mungiu, Alina. Aug. 10, 1990. Vom fi toti egali in fata Legii Presei? *22,* pp. 4–5.

Mungiu, Alina. June 8, 1990. Tara comunista cu presa libera. *22* 4.

Muravchik, Joshua. 1991. *Exporting Democracy: Fulfilling America's Destiny.* Washington, D.C.: AEI Press.

National Audio-Visual Council. July 21, 1995 and Aug. 16, 1995. Lists of radio, television and cable TV license holders. Photocopy.

National Audio-Visual Council. December 1993. *Raport de Activitate (Activity Report to the Romanian Parliament).* Mimeo.

NAVC (National Audio-Visual Council) *Buletin,* no. 1, no. 2, 1992; no. 3, no. 4-5, 1993; no. 7, 1994.

National Republican Institute for International Affairs/International Republic Institute. Sept. 29, 1992. Preliminary statement by the international observer delegation to the Romanian presidential and parliamentary elections. Photocopy.

National Statistical Commission. 1992. *Anuarul Statistic al Romaniei.*

Neuman, Johanna. June 1991. The media: Partners in the revolution of 1989. Working paper, Atlantic Council of the United States.

[No byline] April 14, 1990. New Press Challenge in Poland. *Editor & Publisher* 123 (15): 16.

Nicolaescu, Emilia. July 26, 1993. In 4 Februarie, in TVR, general Sandu m-a amenintat ... *Romania Libera,* p. 1.

Nistorescu, Cornel. Nov. 16, 1990. Este un dictat al preturilor. *22,* p. 2.

Nistorescu, Cornel. July 27, 1990. Libertate amara. *Expres,* p. 6.

N. P. [byline] Sept. 30, 1993. Ulm Spineanu: Starea actuala a transitiei. *Romania Libera,* p.2.

Octavian, Tudor. May 16, 1990. Minciuna—cauza si garantie a adevarului. *Flacara,* p. 8.

Olson, Kenneth E. 1966. *The History Makers: The Press of Europe from its Beginnings through 1965.* Baton Rouge: Louisiana State University Press.

Orwell, George. 1949. *1984.* New York: New American Library.

Palade, Rodica. July 8-14, 1993. Sondind inca o data dimensiunea abisala a Televiziunii. *22,* pp. 8-10.

Paletz, David L., K. Jakubowicz, and P. Novosel, eds. 1995. *Glasnost and After: Media and Change in Central and Eastern Europe.* Creskill, N.J.: Hampton Press.

Parliament of Romania. 1992. *Romanian Legislation: Political Elections* (bilingual edition), vol. 4. Bucharest: Technical and Legislative Department of the Chamber of Deputies.

Passin, H. 1972. Writer and journalist in the transitional society. In *Communications and political development,* edited by Lucien W. Pye. Princeton, N.J.: Princeton University Press, pp. 82-123.

Paulu, Burton. 1974. *Radio and Television Broadcasting in Eastern Europe.* Minneapolis: University of Minnesota Press.

Pavel, Cristian. Dec. 22-25, 1992. Canalul 2- Romania—o afacere scandaloasa? *Expres,* p. 11.

Pavel, Dan. June/July, 1993. Revista Presei Politice. *Sfera Politicii,* p. 31.

Pavel, Dan. July 11, 1991. Cui ii pasa de cea de-a patra putere? *22*, p. 4.

Pavel, Doru, and Corneliu Turianu. Jan. 13, 1994. Ultrajul si presa. *Romania Libera*, p. 7.

Pavel, Doru, and Corneliu Turianu. Dec. 7, 1993. Cenzura sau pedepse aspre? *Romania Libera*, p. 2.

[No byline] April 1995. PDSR's strife for political power already started. *Times-Romanian Monitor*, p. 1.

Peterson, T., et al. 1966. *The Mass Media and Modern Society*. New York: Holt, Rinehart and Winston.

Pilon, Juliana Geran. 1992. *The Bloody Flag: Post-Communist Nationalism in Eastern Europe*. New Brunswick, N.J.: Transaction Publishers.

Pompey, Carmen. Dec. 17, 1987. Romania, in The video revolution in Eastern Europe. *Radio Free Europe/Radio Liberty Background Report* 242:32.

Popescu, Dan. July 15, 1993. De ce ascult in continuare Europa Libera si BBC. *Romania Libera*, p. 2.

Popescu, Rasvan. May 19-25, 1992. Dan Martian respinge Legea accesului la informatie. *Expres*, p. 6.

Popescu, Rasvan. May 12-18, 1992. Pe tapet: Proiectul Legii Accesului La Informatie. *Expres*, p. 5.

Popescu, Rasvan. May 5-11, 1992. Fara legea accesului la informatie, presa va fi obligata sa fure. *Expres*, p. 6.

Pora, Andrea. June 5-11, 1992. Intre imagine si realitate. *22*, pp. 7, 8, 9.

Preda, Eugen. 1993. A comunica—Un verb ce nu se conjuga la forma negativa. Presentation at a roundtable on "Communication, Cooperation and Conflict Between Factors (Involved) in Change," July 15, at Black Sea University, Costinesti, Romania. Photocopy.

Preda, Eugen. Dec. 17-18, 1992. Address to the high level seminar of the EBU on common problems of radio program dissemination in a democratic society. Photocopy.

Preisz, Dan. May 16, 1994. Curtea Constitutionala: Puterea lupta pentru controlul total al Televiziuni. *Romania Libera*, p. 3.

Preisz, Dan. Jan. 17, 1994. "Nu va asteptati sa fac o televiziune dupa chipul si asemanarea mea": Interviu du dl. Dumitru Popa, directorul general al TVR. *Romania Libera*, p. 3.

Preisz, Dan. Nov. 16, 1993. Ramas bun, presa independenta—adio, democratie ... *Romania Libera*, p. 3.

Preisz, Dan. Nov. 12, 1993. Uciderea presei. *Romania Libera*, p. 3.

Preisz, Dan. July 26, 1993. Coruptia in Pericol! Dna Emilia Nicolaescu il infrunta pe dl general Sandu. O sa-i tragem de urechi! *Romania Libera*, p. 11.

Preisz, Dan. July 15, 1993. Greva de avertisment la Televiziunea Romana. *Romania Libera*, p. 3.

[No byline] Dec. 10, 1993. Procesul mitei din Televiziunea Romana. *Romania Libera*, p. 16.

[No byline] Sept. 29, 1993. Program dedicat tinerilor jurnalisti teatrali. *Romania Libera*, p. 2.

[No byline] April 24-27, 1992. Project de lege initiat de reporterii revistei Expres. *Expres*, p. 11.

Pye, Lucien W. 1972. *Communications and Political Development.* Princeton, N.J.: Princeton University Press.

Questor, George H. 1990. *The International Politics of Television.* Lexington, Kentucky: Lexington Books.

Radio Romania. Directia Programe. 1993. Audienta posturilor de radio. Duplicated.

Radulescu, Ilie. 1973. Impletirea activitatii de partid si de stat. *Era Socialista* 22:38-39.

Radulescu-Motru, C. 1936. *Romanismul: Catehismul unei noi spiritualitati.* Bucharest, Romania: Fundatia pentru literatura si arta Regele Carol II.

Radulescu-Motru, C. 1976. Psychology of the Romanian people. *Revista de Filozofie,* no. 2.

Randal, Jonathan C. Jan. 9, 1990. Romanian says patriotic song signaled revolt. *Washington Post,* p. A1.

Ratesh, Nestor. 1991. *Romania: The Entangled Revolution.* New York: Praeger.

Reichman, H. 1988. The last Stalinist. *World Press Review* 35 (11): 22.

Riding, Alan. Nov. 21, 1989. Clamor in the East: Rumanian leader refuses change. *New York Times,* p. 1.

Robinson, G. J. 1977. *Tito's Maverick Media.* Urbana: University of Illinois Press.

Roman, Petre. June 7, 1991. Letter to Marvin Stone, president and chairman of the International Media Fund. Duplicated.

Rompres. 1992. *Partidele Politice din Romania,* 4th ed. Bucharest: National News Agency.

Rosengren, K. E. 1981. Mass media and social changes: Some current approaches. In *Mass media and social change,* edited by E. Katz and T. Szecsko. London: Sage Publishing, pp. 247-64.

Rosenstiel, Thomas B. Jan. 18, 1990. TV, VCRs fan fire of revolution. *Los Angeles Times,* p. A10.

Rosetti, Constantin A. 1889. *Amintiri Istorice.* Bucharest: Editura Vintila Rosetti.

Rosetti, Constantin A. Sept. 27, 1881. *Banchetul oferit lui Ca.A. Rosetti cu ocazia aniversarii a 25-a a fondarii Romanului.* Bucharest: Typographie Romanului, p. 102.

Rothschild, Joseph. 1993. *Return to Diversity.* New York: Oxford University Press.

Ruston, Ursula. September 1990. Index on censorship. Briefing paper no. 354. Index on Censorship.

S., Calin. May 4, 1994. Premiera. O noua revista de informatie culturala. *Romania Libera,* p. 2.

Sandor, Dorel, ed. December 1993. *Sindromul Tergiversarii: Analiza de risc politics.* Orange Report. Bucharest: Centrul pentru Studii Politice si Analiza Comparativa.

Sandulescu, I.V. April 11, 1991. Letter to Razvan Theodorescu, president of RTV. Duplicated.

Schemo, Diana Jean. April 30, 1990. Ceausescu execution film branded fake. *Sacramento Bee,* p. A5.

Schiller, D. 1981. *Objectivity and the News: The Public and the Rise of Commercial Journalism.* Philadelphia: University of Pennsylvania Press.

Schopflin, George, ed. 1983. *Censorship and Political Communication: Examples from Eastern Europe.* New York: St. Martin's Press.

Schramm, W. 1972. Communication development and the development process. In *Communications and political development*, edited by Lucien W. Pye. Princeton, N.J.: Princeton University Press, pp. 30-57.

Schramm, W. 1956. The Soviet communist theory of the press. In *Four theories of the press*, edited by S. Siebert, T. Peterson, and W. Schramm. Urbana: University of Illinois Press, pp. 105-46.

Serbanescu, Tia. Nov. 17-23, 1993. Insulta si batjocura. *22*, p. 7.

Serbanescu, Tia. Aug. 6, 1993. In absenta opositie. *Alternativa*, p. 2.

Serbanescu, Tia. June 3-9, 1993. O complicitate dezvaluita. *22*, p. 3.

Shafir, Michael. 1985. *Romania. Politics, Economics and Society*. Boulder, Colo.: Lynne Rienner Publishers.

Shils, E. 1972. Demagogues and cadres in the political development of the new states. In *Communications and political development*, edited by Lucien W. Pye. Princeton, N.J.: Princeton University Press, pp. 64-77.

Shinar, Dov, and Gina Stoiciu. 1992. Media representations of socio-political conflict: The Romanian Revolution and the Gulf War. *Gazette* 50 (2-3): 243-58.

Shoemaker, Pamela. 1984. Media treatment of deviant political groups. *Journalism Quarterly* 61:66-75, 82.

Shoemaker, Pamela. 1983. Bias and source attribution. *Newspaper Research Journal* 5 (1): 25-32.

Shoemaker, P. J., and E. K. Mayfield. 1987. Building a theory of news content: A synthesis of current approaches. *Journalism Monographs* no. 103.

Siebert, F. E., T. Peterson, and W. Schramm. 1956. *Four Theories of the Press*. Urbana: University of Illinois Press.

Silviu, G. 1936. *Noile legiuri penale si libertatea presei*. Bucharest: Union of Bucharest Journalists.

Skilling, H. Gordon. 1989. *Samizdat and an Independent Society in Central and Eastern Europe*. Columbus: Ohio State University Press.

Socor, Vladimir. Feb. 2, 1990. Pastor Toekes and the outbreak of the revolution in Timisoara. *Report on Eastern Europe* 1 (5): 19-25.

Sparks, Colin, and Slavko Splichal. 1988. Journalistic education and professional socialization. Paper presented at the 16th IAMCR Conference, July 25-29, in Barcelona, Spain.

Splichal, Slavko. 1995. *Media Beyond Socialism*. Boulder, Colo.: Westview Press.

Splichal, Slavko. 1992a. Media privatization and democratization in Central-Eastern Europe. *Gazette* 49 (1-2): 3-22.

Splichal, Slavko. 1992b. *Media Beyond Socialism: The "Civil Society" Paradox and the Media in Post-Socialist Countries*. Ljubljana: University of Ljubljana. Duplicated.

Stanescu, Sorin Rosca. Dec. 5, 1994. Impotriva presei s-a dezlantuit si prigoana legislativa. *Ziua*, p. 1.

Stanescu, Sorin Rosca. Jan. 22, 1992. Coloana SOTI. *Romania Libera*, p. 1.

Staniloiu, Iolanda. Aug. 7, 1994. Note to Peter Gross.

Stefanescu, Crisula. Feb. 22, 1991. Disputes over control of Romanian Television. *Report on Eastern Europe* 2 (8): 28-33.

Stefanescu, Manuela. April 3-4, 1993a. Lege a presei sau cod deontologic? *Alianta Civica*, p. 7.

Stefanescu, Manuela. April 3-4, 1993b. Accesul la informatie. *Alianta Civica*, p. 6.

Stefoi, Elena. Oct. 25-Nov. 1, 1991. Independenta presei si dusmanii ei culturali. *22*, p. 6.

Steriade, S. 1991. Mass communication in Romania: Contradictory effects. Duplicated.

Steriade, S. Dec. 7, 1990. Televiziune si democratie. *22*, p. 4.

Stokes, Gale. 1993. *The Walls Came Tumbling Down*. New York: Oxford University Press.

Stroe-Brumariu, Raluca, and Marian Chiriac. Oct. 4-10, 1995. Votul final asupra Codului penal a fost aminat. *22*, p. 5.

Stroe-Brumariu, Raluca, and Alesandru Ganea. May 20-26, 1993. Scandalul va ramine numai in coloanele ziarelor? *22*, pp. 6-7.

Suciu, Mircea, et al. July 30, 1993. Televiziunea National are o noua organigrama, provizorie. *Evenimentul Zilei*, p. 8.

Szabo, Lucian-Vasile. July 27, 1990. Scurte note despre rolul presei. *22*, p. 2.

Tagliabue, J. Dec. 2, 1987. Romania, ever the maverick, resists Soviet spirit of change. *New York Times*, p. 34A.

Talbott, Strobe. Jan. 8, 1990. Glued to the tube. *Time*, p. 46.

Telegrama (March 12, 1994; March 22, 1994; April 6, 1994; April 15, 1994; April 27, 1994; August 19, 1994; Dec. 2, 1995). News bulletin disseminated by E-mail by Fundatia Pentru Strategii de Communicare, Bucharest, Romania.

[No byline] Televiziunea—procedura de urgenta. Aug. 3, 1993. *Romania Libera*, p. 1.

Thodorescu, Razvan. Aug. 30, 1991. Letter to Mircea Stoian, president of SOTI. Photocopy.

Thom, Francois. 1989. *Newspeak: The Language of Soviet Communism*. London: Claridge Press.

Tismaneanu, Vladimir. 1992. *Reinventing Politics: Eastern Europe from Stalin to Havel*. New York: Free Press.

Tripcovici, D. L. Jan. 22, 1992. Letter (via fax) to P. Gross.

Tripcovici, D. L. April 22, 1991. Report: SOTI—Romanian Society for Creating an Indepedent Television Company. Duplicated.

Tunstall, J. 1971. *Journalists at Work*. London: Constable.

[No byline] Dec. 25, 1989. Two American and two European journalists are shot and wounded. *New York Times*, p. 10.

Uncu, D. June 24, 1993. Puterea si presa. *Romania Libera*, p. 1.

Uncu, D. Nov. 25, 1993. Conflictul Presa-Senat. S-a propus rediscutarea Codului Penal. *Romania Libera*, p. 3.

Uncu, D. Nov. 26, 1993. Fara presa la birourile permanente. *Romania Libera*, p. 3.

Uncu, D. Nov. 29, 1993. Nerusinarea. *Romania Libera*, p. 3.

Uncu, D. July 11, 1991. Vocile presei si urechea puterii. *Romania Libera*, p. 1.

UNESCO. 1988. *Statistical Yearbook*. Paris: UNESCO.

[No byline] Aug. 3, 1994. Un Sondaj Occidental: Audienta Mass-media in Romania. *Romania Libera*, p. 16.

U.S. Commission on Security and Cooperation in Europe. May 30, 1990. *Report on the Parliamentary and Presidential Elections in Romania*. Washington, D.C.

U.S. Information Agency. June 14, 1990. *Romanians Confident About Future ... VOA*

Reled Upon Before the Revolution. Research memorandum.

U.S. Information Agency. March 28, 1991. *Romanians Debate Role of Media in Society.* Research memorandum.

U.S. Information Agency. February 1992. *Romanians' Confidence in Media Steadily Declining.* Research memorandum.

U.S. Information Agency. November 13, 1992. *Supporters of Romanian Parties Differ in Reliance on Media.* Research memorandum.

U.S. Information Agency. November 9, 1993. Faxed note from USIA Office of Research to the author with summary of research on question of confidence in media, 1990-93.

Verdery, Katherine. 1991. *National Ideology Under Socialism.* Berkeley: University of California Press.

Verdery, Katherine, and Gail Kligman. 1992. Romania after Ceausescu: Post-communist communism? In *Eastern Europe in revolution*, edited by Ivo Banac. Ithaca, N.Y.: Cornell University Press, pp. 117-47.

Vighi, Daniel. Feb. 25-March 3, 1993. Teatru TV. *22*, p. 2.

Viviano, Frank. April 22, 1991a. How TV helps shape revolution. *San Francisco Chronicle*, p. 1.

Viviano, Frank. April 22, 1991b. Watching the war on the TV's front lines. *San Francisco Chronicle*, p. A8.

Vlad, Corneliu. Sept. 29, 1992. Inaitea dreptului de a alege, dreptul de a sti. *Romania Libera*, pp. 1,3.

Vlad, C. 1972. Cresterea rolului conducator al partidului in perfectionarea vietii sociale. *Revista de Filosofie* 5:566-567.

Wald, Henri. Sept. 28, 1990. Iarasi despre "Limba de lemn." *22*, pp. 4.

Watts, Larry L. 1993. *Romanian Cassandra.* New York: Columbia University Press.

Weber, Renate. Nov. 17-23, 1993. Dovada relei credinte. *22*, p. 7.

Weber, Renate. April 3-4, 1993. Asigura legislatia penala exitenta descurajarea nationalismului, a mainifestarilor sovine, a insultelor si calomniilor prin presa? *Alianta Civica*, p. 7.

Wilkie, Curtis. Dec. 28, 1989. Television galvanized an old world revolution. *Boston Globe*, p. 57.

Willey, F., and A. Nagorski. Dec. 28, 1987. Down with the dictator—Ceausescu's Romania: protests, not glasnost. *Newsweek*, pp. 27-29.

Williams, R. 1968. *Communications.* Harmondsworth: Penguin Books.

Wolfe, Tom. 1976. *The Kandy-Kolored Tangerine-Flake Streamline Baby.* New York: Pocket Books, p. xi.

Young, Deborah. Jan. 3, 1990. Politics as miniseries: Rumania rapt before TV. *Variety*, p. 7.

April 29-May 5, 1993. Ziaristii au inchis ochii sa nu vada PAC linga AC. *22*, p. 8.

March 5, 1991. Ziaristii isi apara si va apara onoarea. *Romania Libera*, p. 8.

INDEX